AF553739

# Rudiments of Education Sociology and Philosophy

# Rudiments of Education Sociology and Philosophy

**Sankaranarayanan Paleeri**
*Faculty Member*
Department of Education
NSS Training College
Palakkad, KERALA.

**NEELKAMAL PUBLICATIONS PVT. LTD.**
**EDUCATIONAL PUBLISHERS**
**(EXPORTERS & IMPORTERS)**
**NEW DELHI HYDERABAD**

**RUDIMENTS OF EDUCATION SOCIOLOGY AND PHILOSOPHY**

**Sankaranarayanan Paleeri**

---



**First Edition : 2010**
**(Hardback)**



**ISBN: 978-81-8316-210-4**

**NEELKAMAL PUBLICATIONS PVT. LTD.**
Sultan Bazar, Hyderabad - 500 095.
✆ 24757140, 24757197, 24757944, Fax: 040-24757951
*Delhi Office:*
BG5/9B, Paschim Vihar, New Delhi-110 063,
✆ 011-25285894
website: www.neelkamalpub.com
e-mail: sales@neelkamalpub.com; sales_neelkamal@rediffmail.com

---

Published by *Suresh Chandra Sharma* for *Neelkamal Publications Pvt. Ltd.*, New Delhi, Hyderabad and printed at *Sri Vinayaka Art Printers*, Hyderabad, India.

# Preface

This is a textbook. Reflections in a textbook may not be the intellectual contributions of its author, but collection and interpretations on already established knowledge and writings. As this book is packed with authentic facts and explanations, reading needs more attention. The factual explanations given in boxes in certain chapters are important, but may not be actual explanations to the content. They are interesting and supportive to the reading of corresponding area. Try to read the contents carefully. Think on them and think beyond lines. Add and interpret yourself to the content area. Such a mode of reading will be effective and satisfactory.

The title outline is given at the start of each chapter. It will help the reader to get an overall idea on what are the areas of discussion in the corresponding chapter. Furthermore it is a motivation to unfold the content and also a factual support to the matter.

The objective of this book is to render scaffolding to undergraduate and postgraduate students in the area of education, philosophy and sociology. The target group of this book also involves teacher educators who handle "Education in Emerging India" or "Philosophical and Sociological Foundations of Education" as a subject for UG and PG level of teaching.

This book is a support to B Ed, M Ed, MA Education and MA Philosophy students who learn 'philosophy and sociology of education' as a paper for their course. At the same time it is an independent reader for all who like to avail awareness on education, philosophy and sociology.

Keeping in mind the suggestions and advices from well experienced teachers, experts and considering the feedback from classroom students, an attempt is made to make the content matter easy in explanation.

I hope this book will be warmly received by students and teacher educators alike.

– *Sankaranarayanan Paleeri*

**RUDIMENTS OF EDUCATION SOCIOLOGY AND PHILOSOPHY**

## Contents

❖ ❖ ❖

# Education
# Its Meaning and Contents

Man is considered the perfect in the process of evolution. Man has a long period of infancy and childhood. He has educability.

Education is the right of any human being. It is a process of his life. Man preserves and transforms his civilization and culture with the help of education. Education is a social necessity to him like water and air to live. We can't think of a human being of this era without education

This chapter discusses the major aspects of education. Important areas of discussion are:

*Education*

- *Training and education*
- *An art or science*
- *Meaning*
- *Definitions*
- *Functions*
- *Aims*
- *Types of education*
- *Factors of education*

*Globalization or LPG policies and education*

## 1.1 Education

Man has educability. In this world man only possesses this capacity. Development of an individual as a social being is dependent upon the education s/he acquires. Education is tool, which has spontaneous ability to make a man a social being. It makes man a social animal from a biological animal.

Education makes man civilized. Man has become the supreme creature of this universe. He is the master. The culture and civilization of men has progressed very far. Man makes everything for his own better life. Education is the factor that helped him to achieve all his progress. Without education, man is a big zero.

Education is a boon to humanity. It is education that uncovers the ignorance. It leads man from untruth to truth, from the darkness to light and from mortality to immortality. Education is that which emancipates us.

Education is for knowledge. Knowledge enlightens human beings. Aristotle said, "Educated men are as much superior to the uneducated as the living are to the dead". Education is man's beauty and treasure. It is the source of assets and enjoyments. Education nurtures humanity and nourishes human ability.

It is process of learning. By education an individual acquires the knowledge, attitudes, skills, values and socialization essential for an individual's life. This learning paves the way for human development. Education provides preparation for a life. It gives man a job or profession to earn money. The individual is prepared for a remunerative occupation by education. Hence, education is for desirable development. Man is being educated at each and every moment. Education is a process from one's birth to death. Education aims at the perfection of individuality. It is for a 'good life'. It is a process of individual's all-round development – physical, mental, cultural social, emotional, moral, behavioral and even spiritual. Education aims at an individual's specific development in cognitive, affective and psychomotor domains. Thus, education is a continuous process to make a man perfect.

### 1.1.1 Difference between Training and Education

Training and education are different. It is believed that any animal can be trained but only man can be educated. Training leads to performance and does not develop any innate spiritual ability. But education is oriented to develop human being's innate abilities. It facilitates divine perfection of individuality. Education is a concept deeper than training. Training is a process with limitations and it is designed for performance of a skill or certain skills. But education is a continuous process and training is only a part of it.

*Suppose one is trained in pick pocketing. He is trained but not educated. Education is for an individual's desirable development.*

Training focuses on certain skill development and its application. Education aims at an individual's overall development. Education is the source of behavioral change. Training is only a technical aspect of education.

Training usually means preparing a person in a narrow way for some specialized job and not for life in a broad sense. Education implies the preparation of a person for living in a community with all forms of socialization.

### 1.1.2 Is Education an Art or Science?

Education is both an art and a science. It is based on its experiments and observations on its practice. It follows scientific methods to develop all of its aspects like learning, methods, teaching and instruction so and so. At the same time it is an art to the learner and science to the educator in approaches. Education develops as a science and performs as an art.

### 1.1.3 Meaning of Education

Education is a term with wide meanings. For a better understanding, we can consider its meaning from different viewpoints.

### Etymological or lexical meaning

According to Indian thoughts the term that stands for education is *Vidya*. *Vidya* has its root in *Vid*, which means knowledge. One who seeks knowledge is a *Vidyarthi*. The other concept is that the word *Siksha* is education. *Siksha* means to teach and to learn. Lexically the term *Siksha* (education) means teaching, instruction and perception.

It is supposed that the word education has its root in four Latin words such as *educere*(to lead out), *educo(*to lead for, go forward*)*, *educare(*to take care of, to bring up, to bring forth, to nourish*)* or *educatom*(to teach , to train).

### Narrow meaning of education

The narrow meaning education is schooling that refers to school or college or university education. It is education for 3 Rs: reading, writing and arithmetic. It is purposely-oriented programme to get a degree or certificate, and comprises school, teachers, curriculum, methods etc. to educate an individual. So here education means a programme to avail knowledge in certain predetermined area and hence a pathway to get some certificates that testify the education. It is a formal programme to get a remunerative profession.

### Wide meaning of education

In the broad sense education is something beyond the mere concept of schooling. It is not a degree-oriented programme. It is a process of the development of the individual in all aspects. It is a lifelong process of organizing and reorganizing experiences. It is the interaction of the individual with his environment. It is the learning that individual acquires from each and every aspect of life. Through education an individual adopts himself with the environment and also adapts environment to his needs. In its wide meaning, education is life and life is education. Education is both a means and end itself.

## Education as a profession

Of course, education is a process for earning a living. Hence it is a means to an end. As a profession it is not an academic discipline. A profession includes the acquisition of pre-determined knowledge, which can and certainly be utilized in immediate practice for the welfare of the society. Education as a profession draws knowledge from various disciplines for contribution to the welfare of the student community and the society at large. To perform as a profession education needs support from society, culture, politics, philosophy etc. The person who takes education as a profession is known as a teacher.

## A Brief Note on Meaning of Education

As we have seen education can be interpreted in two ways – in a narrow sense and broad sense. Etymologically the more accepted root of the word education is educere. It means *to bring up* and *to bring for.* It is a process of nurturing personal growth, of guiding and modifying the development of individuality. Another one is educo. In Latin *e* means *out of* and *duco* means *I lead*. So education means leading out from within the innate power and virtues. Education is bringing up the innate capacities of the individual. It is not pouring in but drawing out – drawing out the abilities of the child.

Education is for life preparation. Man has to find a job or profession to live in this world. For that he needs education. That education declares him qualified and he can find his own earning for living. Though it is a narrow interpretation of the concept of education, the primary meaning we get by considering the term education is it is a certificate or degree-oriented programme.

Education is continuous organization and reorganization of experiences of an individual. Whatever learning an indivi-dual experiences is his education.

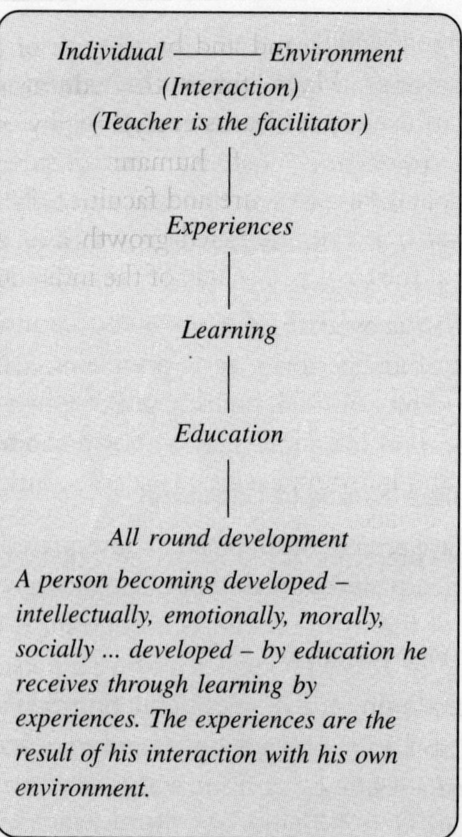


It is the process of development from the cradle to grave. In a wide sense all experiences from womb to tomb are said to be educative. Education can take various forms. It can be deliberate, voluntary, accidental, incidental, formal, informal or non-formal. It is a method to develop man. It is an integrated growth; it is direction, an art of training, influence, adjustment, guidance and integration of activities and experiences of the individual. Education is continuous process.

Education is not a one-way process. To quote John Adams, 'education is a bi-polar process in which the mature personality of the educator tries consciously and deliberately to modify the growing personality of the educand by the direct application of the educator on the educand and by the use of knowledge and skill in all forms'. Many times the educator may be the environment. The educand learns everything by own efforts. It is the natural development of humanity, the very effective development of all innate nature and faculties. Education is not a formal process. It is the integrated growth and the harmonious development of the total personality of the individual.

Education is emancipation. It is the pathway to liberation. According to Indian thoughts education leads a child from darkness to light. '*Sa Vidyaya Vimukthaya.*' – education that emancipate us. It is the emancipation from ignorance. It is a tool to liberate an individual from narrow outlook and self-centeredness. Hence education is not a matter of preparing individual for life, but it is life itself. It is the continuous reorganization and integration of life experience.

### 1.1.4 Education: Definitions

Finding a universally accepted definition for education is like searching for a black cat in a dark room. There is no perfect and universally accepted definition for education. If we turn the pages of standard dictionaries, the word *education* is defined as "systematic development and cultivation of normal powers of interest, feeling and conduct, so as to render them efficiently in some particular form of living as far as life in general".

There are a number of definitions of education. They are the definitions on psychological, sociological, philosophical perspectives and or a combination of all these. The definitions zeroed in on *a)* education is behavioral change, *b)* education is adjustment with environment and *c)* education is the drawing out of the innate abilities. More specifically definitions of education can be classified under two categories:

— Definitions regarding inner potentialities of individual; which stress on a child's inner potentialities and their drawing out.

— Definition which emphasize on interaction and adoption to environmental and social aspects

***Here are some examples based on these views.***

"By education I mean all round drawing out of the best in the child and man – body, mind and spirit". – *Gandhiji*

"Education is the manifestation of perfection already existing in man". – *Swami Vivekananda*

"Education is the complete development of the individuality, so that he can make an original contribution to human life to his best capacity". – *Nunn*

"Education is the development of all the capacities in the individual which will enable him to control his environment and fulfill his responsibilities". – *John Dewey*

"From broad point of view, all life thoughtfully lived is education". – *W H Kilpatrick*

"Education is the natural, harmonious and progressive development of man's innate powers". – *Pestalozzi*

"Education is the organisation of acquired habits of conduct or actions and tendencies of behaviour such as will fit the individual to his physical and social environment".

– *William James*

"Education is the unfolding of what is already enfolded in the germ. It is the process through which the child makes internal, external". – *Froebel*

"Education is the capacity to feel pleasure and pain at the right moment. It develops in the body and in the soul of the pupil all the beauty and all the perfection which he is capable of".

– *Plato*

According to Aristotle "education is the creation of a sound mind in a sound body". Sankaracharya said, "education is realisation of the self".

**Analysis of Definitions: A Brief Note**

Education is the drawing out of the best, that which is possessed by an individual. Education is to be focused on body, mind and spirit. Education is for Sarvodayaya. It is the enlightenment of everything best in the person. Hence it is a spiritual and physical process. Gandhiji's definition is more comprehensive and wide. Education stands for the well-integrated development of human personality – integration of body, mind and spirit. Education is perfect while it is for head, heart, hand and health. According to Vivekananda, education is manifestation of inner perfection. It is the divine perfection. Education means exposition of man's complete individuality. Whatever a man performs is nothing but the manifestation from his own self. Human mind is the source of all educational processes. Divinity is there in all. Education is the manifestation of this divine power. What is happening by education is nothing but the unfolding all power and all knowledge already there in the man. Education is realization. An individual realizes his potentialities he has been endowed with.

According to Dewey, education is reorganization, reconstruction and reconstitution of experiences. It develops individual personal efficiency and social efficiency. Education makes an individual a master of his environment.

Education is for the development of social values and human values. It is to understand the environment and to effectively interact with it. Education is for the all-round development of the individual. Life itself is a process of education. Education is a purposeful activity. Man has to interact with his environment, both physical and social. This interaction makes him a social being. Here comes the importance of education as an effective device to facilitate the individual's interaction with the environment. It is agreed that the individual possesses all capacities within. Education is not a pouring in process. It is a matter of drawing out the potentialities. It provides an effective and progressive interaction. Education makes an individual to render his social responsibilities. Education is not a narrow programme. It is wide. It is not rigid; it is flexible. Education is education to the soul too.

Education has been defined differently by different educationists according to their own point of view. In fact a perfect and last definition to education can't be found. To conclude we can quote the explanation of Tagore, – 'education means enabling the mind to find out the ultimate truth which emancipates us from the bondage of dust and gives us wealth not of things but of inner lights, not of power but of love, making this truth its own and giving expression to it.'

### 1.1.5 Functions of Education

Education is a vast area. So its functions are also vast and wide. Broadly education has two-fold functions. They are individual functions and social functions. By its individual functions education enables the child's overall development. It is the function of nourishment of innate potentialities of the child to the maximum level. It is a function of drawing out from within. It is a child-centered function of education. Here the child receives all personal development to live in this society effectively. It is a function of developing, directing and influencing the educability of the human child.

The second function out of the two-fold functions of education is its social function. More than a personal need education is a social need for a human being. Socialization of the individual is a major function of education. The intellectual, moral, emotional, cultural, social and physical development of individual is a social necessity. Man has to be educated for his better social life in his own society. Education is a functional device to lead a man for effective social life.

While considering education as schooling, a description on its functions is comparatively easy. In school or college or university education has to perform a bi-polar function – the personal and social functions. It is a bi-polar process also. It is a teaching and learning process. It is a function between the educator and educand or the teacher and learner. It is highly motivated to make an educated personality.

The function of education in a narrow sense is the educand's employment. It is a job-oriented programme. The function of education is to bring up children free from anxiety, fear, ignorance, economic dependence etc. Education trains to think, trains to enjoy thinking, trains to feel and enjoy feelings, trains to act and to be active, trains to perform and trains to be self-reliant. Here the pupil is the centre of the education; teacher is the inevitable facilitator and school and curriculum design and establish the relationship between the two.

It is somewhat difficult to draw a line between the functions and aims of education, while we consider education in broad sense. The major functions of education are conservation and assimilation of culture, constructive role, creative and refining role and enlightenment. They are the creative, constructive and refining functions of education. The assimilation of tradition is one of the most important functions of education. The other related function is the development of new social patterns. Such a development is needed for desirable social change. So, social change and social mobility are also the functions of education. Some of the major individual and social functions of education can be listed as follows:

- Giving awareness on humanity
- Make awareness on exploitations
- Ensure individual freedom
- Develop the concept of 'live and let live'

— Develop freedom
— Make a child free from ignorance, superstitions, poverty, disease, insecurity, unemployment, prejudices, and discrimination
— Cultivate values in child's mind
— Develop peace in mind
— Develop national integration and international understanding

Functions of education are not finite; they are infinite and never static.

### 1.1.6 Aims of Education

As philosophers, sociologists and educationists, interpret education differently the aims of education are also defined differently. What we are discussing here is the universally accepted aims of education.

Some of the major aims of education can be short listed as follows,

— Education for complete living
— Individual aims
— Social aims
— Cultural aims

They can be subdivided as follows

— Vocational aim
— Knowledge acquisition aim
— Character and morality development aim
— Citizenship development aim
— Aim of cultural preservation, transmission and transformation

— Education for leisure
— Education for better social adjustment
— Spiritual uplift aim
— Harmonious development aim
— Education for individuality
— Education for social efficiency
— Intellectual development and emotional development aims
— Aims of self realization and self-expression
— Economic development and economic independence aims
— Education for self-preservation – food, shelter and cloth

**An Explanation on Aims of Education**

Mainly the aims of education are placed under the three heads – social aims of education, individual aims of education and cultural aims of education and there is the universal aim put forward by Herbert Spencer – education for complete living.

There is a conflict of individual versus social aims in designing the aims of education. Is the aim of education determined by the individual or by the society? Creation of good man and good society is the overall aim of education. Education aims at all-round development of the individual. No doubt, education must cater to the complete development of an individual. But the individual can't realize his capacities without the support of society. When we say individual development, we mean to bring about the growth and development of an individual in all aspects – physical, mental, spiritual, emotional, intellectual, moral etc. Development of individuality makes an individual a very well adjusted person. Emotional development produces positive personality.

The social aim of education inculcates an individual's social efficiency. The individual qualities like cooperation, cohesiveness, toleration, love and mutual understanding are worthy for success in social life. Man is a social animal. He cannot isolate himself from his society. In all walks of life he is influenced by his society. These influences shape the personality of man. In broader sense social aims of education enable one to utilize his individuality effectively in social life.

> *Individuality develops only in a social atmosphere where it can be feeling on common interests and common activities.*
>
> **– Sir Percy Nunn**

The two aims of education – Individual aim and Social aim – are complimentary aims and not conflicting ones.

All aims listed and to be listed come under the one universal aim of education, that is Education for complete living.

While we go through other aims, we can find that vocational aims, earn a living aim, self-preservation aims, knowledge acquisition aim, character and morality development aim, leisure, spiritual uplift, self-realization and self-expression, economic independence, intelligence development and emotional development aims come under the head education for individual development. They are social aims too.

The major specific social aims are citizenship development, character and morality development, harmonious development, better social adjustment, social efficiency and economic development. Preservation, transmission and transformation of culture are the cultural aims of education.

This classification doesn't mean that the aims of education are strictly segregated from each other. They are mutually related and one aim can be satisfied only with the others. Education aims at making a good man as well as a good citizen; it is the base for the creation of a good society. It is the aim of education to develop individuality through social contacts, influence and social control.

**Knowledge acquisition** is perhaps the oldest aim of education. It is saying that knowledge acquisition is not a means but an end. Knowledge is to save an individual himself from error and to lead to discover truth. Man's progress and happiness are in the expansion of knowledge (Aristotle). It is an essential element for intellectual development, moral development, spiritual development, good character, social efficiency etc. Different philosophical outlooks have different explanation for the aim of knowledge acquisition. However, this aim is treated as one of the major aims of education.

**Vocational aim** is another practical or utilitarian aim of education. Self-preservation is the first need. So education should focus on this aim. It should enable the individual to earn a living by preparing him for an occupation. As education is a preparation for better life we can't deny the importance of bread and butter. A good job or an attractive profession is the major aim of formal education. It is the minimum necessity for **economic independence**. Economic independence will help an individual to pull his own weight, and will not be a parasite or a drag on society. This adds to an individual's social efficiency. Though there is a separate stream called vocational education, vocational aim is treated as a major aim of all formal education systems.

The major work of education is **character development** and **development of morality**. What is the use of education, if it fails to develop a socially accepted character in the individual? Morality is not a direction of religions. It is non-religious. Only education can develop morality in an individual. Morally developed, well-integrated, strong and qualified character formation is an aim of education. Strength and purity if character can be cultivated by education only. Education should raise man from the passionate and brutal nature to the intellectual and human nature. Education is the effective tool in this concern. So character building is one of the significant aims of education.

**Cultural aim** of education has its base on knowledge. Culture draws its essence from the knowledge of past. This is being contributed by education. The passive part of the culture is actively interpreted by education. Culture is passed from generation to generation through education. The knowledge about culture is preserved by the education of the region. All aspects like curriculum, teacher and methods of education preserve, transmit and transform cultural knowledge to the generations. An educated person is considered as a cultured person. He has broad human interests, high attitude on human rights, social sensitiveness, high morality and personal efficiency. It is therefore considered that cultural aim of education a significant one.

Man needs **leisure**. His civilization is envisaged from leisure. Leisure only nourishes his thought and pleasure. Man is not a machine. His aesthetic sense is to be developed to act as a better social being. Leisure helps to select recreation and develop habits. A proper canalization of leisure time is possible by education only.

**Citizenship** training is the focus of any education system. For example, a democratic country aims at development of a democratic citizen through the education system. A religious state like Saudi Arabia aims at development of a Pious Muslim through its system of education. The components like responsibility, civic competence and cultural refinements of citizenship can be effectively cultivated by education. Education should aim at citizenship training.

Education as a device for socialization should focus on the development of child's ability for **adjustment** and **harmonious development**. The education itself may be defined as harmonious development and adjustment with the environment. Integrated development of an individual is necessary to be a social being. Better social adjustment provides better socialization. It will help him to develop, organize, train and express his powers.

Education should help an individual to realize his true self; his **spirituality**. It is something deeper than his intellect. It is mainly envisaged by idealists, but accepted by all. Education should cultivate the values of love, honesty, sympathy, empathy, peace, nonviolence etc. The education, which realizes the unique identity between individual soul and spirituality, is the true education. Man is only a microcosm in the macrocosm. The material development alone will not work. These ideas are to be transmitted by education.

**Self-expression and self-realization** is an individual necessity. There should be provisions for the development of all innate abilities of the individual. It should cater to the physical, intellectual, moral, emotional, social and psychological development of the child. Each child is unique. He needs freedom. Each child has ambitions to realize his own abilities and to express them. Education should enable him to realize his own abilities. Therefore the autonomous development of the individual is the important aim of education. The education system must provide ample scope for free and full self- expression and self-realization.

Development of **intellect and emotion** is a primary focus of education. The emotional development of individual is factor for the development of peace in the mind and in the world. It is necessary for national integration and international understanding. Progressive contributions to the world humanity are the aims of education. Such contributions are possible by intellectually developed persons. Hence education should aim at the development of human intellect. Like knowledge aim, intellectual and emotional development aim is considered one of the oldest aims of education. But to some, this aim is related to old theory of formal discipline, which is now no longer accepted.

According to Dewey education is for social life. Education is one with social life. Man is a social being and a citizen. Whatever his powers, he can't be successful if he is not socially efficient. Society expects an educated individual's unique contribution to its progress and wellbeing. To promote the society he has to develop his **social efficiency** to the full level. An educated individual will have economic efficiency, willingness to sacrifice his interest for others and willingness to use his energy for social progress. Social efficiency means cultivation of one's own powers, abilities and capacities to participate freely in the shared activities of the community. No individual can develop in a social vacuum. Education for social aim is education for social service and citizenship. Education aims at making a 'good man' as well as a 'good citizen. The individual cannot rise to the full stature of his personality nor can he make use of his opportunities unless he is placed within the framework of social institution. For the fullest performance he needs social efficiency. So it is considered an important aim of education.

Herbert Spencer has suggested an aim of education, which is all-inclusive, complete and comprehensive. This aim is education for complete living. All aspects of human life come in the target of educational aims. Learning the art of life is the greatest aim of education. Education helps him to learn all parts of the art of life.

Education must be life in all its manifestations. Spencer's opinions on the aim of complete

*Education must tell us in what way to treat the body, in what way to treat the mind, in what way to manage our affaires, in what way to bring up our family, in what way to behave as a citizen, in what way to utilize those sources of happiness which nature supplies – how to use all faculties to the greatest advantage of ourselves and others. It will enable men to fill their unique and particular function in life. This is complete living.*

**– Spencer**

living are highly criticized by several educationists. He has not always been clear and reasonable. It is saying that this aim is focused on education just as a preparation for adult life. Hence this aim is also considered as one of the major aims of education.

### Conclusion

There are several aims of education. We found that different philosophers, sociologists and educationists have different aims. They differ from nation to nation to a certain extent. Taking all these aims into account, we find there is something in all these aims, but not every thing in any one of them. No aim is a perfect aim and no aim can be expelled. To some education for complete living is an all inclusive and comprehensive aim. To some others social efficiency and adjustment is suggested as an all-inclusive aim. But it is also opposed. There is no one final aim subordinating all other aims to it. The different aims only emphasize different aspects of education. They show broadness of education. They are complimentary rather than contradictory.

## 1.1.7 Types of Education

Mainly there are three types of education; **Formal education, Informal education** and **Non-formal education.** It is a classification for convenience, based upon functions and methods of operations. All the three are needed and relevant for the fulfillment of an individual's educational living.

### Formal Education

When education – learning – takes place in a formal situation, it is called formal education. Formal education is a clearly planned and formally executed education system. It is the education through specified ways and routes, and rules and regulations. It is schooling. Formal education of an individual is completed within a specified age limit.

The system of education with predetermined aims, formal classroom, teachers, curriculum, methods, design and other aspects is formal. It will have a course of curriculum and scheme of work. Formal education is certificate-oriented and aims at awarding of a degree or diploma or other status as per the completion of education. So, the system of education, which aims a certificate of merit after the completion of a specified duration in a school or college or university or any other institution, is formal education. The college education or university education is formal education. Normally, after the completion of the course we may call the man an educated man.

The general concept of formal education is as follows:

- It is the traditional system in which teacher and taught face each other in a classroom in the learning process.
- It has a regular and continuous programme and basis.
- It follows a predetermined and fixed curriculum and syllabus.
- There will be a fixed timetable.
- There will be a hierarchy of class promotion.
- A public examination at the end of the course will be conducted to give promotion from one class to the next higher class.
- The learner will be awarded a certificate after the successful completion of the course.

Formal education is consciously and deliberately planned for the modification of the learner's behavior with a particular aim in view. It is hierarchically structured, chronologically graded, legally designed, practically organized and institutionalized. This is the system prevalent in schools and colleges with a number of formalities such as age of admission, standard, curriculum, syllabus, textbooks etc.

## Informal Education

The individual does not live in a vacuum; he is under the influence of surroundings. He learns all time, from every experience and from every experience. Education received in this indirect manner is called informal education. Education is the result of learning. All experiences provide learning. So the life experiences themselves are education. They are accidental. Hence 'life is education and education is life'. Informal education has a wide connotation. It is the process from womb to tomb. The education we achieve from our life is not a certificate-oriented, preplanned programme. But all such experiences are worthy and necessary to lead a better life. An informally educated man shows more competencies than a formally educated one many times. An individual gets informal education from agencies like family, school, peer group, community, friends etc. All the interactions with the environment will teach him something. There will be no formal classroom, school, teacher, textbook, discipline system, planning, methods or other aspects. But man is effectively being educated at each and every moment. Hence, whatever the individual learns from his life is called informal education. It is a continuous process and lifelong process.

## Non-formal Education

This is a new concept. Non-formal education is formal as well as informal. In this world of competition, time is very important. In the rush of building the life, an individual may be unable to spend a lot of time in colleges to get formal education. He may fail to get formal education within the determined time limit and age limit. Here comes the scope of non-formal education. Non-formal education is a planned educational programme to get a degree or diploma or any other certificate of merit by undergoing a course or curriculum. It is somewhat formal, but highly flexible and lenient. It is the education system of the era. By non-formal method of education, an individual can be educationally qualified at any age without undergoing a formal educational pattern. He can get education from his own house. The education through Distance Education Institutions is an example for non-formal education.

### 1.1.8 Factors Influencing Education

Education is not a single discipline. It is a wide concept with varied interests, implications, applications and practices. The functions of education are varied and different. They vary from assimilation of cultural traditions to development of new social patterns. Education has a creative, constructive and refining role. It has a direct role in the building of nation and desirable development of citizen. The education system of a state is influenced by various factors. Not only as a state's system, but also as a universal phenomenon, education is influenced by various factors. Some of the major factors influencing education are **philosophical, socio-cultural, economic, political** and **historical** factors. They are not perfectly identical, but are complementary to each other. Each one separately and identically influences education system lesser or greater.

A brief sketch on different factors and their influence on education is given below. The list is not complete.

**Philosophical factors** – Determine the aims of education, curriculum, methods, approach to discipline and other aspects. (What should be the aims, curriculum and other aspects of education…)

**Socio-cultural factors** – Influence the selection of educational aspects and needs of its practice. (Which one should be the suitable curricula, method, which are the aims to be achieved….)

**Political factors** – Influence the planning and execution of the educational system and way of practice of educational aspects and directly influence the administrational aspects. (What philosophy and socio-cultural factors should be considered, what should the mode of construction of system and what result to be achieved...)

**Economic factors** – Influence the design of education system, infrastructure and other support and execution. (In what ways the educational system should be designed and practiced...)

**Historical factors** – Influence the whole area of education to be practiced by a state. Historical factors help to give national outlook and organise the future of education. These factors connect the past and future. They provide planning, syntheses and feed back. (How the past can be connected with the present and future for the effective practice of education and when and where a system is to be introduced...)

Man's metamorphosis from food seeker to food producer had taken years and years. The civilizations developed along with man's evolution were not desirable but 'automatic' with the changes in lifestyle. No men or a group of men, in the past, lived with the intention that we have to develop a civilization by living here or there. Civilization emerged with their life, its changes and etc.

Education too developed and got different ways according to their life, culture, philosophy etc. In the early period, as we know, education was not a desirable practice. Slowly education emerged as an inevitable part of human civilization. Even education becomes a synonym with culture and civilization. An educated man is considered as a civilized man. So education is necessary for the present life. Education influences man's culture, social life, economy and politics, etc.

## Socio-Cultural Factors

Culture is the word used to refer to good manners and tastes. 'Culture is defined as a complex whole, which includes the knowledge, belief, art, moral laws, customs, habits etc acquired by man as a member of society' (Taylor).

No aspects of human life can be left without being influenced by culture. Even the biological needs like food, slumber and sex bear the stamp of one's culture. It influences all material and non-material aspects of man's life and of course, education too. Education is greatly influenced by socio-cultural factors. The culture of society determines the pattern of education. It influences very much the formal education. Even the selection of uniform of the school students is being determined according to the culture. It can hamper the ill practices of education as a system. The curricula, method, a teacher's role and behaviour, the organization of textbook and the mode of discipline are being influenced by the culture. Culture determines their selection. An American classroom adopts aspects of education according to American culture and Indian classroom according to Indian culture.

> *A teacher in a class room will not be effective if he or she is ignorant about the culture of the students. Even the wit used by the teacher will fail before the students because of this ignorance. Culture influences the learning, standard of life, Meta cognition and discipline of students. Effective education is that which based up on culture and function according to culture.*

The preservation of culture is an important function of education. The culture of man as a social being is transmitted and transformed by education. Education is, thus, a tool for preservation, transmission and transformation of culture. Acculturation and enculturation is effectively possible by education only. Education has to do these as inevitable functions. Culture and education are interrelated. They contribute to each other. The design of educational aspects is according to the culture. A method should be in accordance with the culture. The mode of discipline will be effective if it has strong cultural base.

The content of textbook and the design of curriculum and extracurricular activities are selected according to the culture where the education system is to be practiced. It is said that components of culture are the cells of education. It is the lifeblood of the body of education.

**Philosophical Factors**

Philosophy and education are two sides of the same coin. Philosophy is the passive side and education is the active side. The philosophy of a society reaches the young generation through education. Education is nothing but the practice of philosophy. The edifice of education is built upon the foundation of philosophical principles. Education without philosophy is rootless and philosophy without education is fruitless. We cannot design an education system without a strong philosophy behind it. It is the life energy of education.

Philosophy as a factor directly influences the aspects of education. The aims of education of a state's education system are determined by its philosophy. It is the function of axiology to determine the aims of education. The metaphysical aspects and epistemological aspects influence the method of teaching and curriculum. A state's education is its philosophy. The teacher in the classroom, the teacher–pupil relationship, the atmosphere of school and classroom, the mode of operation and the teaching morale are determined by philosophy. Philosophy is the cornerstone of education. We cannot segregate philosophy from education and vice versa.

*The method of teaching in an Islamic educational institute, which follows a religious philosophy, is different from that of a democratic secular classroom which follows democratic philosophy.*

A teacher should follow a philosophy, which has a close connection with the philosophical ideals of the educational system. Only then he can transform the philosophical ideals to the pupils. Such a teacher can only mould the students in the desirable way. To enable students achieve the aims and objectives of education a teacher should be philosophically well knit. Philosophy has a role in individualized instruction too. Each and every individual follows his own philosophy of life. This ideology leads his life. He likes to be educated and employed according to the philosophy of life he possesses. It is the same in the case of a state. A state designs and executes various aspects of education like aims, curriculum, methods, discipline and principles of teaching according to the philosophy it possesses.

**Political Factors**

Politics as a factor has strong influence on education scenario particularly in the modern period. Political factors are important in formal, informal and non-formal sectors. The term politics generally refers to the activities of administration of a state. It is also related with the social life of the people. In the modern world, the formal education sector needs huge investments and big support. The support varies from infrastructure to modern technologies. These need the assistance of state's administration. The political ideology and political will of the government are, thus, becoming more important as the factors influencing education. Politics is a phase of ethics, which deals with the duties of a state and its citizens. It can never be divorced from education.

*Fold your little hands*
*Bow your little heads*
*Think of him who gives us*
*Our daily bread*
*Adolph Hitler his name*
*He is our savior claim.*

*This is the translation of a German KG song during the period of Hitler. What evidence do we need more than this to correlates education and political factor?*

The political systems like democracy, totalitarianism, communism, aristocracy etc. influence state's educational planning and execution accordingly. The political administration controls all educational affairs of the state. For example, in totalitarianism the major aim of education is to train the individual to serve for the ends of the state without raising questions. Or, in the case of education in a communist country, the education system follows centralized democracy in planning and administration. The freedom of choice regarding the selection of course, etc. will be of the state rather than of the individual. Education might be for the achievement of national goals with emphasis on social aim rather than the individual goals.

**Economic Factors**

Education in this era is influenced more by economic factors than any other factors. Education as a system cannot stand without the help of economic elements. Economic factor always gives importance to the product. Education has a big role in the state's economic development and vice versa. Expenditure on education is an investment by the state. Educational development and economic progress of a society is highly positively correlated. The economic status of state and individuals influence the forms of education they choose. Industrial growth, agricultural growth etc help economic growth and they influence educational development. Investment in education is not for any direct profit. But it is the base for all progress. Educational development is necessary for the economic progress. Education is an asset forever.

The economic status of a state even influences the aspects of education like curriculum, method and infrastructure. A poor country can never think of the introduction of highly expensive technological devices in the classrooms. The free education and concepts like common education, social justice, education for all and equality of educational opportunities can be achieved with the support of economic efficiency only. An individual's income, economic status, per capita income, economic efficiency of state and financial support of the state are important in the design and practice of education. Education and economics are mutually dependent. Education facilitates state's economic progress and economic condition of the state facilitates educational development.

**Historical Factors**

Education is a continuing process. It is developed along with human civilization and it will exist till the end. Education has a long past and a never-ending future. It has a functioning present. Historical factors connect the past with the present. From these experiences education get its energy to function effectively. The gains and failures of the past educational experiences are considered to design education for the present and future. Historical factors give a universal outlook to education. Education of the contemporary period is different from its past and it will be different in future. Each plan for a period is based upon the past experiences. We cannot go to the future without considering the past.

The historical factors will influence educational design of a state for a long period. For example, Indian education system is based on the British period education of Lord Macaulay. The Vedic, Budhist and Jainist education and Islamic education have influence on Indian education system. Any system of education in this world is highly influenced by the historical factors of the society and region, where the system originates and develops.

**Other Factors Influencing Education**

There are several other factors that influence education. Technological factors, psychological factors and geographical factors are some of them. There might be some other factors that influence education from time to time like policies of international organizations, declarations of national and international organizations etc. For example, the policies of Liberalization, Privatization and Globalization have become a major influencing factor on education all over the world.

## 1.2 Globalization and Education

Liberalization, Privatization and Globalization (LPG) is the neo economic policy of contemporary world. Globalization has become a synonym to trade. It affects all matters of human life all over the world. Education is also experiencing notable changes because of globalization. Education is being realized as a major instrument for economic development. Education is also being considered as a commodity for trade. The International Commission on Education for 21st Century has pointed out the importance of higher education: "Higher education is at one and the same time one of the driving forces of economic development and the focal point of learning in a society. It is both repository and creator of knowledge. Moreover it is the principal instrument for passing on the accumulated experience, cultural and scientific, of humanity".

Every sector of economy including education is subject to tremendous competition in globalization. Higher education is a 'trade' to WTO and World Bank. It should meet the changing needs of global village! It is a matter of trade; hence it is a commodity, which has a big market. A worldwide market! Human capital has emerged as a crucial input for the survival and development of economy (the trade and commerce) in modern period. Hence, commercialization of higher education is a social reality in globalization. Education has become an "Economic Good" rather than a non-economic good.

The tendency of withdrawal of governments from education and investment in education sector is a symptom of globalization. They have been promoting another policy that students must pay for education and free education and universalisation of free and compulsory education for all are merely impractical and not state's responsibility.

## Policies of GATS: Direct Influence of Globalization

The World Trade Organization (WTO), replaced the General Agreement on Trade and Tariffs at the Uruguay Round in 1994. The General Agreement on Trade in Services (GATS) covered in the WTO, also a product of the Uruguay Round, is a legally enforceable agreement aimed at deregulating international markets in services, including education.

The informal WTO Classification List divides educational services into five parts: (a) primary education services; (b) secondary education services; (c) higher education services; (d) adult education, and (e) other education services.

GATS consider education as a business in the service sector. It adopts pay and study policy. Social justice through education cannot be assured while it considered as a service industry. According to GATS, education is not a responsibility of the government. Though predominantly a government supported service, most governments are, as a consequence of neo-liberal economic reforms of globalization, withdrawing from it. The government of India through extensive privatization, commercialization and deregulation is encouraging this process. It considers students as consumers, teachers as sellers and runners of institutions as proprietors.

Higher education is a service sector industry in the area of education as 'service' with a huge global market in which students, teachers, and non-teaching employees constitute resources for profit making. In this industry, the students are consumers, teachers are service providers, and the institutions or companies catering to education services are organizers, and the teaching-learning process is no longer for the building of a nation but a business for profit-making.

When the services in education are entirely provided by the government, they do not fall within the GATS rule. For a service to be out of the purview of the GATS rule it has to be entirely free.

However, when the services are provided either by the government partially or is charged (as happens in education where some fees is charged), or provided by the private providers, they shall fall under the GATS rule.

GATS covers the educational services of all countries whose educational systems are not exclusively provided by the public sector, or those educational systems that have commercial purposes. Since total public monopolies in education are extremely rare, almost all of the world's educational systems fall under the GATS umbrella. In India, we cannot get exemption of education from the application of GATS because education at all levels, particularly at higher education level, is not entirely free (i.e. some fees have to be paid).

As part of globalization policies in education any country can operate educational business in any other country. The widespread opening of universities in other countries will be the immediate effect. The domestic universities of India and in developing and undeveloped countries will face adverse effect, because they are very poor in their assessed quality as per the quality assessment of international agencies. If there arise any purposely-oriented efforts to assure international quality to education in our country, it will be a positive effect of globalization. Except that, the effect of LPG on education is injurious to a country like India.

**Certain specific effects of LPG policies** on education are the following:

a) Education shall become an economic good rather than a social good

b) Investment in education will be treated as a business investment rather than an investment for social service

c) Education will become a profit-oriented business.

d) Ensuring social justice by education and the principle of equality of educational opportunities will become a dream.

e) Pay to learn will become a usual phenomenon

f) Governments will withdraw from general and public education

g) Corporate managements and wealthy investors may hijack education scenario.

h) Designing of educational agenda, curriculum and content will become a task of investors.

i) There may be cultural invasions.

At the same time there will be certain good effects also.

By the LPG policies, there will be a worldwide opening of opportunities. An individual can avail education from anywhere in the world. New and innovative educational programmes will be launched. Colleges and other institutions will get opportunities to affiliate with any university. The quality of education, in higher education in particular, will attain a high status. International quality may be assured. International exchange of students and teachers may foster the values of international understanding.

# Culture, Society and Education

This chapter deals with culture, society and their inter-relation with education.

*Culture*

- *Meaning and definition*
- *Characteristics*
- *Definition to a cultured person*
- *Culture and civilization*

*Culture and Education*

*Socio-cultural Determinants*

- *Cultural diffusion*
- *Cultural lag*
- *Cultural relativism*
- *Cultural pluralism*
- *Cultural conflict*
- *Acculturation*
- *Cultural contact and transmission*

*Society*

- *Social change*
- *Its meaning and definition*
- *Factors of social change*
- *Education and social change*
- *Social control*
- *Social mobility and social progress*

Man is a social being. There is a saying that man a biological animal becomes a social animal by education. Education, rather than any other thing, is a social process. A study of society and culture is relevant in all aspects while we consider education as a social necessity.

**Education** is a social process. Its programmes closely depend upon the socio-cultural designs. Culture, society and education are not isolated notions, but are identical. They are always engaged in reciprocal contacts. One is to be defined in the light of the other. Each one is to be clarified with the help of other.

## 2.1 Culture and Education

Education and culture are closely related phenomena. They are complementary and mutually integrative. It is education that preserves, transforms and transmits culture. Education refines culture and enriches it with contributions. Culture is the designing factor of education. It is on the canvas of culture that the artwork of education takes place.

### 2.1.1 Culture: Concept and Meaning

Culture is an abstract entity. It is a unit to understand through experience and a complex idea that is difficult to define. The term culture in meaning and content is illusive and comprehensive. It is considered as the most crucial subsystem of the social system.

Etymologically the word culture means cultivating the mind. Lexical meaning of culture is 'the quality in a person or society that arises from an interest in and an acquaintance with what is generally regarded as excellence in arts, letters, manners, etc'. Culture is a particular stage of civilization. It is the expression of development and improvement of mind. There is a saying that civilization is 'what we have' and culture is 'what we are'.

Culture is the outcome of the continual effort of the group in its interpersonal living. Through the interaction of the groups, culture is enriched and broadens. Culture includes all that man has acquired in the mental and intellectual sphere of his individual and social life. It includes on the one hand, the whole of man's material civilization, tools, weapons, clothing, shelter, machines and even system of industry; and on the other hand all of non-material civilization, such as language, literature, art, religion, ritual morality, law and even government. Culture may be analyzed in terms of units called traits. A number of traits form a complex and a number of complexes form a cultural pattern.

Culture is a way of life. It includes doing, feeling, thinking, interacting, appreciating etc. It is the ideas, attitudes, values and habits developed by the individual and group in the society. Culture is the things people value, the things and attitudes they do not value, their work, their art, their music, their science, and their history. It includes all values. It is the sympathy, empathy, grasping, communicability etc.

### 2.1.2 Culture: Definition

"Culture is that complex whole which includes knowledge, belief, art, morals, law, customs and any other capabilities acquired by man as a member of society" is the definition given by S B Taylor about culture.

Culture can be defined as the totality of whole performances and thoughts of an individual or a group. According to Andrew Marlaux, "culture is the sum of all forms of art, of love and thought, which in the course of centuries, have enabled man to be less enslaved".

According to L A White, "culture is a symbolic, continuous, cumulative and progressive progress." In this way, culture includes all that man has acquired in the mental and intellectual sphere of his individual and social life.

Some sociologists interpreted Culture in a broad sense, the same as social efficiency. Mathew Arnold suggested that culture is the way of life, the habits, the manners, the very tone of voices, the literature, the things which give pleasure to community, the words, the thoughts which make the furniture of their minds; in broad sense it is sweetness and light of humanity. Culture includes anything that can be communicated from one generation to the other.

### 2.1.3 General Characteristics and Nature of Culture

Some of the major specific characteristics of culture as a social phenomenon can be enlisted as follows:

- Culture is cumulative. All elements of culture grow as a result of years of cumulating.
- Culture includes all social and personal values
- Culture is an organized system of behaviour, molded by social forces and the tide of times.
- Culture is generally an accumulated product and process.
- Culture is not rigid and unchanging; it is flexible and changing according to time and need.
- Culture is inclusive of those elements, which man has created and in which man can make improvements.
- Arrivals of new elements increase the quality and complexity of culture.
- It is transformed from one generation to another.
- Culture is a specific character of human society.

Culture is not an inborn ability. It is an acquired quality. It is communicated from one generation to another and from one man to another. Culture is not static. It has adaptability. It is constantly undergoing change in concurring with the environment. Culture fulfills certain ethical and social needs of individuals and groups. Culture includes ideal norms of behaviour according to which the members of the society attempt to conduct themselves.

### 2.1.4 Who is a Cultured Person?

Culture is expressive in nature. So a man's culture is assessed from his overt behaviour. A cultured person should have broad mindedness, human interest and social efficiency. He should consider and appreciate good ideas and art. He does not manifest extravagance of language. He will not be a flippant. A cultured person will never be meaningless and thoughtless in words or in actions.

A cultured person is considered as an educated person. Education, either formally or informally plays an important role in producing such a personality. A man who is generous in talk and action and interaction with others, does not manipulate facts, tries to accept existing social and cultural norms, contributes to the enrichment of existing culture and a man who practices, produces and maintains knowledge and belief and art of the society can be called a cultured man.

### 2.1.5 Culture and Civilization

Culture and civilization are not the same, though they are identical at many levels. They are mutually contributive and without their collaboration as sociological notions both will become static, undervaluing and invaluable.

More than differences, culture and civilization possess similarities. Culture expresses the essence of civilization. There is a saying that civilization is what we have and culture is what we are. Some say that the material aspects of the society and men's interaction with them are represented by the word civilization and non-material aspects by the term culture. But this is not fully true. Civilization is the life culture of the people and culture is the expressive civilization of the person. Civilization is the advancement in all areas including politics, culture, way of life, and production and exploring of natural resources.

## 2.2 Culture and Education: Scope and Functions

Education has a very significant role in culture. A child acquires his first lesson in culture from the family. The educational influence of family, community, peer groups, associations etc teach him the different aspects of culture. The formal or informal ways of education are to preserve, modify, transmit and transform culture to the individual.

Education is a formal tool to protect the culture in all its aspects. Education is conveying the desirable things in culture by incorporating them in the formal school curriculum. A formal educational institution, being a controlled environment, transmits and promotes in a systematic, conscious and deliberate manner. Education interprets culture appropriately and positively.

The relation between culture and education is not a one-way process. They influence each other. Preservation of cultural heritage is one of the major aims of education. Providing effective education is the primary assignment of any cultured human society. Education without cultural approach is futile and unrewarding. Culture without educational support is of no use.

In specific terms, we can say education has two fold functions. One among them is conservative and transmission of culture. The second function is refinement and transformation. So education, in relation to culture, has to perform

a) conservative function

b) preservative function

c) transmission function

d) transformation function, and

e) refinement function.

Education is a strong factor in culture change. It is the training, the learned behaviour that sets succeeding generations to the pattern. The form of education, the ideas it transmits, and motivation have the impact on a community. Education, as the absorber and reflector of culture, is the best medium for sensitizing the growing generation to the cultural norms and processes of the society.

**An Estimate of the relation between Culture and Education**

Education is closely related with the intellectual, emotional, cultural and social life of the human race. It provides a clear understanding to the individual on his own cultural perspectives and the culture of humanity. Education is an individual's attempt to control his environment effectively and to interact with it progressively. So education cannot ignore the aspects and values of culture, which give meaning to environment. Education is an essential arrangement of social system, which shapes the personality of the younger generation, prepares their social life and adorns them for the society in which they live. These are the processes of knowing and absorbing the culture.

Education can effectively administer the essentials of culture to the younger generation. There is a saying that 'education is corrective for the cultural ills'. Education corrects egoism and wrong appraisal of individualism, those that adversely affect cultural progress. Enlightenment through education gives generosity to each individual and to the whole society. Culture liberates the mind. Culture satisfies human needs of individual in the society. Education paves the way for this attainment. Culture and education are, actually, not two deviated notions, and they are almost same in their *dharma*.

## 2.3 Socio-Cultural Determinants of Education

Education as a device in the field of culture can do a lot to facilitate cultural ends. It can strongly influence the characteristics of culture. Education is not a delitescent 'influencer' in influencing the schema like cultural diffusion, cultural lag, cultural change, cultural relativism, etc.

### 2.3.1 Cultural Diffusion

Culture is not a single 'thing'. It is a configuration, a complex whole. It is a compound of some simple units called traits. Traits always proved significant in the evaluation of culture. The existence of traits can be found in all cultures. A trait may be a single set of customs, beliefs, manners, attitude etc. For example, a style of dressing or eating, a format of discipline, a manner of interaction…..

Different traits combine together to form larger units called complex units, and complex units form the pattern of culture. So, culture is the configuration of traits and whole of the complex units. These traits and complex units are spread from individual to individual, individual to group, from group to individual and group to group. The spread and acceptance of culture from individual to individual or society to society can be called as cultural diffusion. Cultural diffusion does not mean imposing a cultural pattern on the other. It is the acceptance and absorption of some traits by the other. Adaptation and assimilation is the process that brings about cultural diffusion.

Diffusion takes place in two ways –intra society diffusion and inter-society diffusion. Intra-society diffusion is the spread of cultural traits or complex units from one individual to another individual or to a group inside the same society. The factors that influence this type of diffusion are development of mannerisms, learned traits from a distant culture, usefulness of new elements, attitudes which influence the existing ideas, social prestige of a person, policies of individual thinking, inventions, discoveries and forces, etc.

Inter-society diffusion takes place among groups. It is the assimilation of traits and complex units from one social group to another social group. Major factors influencing this type of diffusion are social contact, discoveries, inventions, trade and commerce, international relations, press and other media interpretation, etc.

**Education and Cultural Diffusion**

Education is an important instrument in the process of cultural diffusion. It forms the attitude and assimilates what is acceptable. Education directly influences the factors that influence diffusion desirably. Education functions as a channel and organizer in the cultural diffusion process. Good elements and bad elements of culture are judged in the light of education. Education highly influences rejecting, abstaining, accepting or assimilating cultural traits and complex units.

Briefly, education as an instrument of cultural diffusion, functions through five ways:

a) Preserves cultural traits and complex units
b) Transmits them. Education transmits norms, values, practices, cultural ideas and social values.
c) Interprets culture appropriately
d) Helps continuity of self-reviewing process of culture
e) Helps the filtering of cultural factors and traits
f) Promotes the specific three-fold processes of culture – transmission, promotion and enrichment of social life.

The desirable aspects of cultural diffusion are the contribution of education. Education is the instrument and platform for the diffusion process. The significance and scope of cultural diffusion is determined by the education of the society.

## 2.3.2 Cultural Lag

Cultural lag is a socio-cultural concept. The term cultural lag refers to the degree and speed of cultural diffusion. Some aspects of culture may change to a high degree and speed. But certain aspects do not change at the same rate. A part of the culture may be changed, but some other aspects remain unchanged. This phenomenon is known as cultural lag.

In other terms the gap between material culture and non-material culture is known as cultural lag. The various patterns of culture do not change at the same rate. Some patterns change rapidly and some slowly. This creates imbalance between different parts in the case of cultural change. Education is considered as an instrument that bridges cultural lag.

As an example of cultural lag, Sociologists say that, the production of oil helped material development of Arabian countries. But they lagged behind in the non-material development. It is difficult to change man's concept of values and practices.

Every day there are modern inventions in science and technologies. The development of information is drastic. There are sudden changes in the lifestyle of people. Today is different from yesterday and tomorrow will be totally different from yesterday. Society has undergone a total change by adopting the gifts of scientific achievements. So, great changes are acquired in material aspects of culture. At the same time non-material aspects of culture like values, customs, practices etc have been left behind. This gap that can be observed and

*The effect of cultural lag can be experienced in our village life. We have drastic development in communication technologies like telephone or e-mail. It is material change. But, especially in village community, these changes are not assimilated with the social practices of the culture. No closely related family or kith and kin will attend a marriage function, if they are invited by e-mail only. They expect a direct invitation or letter of invitation! Though there have been material developments, values and practices may lag behind. It will take years to change them.*

experienced between material and non-material culture is called cultural lag.

Rigid and conservative outlook of the people, vested interest of leaders, attempts to protect group interests, interests of capitalists, cultural inertia, undesirable attitude of mind, fear, religious beliefs, hesitation to welcome changes and cling with the 'good old' practices, philosophical thought and cultural isolation are some of the factors fostering cultural lag.

Education can bridge the imbalances in cultural aspects. It is the effective way to introduce the modern changes in the society. Curriculum in schools should welcome changes. People can be oriented to the constructive use of technology and its development can be availed by the society through education.

### 2.3.3 Cultural Relativism

Culture is a complex whole. It is the combination of complex units and traits. The existence of cultural traits of unknown origin has been found in all cultures. In a cultural pattern, certain traits or subculture, or alternatives may change from time to time. This change is an adjustment for the smooth running of social relations. Normally these changes or alternatives will not affect the totality of the whole of cultural pattern. The change in trait or adoption of alter-natives is being accepted by the culture of the community. This acceptance is based on cultural relativism. Hence, accommodating harmoniously a change or subculture with the existing culture is cultural relativism.

Sociologists show the abortion in Christian community as an example of cultural relativism. Abortion is against to Christian belief. But they do it to protect individual health or socioeconomic conditions. Then it becomes acceptable to their cultural pattern. People reject disharmonious elements and try to retain useful characteristics.

Every subculture or any change in a culture must harmoniously fit in with the rest of the culture. This harmonious acceptance of change is called cultural relativism. It is an adoption of reality, in order to maintain smooth social life.

Education has significant role in accommodating new traits to the existing cultural pattern. It functions as a filter in selecting alternatives and solutions to the problems. Education defines the need and significance of changes from the existing way of complex units. It preserves, transmits and enriches the traits and complex units of culture. Education transforms the cultural patterns from community to community and generation to generation.

### 2.3.4 Cultural Pluralism

The concept cultural pluralism reveals the pluralism in the culture. Culture is not a single or isolated concept. It includes the physical world, the mental world, the world of thought or idea, the world of beliefs and customs, the social world and the emotional world. Culture is the result of the combined function of all these factors. Culture is not the development of a single factor, but the development of all of these (plural) factors. The plurality of aspects is the basic characteristic of culture. Culture is a collective result of all aspects. This special behaviour of culture with equal importance to all aspects in the whole of culture can be called cultural pluralism.

### 2.3.5 Cultural Conflict

Cultural conflict is he conflict between two groups in the same cultural pattern. The conflict may arise between groups like one group exploiting the society and another trying to reform the society. The conflict may arise between groups in connection with the practice of trait. This is known as cultural conflict. The dispute between two or more groups on a trait or complex unit in the same cultural pattern is called cultural conflict. It is also a conflict of individuals or a group with the social environment while one fails to adjust with new social reforms. Cultural conflict may be the conflict between two different cultural patterns with regard to the assimilation of reforms or invasions. Right education can only bring about solution to conflict.

### 2.3.6 Acculturation

Due to cultural contact, the traits of one culture may dominate the pattern of the other culture. This process can be called acculturation. More than eighty years of rule of British in Kenya changed the cultural pattern of Kenyan community according to the British culture. Not even a single unit of culture spread to the British community from Kenya. This is an example of acculturation.

An individual in the community may absorb the traits and practices. He is acculturated by the society. Normally the acculturation process denies filtering. It is the direct acceptance of cultural traits by the existing social behaviors. If a forest dweller lives in the city for years and absorbs the urban culture, we can say his social behaviour is acculturated. Acculturation is a type of cultural invasion.

### 2.3.7 Enculturation and Transmission of Culture

Enculturation is basically synonymous with the word socialization. It is conscious or unconscious conditioning occurring within the learning process, where man as a child and adult achieves competence in his culture.

M E Goodman describes the term enculturation as a process of transmitting a culture to the young. It takes place through an informal and unconscious process and transmits to the present and also to the following generations.

Transmission of culture is a process, which helps an individual to understand the culture of the society in which he lives. It is a type of cultural diffusion. Transmission of culture ensures the continuity of culture from one generation to the next.

**Transformation of Culture**

By transformation, a culture modifies itself by acquiring more and more aspects, traits and complex units. The Indian cultural practices like Sati are not practiced any more because of the impact of Western culture on Indian culture.

Transformation is conscious or unconscious spread of culture. By transformation a culture receives new traits. It avoids some practices from the existing pattern. Transformation of culture is an educational and social process.

**Culture Contact**

Man is born in cultural isolation, but grows within the walls of culture. Culture grows within the geographical bounds. But it flourishes through assimilation. No culture can withstand isolation. Culture is not a static entity. A great culture is always dynamic. It will be eclectic. Its door will be open to welcome whatever is new. Intolerance of and indifference to the changing conditions is non-cultural and destructive. To ensure dynamism of culture, it needs cultural contact. Cultural contact is a reciprocal contact between different cultural systems. Carrying of cultural traits or sub-culture from one culture to another culture through interaction is termed cultural contact.

Some traits in any culture might be the contribution of another culture. Culture contact has always been in operation. This has certain conditions like desire among people, geographical unity, possibility of communication, possibility of acceptance of new traits etc.

For example, India, long ago, had established commercial relations with the South Asian countries. The traits they mutually transmitted can still be seen in the culture of South East Asia and in India.

## Specific Role of Education in the Socio-Cultural Processes

Seeking the help of the pre-phase of the Kothari Commission report on Education, we can say that the destiny of a country is to be shaped by her education. Education is the most basic medium of cultural changes because of the three-fold functions such as conservative, transmitting and progressive functions. Education preserves the cultural heritage, transmits the conserved culture to the new generation, and stimulates positive cultural changes in the society. Education can trans-form cultural aspects of society by providing opportunities and experiences through which the individual can nurture himself for adjustment with the emerging needs and socio-cultural principles of the changing pattern. Education is the one and only accepted instrument to make these changes desirable.

## 2.4 Society

Society is an abstract concept. Sociology makes a scientific study of society. The term society is used in different ways. For example, a group of women is called a women's society. Society is considered as a corporate body. It is defined separately from the terms groups and community.

F H Giddings defined "society is the union itself, the organization, the some of formal relations, in which asso-ciation of individuals are found together." From the definition we can see that society is a voluntary union. It is the total complex of human relationship. Men with common attitude form the society. 'Society may be visualized as the behaviour of human beings and the consequent problems of relationships and adjustment that arise.'

A society is a collection of individuals united by certain relations or modes of behaviour. These relations and modes of behaviour differentiate them from others. Others may have no chance to enter into these relations. According to E B Reuter 'society is an abstract term that can note the complex of interrelations that exist between and among the members of the group'.

Society is a complex of forms or processes each of which is living and growing by interaction with the other. The whole being unified what takes place in one part affects all the rest. Society means the whole system of social relationships. It is a system of usages and procedures of authority and mutual aid, of many groupings and divisions, of control of human behaviour and of liberties. Society is a web of social relationships. Some of these social relationships are simple, some are complex, some are temporary and some are permanent. These relationships include behaviour, customs, modes of operations, authority, assistance etc.

'Society is a system of usages and procedures of authority and mutual aid, of many groupings and divisions, of control of human behaviour and liberties'.

### 2.4.1 Social Change

Society in its aspects has never been absolutely static. It changes from time to time. The change that occurs to the social pattern is called social change.

Social change is social evolution. Whenever there are changes in mores, beliefs, customs, habits, purposes and attitudes, it is called social change. It is the change in the social relationship, social process, social pattern, social interactions and social organizations. It is a continuous process. Social change may be:

a) **Exogenous change** – when change arises from outside the social system. For example, in India the British rule had considerable role in making social change.

b) **Endogenous change** – when change in the social pattern arises from the existing social system. For example, revolution in the society makes drastic changes.

Social change is the result of intermingling of traditions, practices and innovations. It occurs from the interaction of factors with the existing social pattern – historical, environmental, technological, literal, personal contributions and so on. Man is a dynamic being, hence society, which is constituted by men, can never remain static. It undergoes constant variation.

Human society is constituted of human beings. Thus, whatever apparent alteration in the mutual behaviour between individuals takes place is a sign of social change. Man is a dynamic being; hence society can never remain static. It undergoes constant variation. In other words, since man changes, society has automatically been changed.

## 2.4.2 Definition of Social Change

Social change is defined as a change in social structure in the form of the size of the society, its composition, and balance of its parts or the type of its organization. "Social change is a term used to describe variations or modifications of any aspect of social processes, social patterns, social interactions, or social organization" – Jones

Another definition of social change is that (by K Davis) 'social change is meant only such alterations as secure in social organization, that is, the structure and functions of society'.

Ogburn defined "social change means change in the culture and its chief factors; material culture and non material culture"

**How does Social Change Occur?**

There are several theories that explain the phenomena of social change. The teleological explanation to change says that every change in this universe occurs on the basis of certain predetermined design.

Another explanation is that social change takes place in logical cyclic evolution. Change is an inherent characteristic of the human society.

Sometimes the thoughts and efforts of some great men may bring about changes. The exploitation of natural, industrial, agricultural or any other resources of a country may greatly affect the environment and thereby the social life of the people. The major factors that determine social change are:

a) Influence of exceptional or great men
b) Impact of ideologies and ideals
c) Effect of cultural diffusion
d) Impact of changes in physical environment
e) Impact of science and technology and inventions
f) Change through collective actions (a collective attempt by members of legislative assembly can make changes in social life)
g) Impact of war and calamities
h) Contributions of heredity and environment
i) Economic impact
j) Education

Other factors influencing social change, especially in states like India, are population, development of means of communication, rapid progress in the connection between villages and cities, growth of cities and suburban areas, judicial interpretations, growth of mass media, social legislation and social awakening, lessening of caste system, inventions. The policies of Liberalization, Privatization and Globalization and psychological factors are also having an important role in creating social change.

### 2.4.3 An Explanation of Factors or Determinants Influencing Social Change

Social change results from the interaction of various factors – historical, environmental, cultural factors, technological and scientific developments, voluntary actions of individual, cultural diffusion and so on.

**Ideological factors:** Social changes may occur due to ideological changes, sometimes without the society being aware of it. For example, the Nazi rule changed the social life of Germany. The Islamic rule in Pakistan created social change in that country. The principles of non-violence and tolerance have influenced attitude and created changes in political and social life in India. Thus ideological factors are very important in social change. Ideas related with various areas like philosophy, religion, politics and economics are causing many social changes

**Historical factors:** Historical factors may totally change the social system in different ways. The historical partition of India created a new way of life and abstinence in Pakistani Muslims. The historical decision to ban slavery in USA changed the social stratification of that country to a great extent.

**Environmental factors:** physical environment may change the pattern of community. Volcanic eruption, earthquake, tsunami, storm or any other natural calamity affects the social life pattern of the community. The bombing on Hiroshima changed the pattern of the life of Japanese society.

**Cultural factors:** The main cause of social change is the cultural factor. Changes in culture are accompanied by social change. Any changes in culture inevitably influence the social relationships. Actually the limit and direction of social change are determined by culture.

Cultural diffusion is a significant factor in social change. Society, which is isolated from outside, tends to be static. The society, which is communicates and interacts with others acquires new elements and patterns. They are responsible for social change.

**Technological factors:** Technological factors have immense influence on social change. Technology changes society by changing our environments to which we in turn adapt. This change is usually in the material environment and the adjustment we make to the changes often modifies customs and social practices. The scientific discoveries and technical or technological inventions like electricity, solar energy, atomic energy, and computer and the dominant aims and aspirations of society are major determinants of social change.

Language, both written and spoken also has considerable role in bringing about social change.

Demographic factors like migration, birth and death rate and population explosion are important in social change. The size and composition of population determine the regular life structure of the society. In India, for example, the population explosion is becoming a barricade for desirable changes in the society. Changes in the quality and size of population have an effect upon the social organization as well as customs and traditions, institutions and associations. Increase and decrease of population, a change in the ratio of men and women, young and old etc have effect on social structure and relationships.

**Biological factors (heredity):** This factor has some indirect influence upon social change. There is a saying that the qualitative aspect of the population is related with heredity. The 'qualitative birth' is dependant to a large extent upon heredity and mutation.

Most of the sociologists consider psychological factors as an important element in social change. The psychology of change is important in social change. Man is always trying to discover new things in every sphere of his life and is always anxious for novel experiences. As a result of this psychological tendency, the values, mores, traditions, practices and etc of human society are perpetually undergoing change. Change is a psychological law of human mind.

### 2.4.4 Education and Social Change

Social change is a fact of social life. All social changes are not progressive or for the good. Some changes may adversely affect the preservation of traditions, cultural heritage and old practices. It is education that brings about progressive and desirable social change. It is education that preserves cultural heritage and practices while changes come into form. At the same time, while preserving, conserving, assimilating and transforming, education can modify culture effectively.

A sound system of education, as an agency of social change, renders social progress, social mobility and social control. Education and social change are interactive social phenomena. An aptly developed individual through right type of thinking and right type of knowledge is necessary for desirable social change. Education supplies that knowledge and that type of thinking. Teachers, as the vital part of educational processes, are the great architects who can bring about desirable social change.

Education can transform society by providing opportunities and experiences through which the individuals can cultivate them for adjustment with the emerging needs and philosophy of changing society. Education must make pupils socially conscious. The curricular and other framework of education must familiarize pupils with the problems of society.

Some of the specific roles of education in promoting social change are the following

— Education is the best device that can be used for desirable social change

— Education familiarizes pupils with social change and makes them socially conscious

— Education emphasizes on social behaviour and social values. These are a must for desirable social change.

— Education provides better employment opportunities. It is a subjective necessity for positive social change.

— Schools adopt modern methods of teaching, which emphasize social behaviour and social values.

— Education gives opportunities for an individual's development according to his own capacity and environment. At the same time it teaches an individual to live according to the social norms. Education develops the personality of child and prepares the child for the effective membership in the society.

Education as an instrument of social change brings about desirable and effective changes in the society through its centers and ways of learning – formal, informal and non-formal. But it is felt that 'it is easier for society to change education than for education to change society.'

### 2.4.5 Social Control

Society is a collective form of individuals and groups. There have certain norms and practices among them in forming the society. Social control is the control over the tendency of the individual to deviate from the approved standard norms of the society. It does not mean fencing of individual freedom. Social control is a control on the unsocial and anti social behaviour of the individual. This control is exercised when there is deviation from the approved standards of society. Social control, which implies the social intercourse is regulated in accordance with established and recognized standards. It is comprehensive, omnipotent and effective in stimulating order, discipline and mutuality. Social control is effective in discouraging and if need be to punishing the deviance.

Each society has its own cultural practices, norms, customs, beliefs, subculture and conventions. Each society develops its own social discipline. At the same time each individual member of the society may have different attitudes towards these social values and norms. An individual may possess his own self-discipline. This may create conflict and hence raise the tendency to get rid of the social norms. Social control is an attempt to develop positive approach towards social discipline. It is the control on attempt to deviate from the standard norms. In a complex society, there might be harmful factors and forces. They have to be controlled effectively. It is here that social control has to be exercised in order to keep within the accepted and desirable practices.

There are different types of social controls like direct social control, indirect social control, formal social control, informal social control, positive and negative control and social control by sanction and control by socialization and education.

Norms, values, folkways, mores, customs, beliefs, established systems, ideology, public opinion, technological advancement, law, education, mental attitude or psychological factor and compulsion or oppression are the major factors and means of social control.

## Definition of Social Control

'Social control means the way in which the entire social order coheres and maintains itself, how it operates, as a changing equilibrium.' MacIver and Page.

According to Brearly, "social control is a collective term for those processes and agencies, planned and unplanned, by which individuals are taught, persuaded or compelled to conform to the usages and life values of the group they belong."

According to Moore "social control can be defined as the sum total or whole of cultural patterns and social symbols with collective meanings. It attempts to maintain equilibrium and takes steps for creative adjustment."

### Social Control and Education

Education is major means of social control. It is a device to preserve and transform the norms of society. Education inculcates the social discipline amongst the individuals so as to protect the interests of society by trying to avoid antisocial and unsocial behaviour. Education is a social process, which attempts to eliminate inhuman activities and brings about virtues in the society. Education impels man to grow in the context and realities of the society and not to deviate from the accepted social norms. It develops social discipline and self-discipline among members of the society.

Education is a great vehicle of social control. It inculcates socially approved moral, intellectual, personal and social values in individuals. Education imparts a sense of continuity of values, customs, beliefs, system etc. Hence, education functions as an effective formal means of social control.

## 2.4.6 Social Mobility

Social mobility is a social phenomenon. It means movement within the social structure. Social mobility is the phenomenon of movement of a person within the social structure or social space. It is a change from one category to another. For example, a schoolteacher becoming the director of state's curriculum construction committee is a movement or change. It is a change from one category to another.

In most of the societies people are classified into different strata or categories. These categories are ranked from higher to lower order. This process is called social stratification. Stratification may be based on caste, religion, economic and socio-cultural background and so on. Social mobility is a movement from one stratum to another due to several influencing factors.

Social mobility takes place when there is a change in occupational level, educational level, income level, style of life etc. Change in occupation is the best indicator of social mobility. Mobility is a specific kind of social change. Evaluation of social mobility is applicable. Movement from one category to another seems to be an upward mobility to one society but may not be a mobility criterion to another society.

## Types of Mobility

Mainly there are two types of social mobility: Vertical mobility and Horizontal mobility. Special movement is also considered as a type of mobility. (It is a type of migration. A family change their residence from rural locality to urban area, is a special movement.)

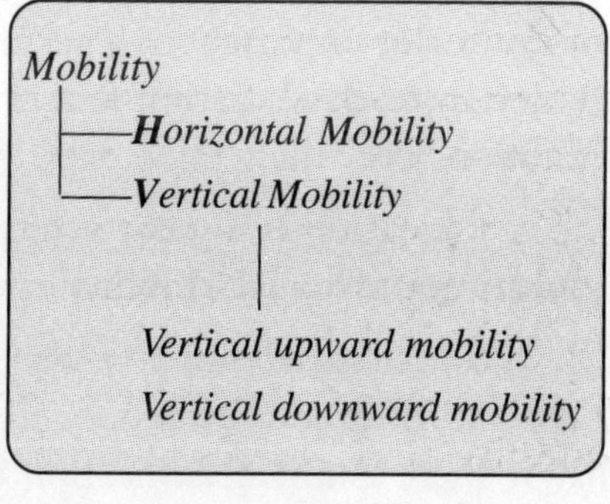


Change or movement of a person from one situation to another, without experiencing further change in his social life level is horizontal mobility. Here the individual move from one situation to another without any change in his status and there is no rank difference between two situations. For example, the proprietor of a confectionary shop changes his business to a stationery shop is a movement. It is a horizontal mobility. When an industrial laborer becomes an agriculture laborer or vice-versa, without drastic change in income, he has moved horizontally within the social structure.

Vertical mobility is not a simple movement from one situation to another. It is a movement from one stratum of society to another stratum with notable changes in the life of the individual who moves. An alteration in position or status upward or downward is called vertical mobility. Movement from existing stratum to a higher order stratum is upward vertical mobility. Movement from existing stratum to a downward stratum is downward vertical mobility. If a shop-keeper becomes an exporter, it is upward vertical mobility. If the shopkeeper becomes an unemployed, it is downward vertical mobility.

Personality pattern of social mobility is an important subject of study. Values, aspirations, IQ, EQ, DIQ and achievement motivation are positively correlated with social mobility. The occupational status of parents, values and aspirations prevailing at home are also important in a person's social mobility. A student of a lower caste\class\stratum and or rural area tends to have lower aspiration level than those who hail from upper class or urban area.

## Education and Social Mobility

Positive social mobility is a good element of an ideal society. It is possible by education only. Education emphasizes a principle that if there is any classification of individuals it must be done keeping in view the capacity and ability and not the class or caste of birth. Education enables people to realize the best of their capacities and abilities so as to overcome the hindrances arising from family and social stratification. It also helps individuals to realize what they are and what they can be; this realization is a must for accelerating upward vertical mobility.

Upward vertical mobility results from advancement in education. Education imparts essential skills and competencies, which may help an individual to achieve mobility. The adverse effects of aspiration level of family and community can be eliminated by education. Education is the only effective possible solution to eradicate the problems of social stratification. Education directly influences getting a better job and raises income, thus raising social status. Achievement of higher education itself is a social mobility.

Education works as a filter of social norms. The conflict between an individual's urge for mobility and control of society is smoothly handled by education. It can change the situation by changing the values and norms of society in desirable ways. Education has two-fold functions in an individual's social mobility. It functions as a stage setter to achieve mobility. At the same time education is a device that can directly contribute to social mobility of persons.

### Social Progress

Social progress is a type of social change. All social changes may not be desirable or progressive. For example, change of a society from its secular outlook to religious is a social change. If a well-governed society falls in to anarchy, it is a social change. These are not desirable or positive social changes.

Social progress is desirable as a positive social change. Social progress is possible by developing a sense of equality and self-esteem in the members of the society. Social progress is the necessity of any civilized society. It is the process that takes place in dynamic social groups.

### Education and Social Progress

Education plays a vital role in social progress. In the case of positive social change like social progress, education has to perform three fold functions: a) conservative b) transmission, and c) progressive functions.

Conservative function of education in social progress means preserving the cultural heritage of a society. It preserves the cultural heritage, which is worthwhile and with standing. Transmission function means transmitting the preserved culture to the new generation; i.e., acculturation. Progressive function means progressive by distributing new knowledge to generate dynamism in cultural life and stimulate positive and desirable change in the society.

Education has some other specific formal and informal functions in providing social progress. School as center of education becomes a laboratory to formulate the elements for social progress. School ensures all-round growth of a person so that he is able to formulate the requirements of social progress.

Education is a motivating factor of social progress. It motivates the rising generation to adopt new elements in order to remain dynamic and forward looking. Such a society attains social progress. Education takes initiative and responsibility of social progress.

Mind is an important element in social progress. Mind develops through right type of thinking and right type of knowledge. Education supplies these two factors. Teachers have a great role in bringing about the progress in the society. In short education is the best instrument to postulate social progress.

# Introduction to Educational Sociology

Educational sociology is comparatively a new subject. But it is an inevitable subject to understand the discipline of education and its interrelations with social processes. Sociology of education helps to understand the influences of social units in education also.

This chapter deals with the Educational Sociology. The reader can easily grasp the major content aspects of sociology and educational sociology from this chapter. Outline of the content is given under:

*Sociology*

- *Meaning and definition*

*Educational sociology*

- *Nature, scope and Impact of educational sociology*

*Agencies of education*

- *Educational functions of socializing agencies –*
  - *Family,*
  - *Peer group,*
  - *Community,*
  - *School and state*

*Community school*

*Concept of socialization*

Sociology is a science dealing with man and his life in his society. It has tremendous influence on education. This chapter deals with sociology, sociology of education and educational sociology.

The first introduction to mankind is that man is a social animal. He lives in the society. The social life makes a man a man. He has no 'life' outside the society. Man leads his life as an individual and as a member of the society. He carries out his social life as a member of groups and organizations like family, peer groups, community, clubs, schools, political parties, political and non-political associations, guilds etc. This fulfills his safety, economic interests, security, personal development, culture, common interests, ambitions and aspirations. There are inseparable connections between an individual and his groups; in vast sense with his society. Every individual is born and bought up in some primary social groups like family, peer groups and community. The study of these social relations of an individual is necessary for the effective launching of education. Here comes the significance of educational sociology.

## 3.1 Sociology

### 3.1.1 Sociology: Meaning and Definition

Sociology is the science of society. It studies the society and social institutions, as they exist. So, sociology is a social science that concerns man and society as they are. Its subject matter is society: society as an organic whole, group living of human beings. The interrelations of social institutions, the social relations and social structure are part of its field of study.

Auguste Comte is known as the father of sociology. Auguste Comte coined the term 'social physics' to study the society and he himself replaced it with the term 'sociology' later. Sociology as a discipline is comparatively of recent origin. Comte believed that the study of sociology would remove the ignorance about the social institutions. Sociology is social consciousness, because it is the study of the interactions of human minds and social actions. According to Max Weber 'sociology is a science which attempts the interpretive understanding of social action in order, thereby to arrive at a casual explanation of its course and effects'.

A better understanding of the nature and scope of sociology can be understood from the following definitions:

LF Ward, "sociology is the science of society"

JW Bennet and MM Tumin, "sociology is the science of the structure and function of social life."

K Young, "sociology deals with the behaviour of men in group"

T Abel, "sociology is the scientific study of social relationship, their variety, their forms, whatever affects them and whatever they affect."

From the above definitions we can avail a clear picture that sociology is scientific study about man and his social relations. Education is considered as a device to develop man's socialization and social efficiency. Hence sociology of education is important in the planning. design and execution of education. The subject matter of sociology of education is relevant and important. As a product of the sociology of education, educational sociology is important in determining the role of education in present society.

## 3.2 Educational Sociology

Educational sociology is the sociological approach to educational phenomena. It is the sociological studies in the field of education. Education is a device for social change. The effective use of education as a desirable and effective instrument for social changes is possible through educational sociology. It tries to find solutions to sociological issues and problems in education.

Education is the interaction of the individual with his environment. Environment has a wide connotation. Educational sociology, as a branch of sociology, studies the interaction of an individual with his social and cultural environment. It studies the effect of these environments on the individual and ways and means for its desirable changes. It is not a theoretical study, but a practical science. Educational sociology gives suggestions and provides practical ways for reforming and restructuring education with sociological perspective. It is the application of sociological principles in education. Educational sociology as suggested by experts "starts with the assumption that education is an activity which goes on in society and the society in its turn determines the nature of education.'

**Why educational sociology?** Educational sociology has an important role in developing the standard of social life, because it focuses on the social development of the individual. Education must train an individual to carry out his social responsibilities. This is the aim of educational sociology. Social progress is the ultimate aim declared by sociological view of education. Sociology influences education in its all aspects. The planning, process, aims and objectives, functions, curriculum, methods, freedom and discipline and teachers role are highly influenced by education. Actually sociological analysis is the resource for determining these aspects.

Educational sociology studies the relation between education and society. As a science educational sociology tries to explain interactions of individual with social environment and social groups. It determines the social need of educational system. It is a detailed discussion of effect of education on society and vice versa. Its major aim is the attainment of better personality by effective social interaction. So, *educational sociology can be defined as a scientific study of relations between education and society, and action and interaction of individual and his social groups.* It is the sociological explanation for educational aspects, problems and issues.

### 3.2.1 Nature, Scope and Impact of Educational Sociology

According to John Dewey, 'curriculum and methods are the products of social situations'. Educational sociology does not allow education to get aloof from the social affairs. It comprises areas concerning social realities.

Education is not a process happening inside the classroom. It must be related with child's experiences in the family, community, organizations and society at large. Educational sociology opposes the emphasis on individual's growth development by education. It concentrates on education as a means of social change, social control, social progress, cultural progress and mobility.

Educational sociology has wide scope in education scenario. It studies the impact of formal agencies (church, temple, school, state, club, TV, radio and etc.) and informal agencies (family, peer group, community and etc.) on the educational development of individual. Socialization and social efficiency of individual also form a part of educational sociology. Thus, scope of educational sociology varies from the study of individual's social development to the agencies that influence education. It also discusses:

a) social interaction
b) group living
c) cooperation and cohesiveness
d) social adaptation and assimilation
e) social conflicts
f) social norms
g) culture and related aspects, *and*
h) social values

These influence the education system and development of individual and society.

Educational sociology attempts a sense of active participation of individual in social life and cooperation with social order and norms. It is the resource data for determining the various aspects of education such as aims, curriculum, methods, discipline and role of teacher.

Aims of education are connected with conditions, norms, trends and system of existing society. Social life and culture of society influence the aims. The need of education itself is aroused out of man's social life. For example, promotion of social unity and development of secular citizenship should be the aims of education in India. It aims at social unity irrespective of caste, creed and other factors, as social stratification based on caste and religion so strong in India. Education must aim at the preparation of an individual to adjust with the society. Education is an activity, which goes on in a society and its aims depend upon the nature of the society. The aims of education like education for citizenship, education for social effectiveness, for democracy, for social integration, for socialization, for cultural transmission, cultural transformation and education for individual's social development are directly developed from the area of educational sociology.

In the case of curriculum and methods, educational sociology has vital roles. John Dewey said, "Curriculum and methods are the products of social situation." The influence of the social situation on education is the content matter of educational sociology. Curriculum should include the realities of social life. A good curriculum and adopted method for its transaction should reflect the realities of social life concerned. Needs, demands, conditions and aspirations of the society contribute to design the structure of the curriculum. These contributions are determined by educational sociology. The curricular content and methods have to be active in realizing the social aims of education. It should reflect the social values. To educational sociology, education is a social process. Learning is not a teacher-pupil business, but the result of social interaction and social motivation. Yet it so, the methods should be changed according to the conditions and needs of the society. The emergence of new methods like project method, socialized recitation, simulation techniques, seminar symposium, group discussion are the contribution of educational sociology.

Discipline of an individual emerges out of his social life. Qualified freedom and discipline are to be inculcated by all types of social institutions. It is the result of social interaction. In fact many disciplinary problems depend upon the social life. The realities of discipline can be grasped from the social life and conditions.

Educational activities will be inadequate unless the teacher conceives the social realities in terms of educational sociology. A teacher must be up-to-date about the social order in which he lives. He should be aware of the possibilities of educational sociology in educational scenario. The realization of why education is being provided to the teacher by the educational sociology.

An educational system which meets the socio-cultural, physical, economic, emotional needs of the society and which considers complete development of individual in social context is the perfectly organized education system. Such an organized system can be organized only with the help of educational sociology.

## 3.3 Agencies of Education

There are several social agencies of education like family, school, peer groups, community, organized clubs, associations, technological agencies like TV, radio and the state. Some of them are formal agencies and some are informal. The may function formally and informally at the same time. They are the agencies through which the aims of educational sociology are satisfied. The importance of these agencies is discussed here to get a clear picture of the wide scope of education in social context.

Mainly there are two types of agencies; primary groups and secondary groups. Family, peer groups and community are known as primary groups. They are 'we' groups or in groups. School, associations, clubs, states, etc. are known as secondary groups or 'they' group or out groups. 'In group' is an association towards which an individual shows a sense of loyalty and commitment. The members have great respect, confidence and attachment to this group. In out group an individual views the other members with indifference and disrespect. An individual is able to take part in social life by the interaction effects of all these agencies.

"Man is man, only when he lives in society", says Durkheim. Man is being socialized through action, interaction and reaction among individuals and these social units. Through interaction an individual develops social personality and thus he is socialized.

### 3.3.1 Family as Agency of Education

The first primary group the individual enters is the family. It has great responsibility towards an individual's personality development and socialization. Family is a social unit. It is an informal agency of education. Membership of an individual in family is by birth.

There are two types of families, a) *conjugal family* and b) *consanguine family*. Conjugal family is the marital family. It consists of married pair. Husband, wife and children are the members of a conjugal family. It is a type of nuclear family or micro family. Consanguine family is based upon blood relations. There will be a large number of members in this family who might be kith and kin. Family connections make this family united. They are the joint family or extended family.

On the basis of marriage also some distinctions of family have been made such as a) polygamous family, in which one marries two or more women, b) polyandrous family, in which one woman marries two or more men and c) monogamous family, in which one man marries one woman only.

Family functions are divided under six heads. They are affectionate, economic, recreational, protective, religious and educational. Of these all sociologists accept reproduction maintenance (family being a structural arrangement, its function is the maintenance of its members), socialization and placement (through family child gets social placement, status and social role) as the essential functions of family.

## Characteristics of Family as an Educational Agency

Family is considered as a unit of economic production and social life. Unity is its major trait. Each family has its own traditions, mode of living, interests, ends and even mannerisms. Family functions as an institution at many times. Family is a formally constituted unit with informally delivered functions. It is highly informal in all functions. It is the group for rearing of children! Certain families function as formal centers of learning. They give special stream of education to the students who seek education.

There is a saying that charity begins at home. Almost all values are acquired and practiced in the family. Along with educational functions, the family has to perform several other functions. It gives security, entertainment, free feeding and suitable environment to children. The family is a unit of economic production and social life. Democracy has its strong roots in the family. Family looks after all aspects of child's development, physical, emotional, intellectual, cultural, moral and social. Hence we can say that family is the most effective agency of informal education.

## Educational Functions of Family

Education is a process that starts from the birth. Mother is the first teacher and family is the first school. There is a saying that education does not begin with reading and writing, but begins with mother's look, father's nod of approval, sister's gentle interaction and brother's noble act of moderation. The values and ideals are developed from the family. A child develops the qualities of love, tolerance and democratic way of interaction from the family. Family is the nursery of human nature. The learning from family will be effective and ever existing. Home educates not only the growing child but also adults. Members in the family are always in reciprocal contact. They teach each other indirectly. They learn indirectly from others expressions. "We" feeling, love, affection and consideration bind the members together. Communication in the family is deep and all-embracing.

Family can be considered as the first school in the history of human education. Even the formal education had taken place in the family for several years. Family functions provide the members with security, emotional integration, and social recognition. Family is the premier agency of an individual's socialization. The primary function of family is, thus, the child's socialization. It is the source of the child's physical, intellectual, emotional, moral and social development. The process of socialization starts in the family. Family is the premier non-formal agency that teaches the child his social role and identity.

Some other specific functions of family are the following:

— Family provides nourishment of individuality, health practices, value development and also adequate care

— Child develops adjustment mechanism from family.

— Child learns to learn from the family.

— It provides provisions for developing virtues and moralities.

— It provides an informal training to all members for a better and well-knit life.

— Family trains to give and take love, respect, obedience, affection and a sense of security. Democratic sense, democratic principles, good manners and habits and way of life are taught in the family.

— Effective socialization through informal methods.

Family atmosphere has an important role in a child's personal and social development. The functions, dialogical actions, rituals, traditional practices, conversations, incidental or accidental directions and other activities function as source of knowledge, values, ideals, attitudes etc. A child develops a sense of consideration from this informal atmosphere. Family is the suitable environment for emotional development and emotional learning. It is the agency for cultural preservation, transmission and transaction. Family is the centre for physical development too. The famous sociologist CH Cooley considered family as "the nursery of human nature". Home educates not only the child but also the adults. It is the source of income for child's formal education. Family invests in child's formal education, social life, recreation, and all other development. Family educates an individual in all senses. It makes an individual a social animal from a biological animal.

### 3.3.2 Peer Group as Agency of Education

Peer group is another primary agency for a child's socialization and education. It is an informal agency. Peer groups are voluntarily formed effective groups. Members of peer groups possess 'we' feeling. Playgroups, gangs, school friends, neighborhoods, friendship groups and club associates belong to peer society.

The members of a peer group may be equal in maturity, age, status and prestige. Usually a peer group is not a formally or purposively organized group. Members share common interests. Recreation and play are the major aims of their association. There is no hierarchy of status and predetermined role among members within a peer group. Keeping separate individual identity in a peer group is possible, but difficult. Membership in groups and relationship between members are not permanent or long lasting.

## Types of Peer Groups

There are different types of peer groups. Some are

a) playgroup

b) gangs

c) cliques

d) youth membership groups.

### *a) Playgroups*

Playgroups are informally organized groups of young children. They are neighborhood groups mainly formed for play and enjoyment. This might be the first group that children form outside their family. Child's association with a playgroup or membership in a playgroup will not be a deliberate selection but a matter of chance. Normally there is no chance to consider caste, creed, color and sex to for a playgroup or to consider one as a member in the group. Children are least bothered about these factors. Members in the playgroup will have strong relationship among them. Parents have a vital role in determining the 'time of function', plays and interaction possibilities of the playgroups.

### *b) Gangs*

The groups formed by children above twelve years of age are called gangs. Ganging is a teenage characteristic. Ganging tendency is an adolescence tendency. Diffused, conventionalized, solidified, creative, criminal and secret society type gangs are the major six types of gangs. Gangs are formed formally and informally. The members of the gang consciously try to keep their individuality in spite of their wholehearted association with the gang. Members might have common interests and common aims. Gangs may be organized in classrooms, schools, colleges, hostels and in residential areas.

Generally gangs are formed with the same sex. Gender difference is significant in its organization. This group may have a leader. Such leadership is not a formally placed candidacy and is not a stable post.

Gangs have several positive effects. It is a powerful device for an individual's socialization. Ganging is a social recognition. Members experience and share love, consideration and other personal and social values in this grouping. At the same time, gangs have certain adverse effects too. Gangs may be organized, either formally or informally for carrying on antisocial activities like gambling, blackmailing, kidnap, ragging, street harassing and etc. Occasionally they may function as counterparts of secret associations and under-world dons. Such gangs do anything for their own selfish ends.

*c) Cliques*

Cliques are smaller groups. Members of clique possess strong 'we' feeling. They have close intimacy with common attitudes, interests, opinions, ideals and values. Cliques are formed in neighbourhood, in joint family, in classrooms, schools and in hostels. Members of this type of group try to be aloof from others. They have a tendency to confine themselves to their own shells.

*d) Youth Membership Groups (Clubs)*

These types of groups are secondary groups. Clubs, organizations like YMCA, NCC, NSS and Scouts & Guides are the examples. They are formally organized groups with youngsters as members. They are formed sometimes by themselves and sometimes by others. Generally they are formed for certain social programmes.

**Educational Functions of Peer Groups**

Peer group acts as an instrument for socialization, which is an important aim of education. It develops leadership qualities, cooperativeness, love, toleration, cohesiveness, group living, group attitudes, social vocabulary, adjustment with social norms and a spirit of oneness. Proper channeling of peer group activities can function effectively for individual's social and personal development and full expression.

Peer groups are effective devices for socialization of the individual. It is an informal educational agency. As instruments of socialization these groups develop love, cooperation, sympathy, empathy and all personal and social values. Peer groups do not have any formally designed educational function. The members informally learn all social norms from the group living. They learn, sometimes modify or even create sub-culture, rules, principles, customs, practices, conventions, beliefs, manners and, if needed, own language. These informally organized and freely functioning groups provide opportunities for self-expression, creative interpretation and social participation to its members. A child develops imagination, idea formation, concept formation and positive interactions from peer group life. Peer group provides a reciprocal contact between members.

There will be no class discrimination in a peer group. Children form the groups themselves, except secret groups or groups aimed at social evils, irrespective of social strata. The factors like class, caste and creed are not important in forming a group. It helps social mobility of members. It is an agency to impart social justice, citizenship training, democracy, secularism and human rights education.

Peer groups reflect culture of the society. They help in cultural preservation, transmission and transformation. Groups informally assign social roles to individuals. They help individuals to reach educational aims like self-expression, social efficiency and emotional integration.

Children enjoy freedom and leisure in peer groups. This freedom effectively supports the individual member to select his own social role.

**Specific Educational Influence of Peer Groups**

— Peer groups reflect culture of society
— Social learning and language efficiency
— Satisfy cultural aims of education
— Value acquisition and development
— Knowledge acquisition and sharing of knowledge
— Effective socialization, opportunities for social experimentation, self-expression, interaction and adjustment with social norms
— Foster self-realization and social role
— Help to eradicate self-motives, selfishness, arrogance and prejudice
— Satisfy psychological needs like recognition, achievements, appraisal, approval and reinforcement
— Members can learn social formalities, customs, etc.
— Leadership training and follower training

We can find immense educational influence of peer groups. Peer group informally educates its members in almost all social aspects.

### 3.3.3 Community

Community is a group of individuals who live in a definite territorial area or in a definite segment and share a common way of life. Generally, the members of a community exhibit similarity in beliefs, customs, practices, mores, traditions, language, attitude, etc. Members of a community possess a strong 'we feeling'. We feeling is an essential trait of the people belonging to a community.

Specific locality, homogeneity, we feeling, name (every community has some definite name), neutrality, naturality, sincerity and permanence are some of the ***major characteristics*** of a community.

Neutrality is approach of community as a whole towards it members. As a social organization community is impartial in its treatment of members.

Naturality means that communities are not made or created by an act or purposively-oriented task. It has a neutral emergence. An individual is born in a community. Membership of a community is compulsory to the individual. He is born and dies in a community. Community does not have any property of its own.

A community is not a temporary arrangement. It is a permanent social unit. Members may come and go, but community exists forever. It is 'an intimate, private and exclusive living together'. It is based upon community sentiment and sincerity among members.

A community is

— a population aggregate
— sharing a historical heritage
— living in a particular locality or segment
— possessing same cultural beliefs, practices, customs and traditions
— motivated with same ends, and
— participating in a common ode of life.

A community has an area of common living, having common values and even dress code, having common community sentiments and awareness of sharing a common way of life.

**Educational Influence of Community**

Community is an informal agency. It is the largest social unit. Informally it educates individuals through group functions, festivals, social motivation, functions etc. Sometimes community acts as an agency of other agencies. It constitutes and encourages formal and informal agencies of education. Certain communities run their own educational institutions.

The specific educational functions of community are:

— Community provides an opportunity for effective socialization.

— It informally activates the cultural functions of education – preservation, transmission and transformation of culture and acculturation and enculturation.

— It considers educational needs of its members unconditionally.

— Community itself establishes school, colleges and other educational institutions.

— Gives opportunities in needed vocational training

— Functions as a co-coordinator of several educational efforts.

— Provides financial support and needed guidance.

— Develops values and social and personal mores.

— Gives opportunities to individuals to interact with social customs, norms, practices and traditions.

— Helps to develop social adjustment.

Community develops values of cooperation among members. It also helps in adult education, social education, developing democratic way of life, secular outlook, group living and establishing and guiding formal organizations like clubs, associations, libraries etc. Community also provides health education, environmental education, and population education to members. It introduces informal methods of leadership training and citizenship training to individuals. In short, by its informal and formal educational functions, the community serves the individual as a steppingstone for his future social life.

### 3.3.4 School

Etymologically, the term school is derived from a Greek word 'schola' which means leisure. The patricians – leisured class – of Greek society, who did not have to work for their livelihood, were privileged to acquire Greece education. It was a liberal and voluntary engagement of that group in arts, cultural and recreational search to enjoy their leisure. These leisure-spending centers contributed to the development of schools! Now the term school stands for the centre for formal education.

The generation of schools varied from Ashram of ancient sages (Gurukula) to the modern international schools. Schools have a large number of educational functions to practice. They have a lot of responsibilities to perform in the process of education. A school is a centre where education is provided to all those who seek it. The modern world considers school education as a must for all children. Formal school education is not a matter of selection but a matter of necessity now.

A school is the sum total of organized educational functions. It has to follow certain rules, regulations and principles in its function. It is a formal agency that imparts education directly. School aims modification of the behaviour of learners in socially desirable directions.

A school is a resource center. Schools function with preplanned and predetermined educational programmes. There is a saying that 'school should be an idealized embodiment, a model of the community, not merely the world of ordinary affairs, but the whole of humanity with its body and soul, past, present and future'. School is a miniature of the society. Infrastructure facilities like buildings playground, library, laboratory, classroom, furniture, teachers, students and administration system are the main factors that constitute the anatomy of a school. As the centres of formal education, schools systematically follow curriculum, syllabus, extracurricular programmes, classroom teaching methods, textbooks etc.

**Major Educational Functions of Schools**

Schools have to perform formal educational functions. It is a formal agency of education. Schools follow formally designed educational functions. The formal education programme with predetermined aims takes place in schools. Community and state use schools to impart formal education. Schools are the nationally accepted input device of education. It is the arena to practice education. Schools are the centers where the philosophy of a state is activated and experienced.

Main educational functions of schools are

- School is a centre of formal education, which functions according to the philosophy that the state education system follows.
- School imparts useful knowledge in all desirable areas to pupils
- It is the place of practical education and education in 3 *R-s*
- It liberates children from ignorance and prejudice and tries to foster individual efficiency in all matters
- Develops and encourages physical, intellectual and moral powers, knowledge standard, and character formation of children
- School provides desirable effective socialization
- School promotes social efficiency and responsibility in children through varied academic and non-academic activities.
- School promotes harmonious, well-adjusted personalities and ensures all round development of individual

- Effective teaching and learning is planned and practiced in schools for better knowledge acquisition and development of the child
- School develops self-discipline, social discipline and moral values and promotes an individual's capacity for self-direction
- Develops abilities in an individual to adapt and adjust himself with his social environment; hence it prepares him for complete living
- Provides citizenship training, promotes emotional integration, national integration and international understanding
- Training in leadership qualities
- School as a social unit, understands needs, interests, aims and ways of community and individuals and foster them
- Preserves, transmits, transforms and expands culture
- Schools provides awareness and cultivates in children the spirit of service, dignity of labor, spirit of sacrifice and self-reliance
- Cultivates strong attitude in children in democratic way of life and secularism
- School functions as a center of social change and social control

School is the formal education center where the formal teaching and learning take place in all their preplanned forms. And these teaching and learning are the premier aims of schools. They have direct and formal educational assignments to perform in teaching and learning. Schools provide opportunities for exact learning to the learner. Schooling is the synonym with availing formal education.

### 3.3.5 State

State is an organized whole. It is peoples' totality within a territorial area. It is a political grouping of people to protect common interests. The idea of state as an agency of education is as old as Plato. With the advent of democracy and welfare state, education became an essential function of state.

**State as an Agency of Education**

The role of state in the education of its people is the subject of great importance. It is admitted by all that the public education is a state responsibility. Education at the expense of state alone satisfies the social necessities like education for all and equality of educational opportunities. The welfare of the citizens and future of the country depend upon the education provided by the state. Hence, education is an essential function of the state. Educated citizens are the productive assets of the state.

Making of policies and administration of education is effectively possible by state. Educational aspects such as aims, content, curriculum, method, textbooks, appointment of teachers, etc fall under the broad framework of the state. It provides guidance, control, financial support and management of education. The educational system of a state depends upon the administration policies, political ideology and the philosophy that state follows.

Some Specific Functions of State as Agency of Education

— State as an agency of education acts formally, informally and non-formally in education.

— It designs policies pertaining to educational matters.

— Committees, commissions and experts for revamping education are appointed by the state.

— All types of education such as vocational, professional, technological and general education and public education or mass education are planned and executed by the state.

— State makes legislation for the development of the state.

— It functions as an agency of other agencies. State constitutes other agencies like schools, universities, institutions and organizations and supports them for educational development.

— Provides financial help and scholarships to students

— State undertakes responsibilities of education, promotes, coordinates and evaluates educational functions and suggests modifications.

— State's functions are: Organization
Supervision and monitoring
Planning and execution
Assessment,
Financial and other aids and support.

**Other Agencies**

There are several other agencies of education. They may be formal, informal or non-formal in their approach. They influence the educational development of individual and society.

Churches, temples, religion, religious institutions, museum, centers of functions like club, organized recreational and cultural centers, press, TV, radio and the Internet are some of them. Among them, some are functioning as direct agencies of education. For example, the Internet is a direct source of education. Museum gives direct information to a leaner on many things.

Churches and temples were the only formal centers of education sometime before. Now also they undertake a lot in informal education. They are the places of religious education. Culture is being preserved and transmitted by them. Value education, moral education and character formation are possible by these agencies. Some churches run their own educational institutions like schools and colleges.

The radio and television are directly partaking of education. They are the best ways of imparting non-formal education. The educational functions such as knowledge acquisition and training are possible by them. They give relevant and updated information to the learners and learners can make use of them at any time. They refine knowledge, vision, sensitivity, taste, interpersonal abilities, appreciation etc. They are helpful to develop personal skills. Mass education and public education are effective via radio and TV.

The Internet has become an inevitable source of education now. It provides all information at our fingertip. The collec-tion of information has become very easy by this revolution in information technology. The Internet is useful to provide knowledge, the student can avail information; educator or educationist can supply innovative ideas. Online education and online schooling have become a habit of the era through the Internet. The Internet is a source of knowledge; a source of formal and non-formal educational degrees and provider of educational opportunities.

All these agencies influence the educational development of individuals by and large. As agencies of education they enrich the educational development of the state and human society.

## 3.4 Concept of Community School

A school is not a complex of buildings, classrooms and land. School is not an isolated institution. It is not a closed or segregated social unit. School is an 'open forum' admitting school-community cooperation.

In the community school schoolteachers and students live and work hand in hand with local community. Community school undertakes follower-ship and leadership of community.

The school gives real experience of community life. Student will always avail opportunity for selected field of living in community. Unit of work in community projects coined with social life shall be the ways of learning experiences. The unit of work with community involves surveys, social work, fieldtrips, interactive functions, etc.

The community school runs with social-centered curriculum and is not book-centered. It functions according to the convenience of the community; the community does not fit according to the needs of school. Teachers may be the members of the community and not isolated schoolteachers. It fosters hope for socially desirable changes in the outlook and behaviour of pupils. The curriculum, method and other functional strategies of community schools are not formed by the state or its agencies. Such aspects are developed as a cooperative venture of school and community. Community school satisfies the role of school as a social unit. Community school is not a traditional school system with community cooperation, but a system that provides education along with community life.

## 3.5 Socialization and Education

Socialization is the fundamental aim of life; hence it is the aim of all educational processes. In general sense socialization means a tendency to be like others. It is the living as a member in the society. Socialization is the process by which man – a biological animal – becomes a social animal. Through socialization process the individual learns to conform to norms, values and practices of the group. By this the individual accepts ethics and practices of the society to interact and to behave in a socially acceptable manner. Socialization is the result of interaction between individual and individual, individual and group and between group and group.

## Socialization

Socialization is a continuous process, not a concrete object to be achieved. It is a process of acculturation. According to Linberg "The process of interaction through which an individual learns the habits, skills, beliefs and standards of judgment required for effective participation in social groups are collectively called socialization". Drever said, "Socialization is a process by which the individual adapts to his social environment and becomes a recognized, cooperative and efficient member of the environment". Sorokin tried to clarify socialization 'as a process of internalization of ideological and cultural factors, which transforms the biological individual into a social being.' The process of socialization may be through competition, cooperation, conflict, accommodation, assimilation, suggestion and imitation.

## Socialization and Education

The process of socialization starts in the family. But the effective socialization is widely possible through education only, because the scope of family to provide a controlled environment in all aspects of life situations is limited. Natural development socialization process can be practiced in schools rather than in family. School is the miniature of the society. Schools, as specific formal agency of education, are helpful to acquire effective socialization. Schools provide training for social existence. There are opportunities for forming groups, and facilities for mingling and growing up with similar age groups of both sexes. Through the teachers, a child gets the status of adult role. Ideal social rules like equality, justice and fraternity can be directly experienced in the school life.

Education is a formal way of socialization. Education functions as a 'source' for socialization. It is helpful to provide all socially desirable behavior to the educant, which are inevitable for better socialization. Education, through its varied functions, leads individuals to acquire socially desirable knowledge, skills and experiences. It also gives opportunities for participation in group life, social learning and community living. Educational centers function as extensions of the social life. Education is preparing students to perform various roles in life. Along with making individual a social being, education helps him in developing his own personality. By education an individual acquires personal independence while he acts as a socialized individual.

Education is an external control over an individual's unsocial behaviour. It prevents him from social evils. Education 'makes effective participation in total process of interaction in terms of various socially desirable values.' Hence, socialization means progressive learning of desirable roles in the social life. Socialization and education are not different processes. They are complementary and reciprocally integrative. Education is a purposive, formal and conscious effort for socialization. Socialization itself is mostly an unconscious process of an individual and or group. Education is the one and only effective tool to provide socialization in formal ways to the growing child after his family.

# Democracy and Secularism as Educational Determinants

This small chapter discusses the concept of Democracy and Secularism. The explanations are zeroed in on educational aspects of these sociological factors.

*Democracy*

- *Meaning and Concept*
- *Education in a Democratic Society*
- *Democracy in Classroom*

*Secularism*

- *Concept of Secularism*
- *Education in a Secular Society*
- *Secularism and Education*
- *Secularism in Schools or Classrooms*

The reader can get information on democracy, its meaning, interrelations of democracy and education, and its practice in classroom.

From the second part the learner can avail knowledge on secularism, its Western and Indian concepts and its meaning. The readers can also gain insights on secularism in education, education in a secular society and importance of secular practices in classrooms.

**Ability** of education to nourish desirable social outlook is great. Education is a wonderful instrument used to develop social behaviour positively. The pattern of a society can be identified and interpreted with the multiple functions of education. It is a determining factor in developing the social and philosophical outlook of democracy and secularism. Both of them are essentially the needs of the hour. Education must be designed with the view to develop these two social phenomena.

## 4.1 Democracy

Democracy is a term that carries the spirit of cooperation, humanity, love, consideration and renunciation. It is social philosophy influencing modern life greatly as a way of life and form of government. It means democracy stands not only as a political concept but also as a way of life. There is a saying that if any three things influenced modern social life of human beings they are science, industry and democracy. "Democracy is a current think up, a legal tender in many walks of life –economic, social, political and educational." Democracy is democracy in thought and action.

### 4.1.1 Democracy: Meaning and Concept

The word democracy is derived from 'demos', which means people. It denotes the power of people. There is a saying that democracy has its origin from Greek city-states. Some historians believe that democracy has developed as a system in India in some of the ancient Sixteen Mahajanapathas even before the period of Greek city-states.

Usually, democracy is considered as a system for political administration. In the words of Abraham Lincoln 'democracy is a government for the people, by the people and of the people.' But this is a definition for a democratic government. The modern connotation of democracy cannot be limited to this definition.

Democracy is a way of life. We can interpret Lincoln's words to justify modern connotation of democracy, as 'democracy is a society or social system for the people, by the people and of the people.' In this social order every individual finds his scope of development and self-expression according to his own potentiality. It provides opportunity to an individual to nourish himself according to his capabilities and interests. It ensures equality in opportunities to all citizens. It is cultural, social, economic and political equality. Democracy is liberty, fraternity and equality. It is a sense of responsibility. It ensures equal justice and equal considerations.

Development of democracy is development of democratic values like love, tolerance, nonviolence, honesty, truth, appreciation and etc. The perfect perception of democracy is economic democracy, social democracy, educational democracy and cultural democracy. In such a condition, no one is overexploited for the material and economic benefit of others. The economic asset of state will be well distributed in the society. To ensure the social democracy a democratic society assigns individuals duties and responsibilities. Individual freedom will be ensured. In social democracy it is recognized that each individual is of supreme worth as a citizen and that he is sovereign with power to govern. It means, in a democracy human personality is judged as supreme and of measureless worth.

There are several **democratic values**. Love, cooperation, cohesiveness, toleration, sympathy, empathy, mutual respect, consideration, truth, honesty, peace and nonviolence are some of the democratic values. They are democratic social values, personal values and human values. What we mean by development of democracy is the accurate perception, practice and development of these values. Where there is the prosperity of these values there is the prosperity of democracy.

An explanation to democracy can be noted as follows:

Democracy is –

— A way of life

— An order of social relationships

— Collective interest of common people
— Dedication of individual interests for collective welfare of society
— Spirit of understandings and sympathy
— The cooperation of groups and communities
— Strong belief in humanity
— Democratic attitude in thought and action
— Practice of democratic values
— Education and Democracy

Education lays sound foundation for democracy. It is an effective instrument for creating and developing desirable attitude towards democracy. The whole education system, its administration, organization, formal centers, aims, content, methodology and all other factors should breathe out the air of democracy. Democracy at its best is the result of education. Democracy without education is worthless. Educated people are the effective pillars to protect democracy as a social and administration system. Properly educated people can only protect and make democracy rich.

Education is to plan for the maximum utilization of minimum resources and equal distribution of resources. It is education to make individuals who can discover their potentialities and can express them in full. These two functions – recognition of potentialities and expression of individual in full – are treated as minimum requirement of democratic practice and they can be developed by education only. Education gives awareness to pupils and people about the need of democracy and its various ways of functioning. It inculcates correct knowledge of the political, social, religious, cultural, educational and economic problems. This knowledge is necessary for the renunciation of individual to protect collective interests of the society. The formal inculcation and cultivation of democratic values are possible by education only. Democracy cannot develop effectively unless democratic principles are reflected in education. The broadmindedness, democratic attitudes, awareness of duties and responsibilities, need of social adjustment and contributions for the social welfare can be achieved by education.

### 4.1.2 Education in a Democratic Society

Education in a democratic society should be based on democratic values. In imparting education to citizens, democracy should keep the spirit of liberty, equality and fraternity and justice to all. It should have to ensure equality of educational opportunity. Opportunities are to be given to all citizens in such a way that each individual is provided an opportunity to nourish himself according to his own abilities, capabilities and interests. Consideration of individuals in a democracy should not take into account religion, caste, class, economic disparity etc. Individual's right to avail education should be protected.

Democratic organization and administration of educational system envisage a life attitude of give and take and a balance between rights and duties. Democratic educational aims, methods, curriculum, textbooks, curricular and non-curricular activities should be planned in accordance with the way of life. 'Democratic education must be well planned in which all members work effectively, cooperatively, harmoniously and economically. With the collective interests they should undertake responsibility, beneficial to the individual as well as to the society at large.

Democratic education has to keep ethical dimensions such as

— Dignity of individual

— Equalitarianism

— Spirit of brotherhood

— Spirit of freedom

— Good citizenship training
— Cooperation, cohesiveness and other values
— Appreciation of the contributions of individual (it is a motivation for socially desirable activities and protection of collective interests)
— Development of social character and standard of judgment
— Equality of opportunities
— Social justice, and
— Faith in educability of man.

Democratic curriculum has to be planned in such a way that the individual in the society gets clear awareness in democratic values. There should be provisions to practice democratic values in day-to-day life. To develop democratic attitude in children, schools should follow democratic principles. The classroom, school atmosphere, teacher behaviour, methods to maintain discipline, etc have to follow democratic spirit in operation. The students have to recognize their own rights and duties. They should ensure the practice of democratic policies and principles. Others rights and values must be protected. They should ensure the atmosphere to practice others rights also. In short, the whole educational programme in a democratic society should breath the spirit of democracy in all aspects.

### 4.1.3 Democracy in Classroom

Democracy is not a matter of recitation but a matter of practice. School is a laboratory in which children learn, test and practice the art and skill of democratic social living. The spirit of give and take and the balance between rights and duties have to be nailed on school organization, administration and on the education system in total. Atmosphere, teacher behaviour, interaction between students and teachers and total programmes must be maintained with democratic spirit.

Both students and teachers should have freedom in school. Students must provide opportunities for self-expression. Teachers should identify and recognize children as individuals and have to ensure their rights. Teachers should respect children. Both students and teachers should follow the principle of 'give respect and take respect.' The concept of equality, fraternity and liberty should be developed in classroom. There must be perennial attempts by the school system, especially by teachers, to protect and promote democratic values like love, tolerance, peace etc in classroom.

A teacher must be democratic in his or her approach and outlook. Autocratic teachers can never develop democratic values among pupils. A democratic teacher never denies rights of his pupils. He must respect child as a separate individual with all rights. One great attribute of democracy is freedom –freedom for speech, action, movement, organization etc. A child loves freedom. A child has to enjoy freedom for realization of potentialities. A democratic teacher must ensure freedom of children in classroom.

Democratic approach of teacher is very important in developing democratic values in children. He must be 'democratic' towards his students in all respects. A teacher who preaches democracy and follows totalitarian principles will spoil the democratic atmosphere. Such a behavior adversely affects the development of democratic values in children. A teacher should maintain democratic atmosphere in classroom in all aspects like method, interaction, dealings etc. A democratic teacher should recognize that every individual is different from other individuals; everyone is capable of making moral choices, of deciding what is true and false, good or bad; every child has the right to freedom, to think, to choose and to equality of chances. There is a saying that democracy comes not from a course of study but from a teacher, not from a curriculum but from a human soul.

The teaching learning process must follow cooperation and participation programmes. A student in the classroom is human with all democratic rights and hence he is to be judged as supreme and of measureless worth. There should be spirit of understanding, tolerance, sympathy and cooperation between teachers and students. A teacher has to frame democratic condition by which every child finds full scope for development and self-expression.

Methods of teaching have to follow the democratic spirit. Students must have opportunities to interact. Classroom should not be a teacher-centered classroom. Methods, which envisage cooperative learning and child-centeredness, are to be practiced.

Discipline in classroom is based on conviction of doing right thing in the right manner at the right time. It is a process of give and take; give respect and take respect, give love and take love! There is no scope for corporal punishment in a democratic classroom. Discipline should follow a general principle that no child is absolutely wrong. Discipline in a democratic classroom is based upon proper understanding of the nature of human relationships. As Montessori said, "to obtain discipline, give freedom".

Flowering of human personality is important in democratic education. Men prosper best in an atmosphere of freedom. Rigidness and suppression hold back the growth. Democratic education is a social system dedicated to development. The institution, which ensures encouragement and development of creative qualities of each and every person, has democratic atmosphere.

According to John Dewey 'the devotion of democracy to education is a familiar fact. It is a social necessity. Since democratic society repudiates the principle of external authority, it must find a substitute in voluntary disposition and interest; those can be created only by education.' These words undoubtedly clarify the relationship between education and democracy. The purpose of education in a democratic society is to support, enable, enlarge and strengthen the democratic way of life. Education will be the foundation for the democratic way of life. Education can change the society in a democratic way with all efforts and strengths.

## 4.2 Secularism

The word religion takes our mind to the idea of god, spirituality, supernatural beings and our relationship with such powers. Religions are discussing the matters like religious life, spirituality and godliness. Naturally religion has infused and governed many significant aspects of human life. It is the instrument of social control. Religious teachings and practices have the greatest role on an individual's life. Moral values and social obligations have their sources in religions.

Religions are playing an inevitable role in a country like India. They have immense influence on Indian social life. Beliefs, customs and social practices of individuals are penetrated by religions. According to MC Chagla, who was former Indian education minister, religion is something individualistic, personal and intimate to Indian society.

Eliminate all religious practices from social life. In a multi-religious country like India it is difficult; and to a certain extent impossible. Religion is a significant force in the life of individuals as well as communities. At the same time religions should stand apart from the state's regular systems. Interference of religions in state affairs will create adverse effects. The concept of secularism is important in these circumstances. Secularism is a panacea to almost all social evils caused by religions.

### 4.2.1 Concept of Secularism

Concept of secularism is different in its Western and Indian interpretations. Western secularism is based on the strict separation of the state and church. They follow the principle of noninterference of state in religious matters and religions in state's political and social matters. Western secularism segregates religions – churches – and state governments in their own way of operations.

The Indian concept is different. In India it is social phenomenon rather than a political adjustment. Indian constitution authorizes the state to interfere with the time-honored practices in the religious matters in the interest of social justice. The concept of secularism is different from that of Western idea, because India is a country with a number of religions. Indian constitution recognizes the existence and practice of all religions in the state. The essential features of secularism are explained in Articles 15, 25 and 26. In India secularism, socialism, democracy and nationhood become indistinguishable in social life. All these four factors are necessary to define each one in Indian situation. Constitution ensures right to profess, practice and propagates any religion freely without fear or favor.

A secular state is neither religious nor irreligious and never anti-religious. Such a state possesses a type of religious neutrality.

More specifically major characteristics of secularism are:

a) There is no state religion

b) State government shall not interfere in religious matters and religions have no direct role in state administration.

c) State must be impartial to all religions

d) Practice and propagation are religions responsibility and the state has no role to play in it

e) State will not entertain or discourage any religion particularly

f) Every religion is given equal status

g) Secularism is not an antireligious approach or irreligious.

h) 'To be secular is not to be religiously illiterate'

i) An individual can believe and practice any religion which he likes

j) An individual has right to not to believe in religion

k) Secular state considers human nature as one and it defines man beyond his religion

Secularism is social life of man above all religions in a state, where there is religious pluralism.

Religious pluralism may create terrible problems in the way of national unity. Pluralism is a social reality and closing eyes towards this is foolish. To keep human unity in a society with religious pluralism, the best way is secularism. Secularism recognizes all religions, giving equal consideration to all religions and gives no special preference to any one of them.

Secularism, particularly in the Indian perspective, is religious neutrality. A secular state has no responsibility of protecting any religion; at the same time it tries to protect the religious freedom of all. A major objective of a secular state is to safeguard and foster human values. Secularism is impartial to all religious values. The state has no religion and all religions are treated equally by the state. Social values, personal values and human values are more important than religious values.

Secularism is the need of the hour. A properly perceived practice of secularism is essential in a society, which has religious pluralism. It is inevitable for national integration. There is the freedom to practice religion. This freedom should not be used as a license to interpret the matters of other religions. The state should keep itself away from religious agenda and vice-versa. In short secularism is the belief that the state, society, moral education etc. should be independent of religion.

### 4.2.2 Education in a Secular Society

Secularism as a social system and education must be reciprocal and interactive in a secular society. All the aspects of education like planning, administration, teaching morale, atmosphere, and so on must express the nature of secularism.

Education in a secular society will be more effective if it is under the public administration. Rights of all religious groups in education must be protected, but no religious group should be permitted to run its institutions to impart public education. The religious interpretation in education must be discouraged.

Education in a secular society must possess secular outlook in educational planning, administration, organization, curriculum development, curriculum transaction, teaching-learning methods, textbooks, and content and in all aspects.

More specifically a system of education in a secular society must be

a) Irreligious
b) Non-religious
c) Equal to all religions
d) Preach secular outlook
e) Organizationally secular
f) Practically secular
g) Effectively planned to protect the secular culture of the society.
h) Democratic

Such an educational system can emerge from the social life only. It should develop all democratic and secular values like love, tolerance, peace, cooperation, nonviolence and the like. The teacher education scenario in a secular society also has to be secular in all aspects. A religious teacher will be a failure in developing secular outlook among children.

In school the regular routines and practices also should be secular. Dress code with religious mode, emphasis on a particular religion, integration of religious rituals into school practices, religious preaching and prayers, and religious education must be discouraged from the school practices. But education on religions can be introduced.

### 4.2.3 Secularism and Education

Education has great contributory role in the development of secularism. Cultivation of secular values is being done by education. The pivotal role of education in creating a sense of emotional integration is significant. This emotional integration of individuals is a basic factor for the practice of secularism. It is possible effectively by education only.

Education on religion is a must in a multi-religious society. At the same time religious education should be discouraged. Knowledge of all religions is essential to facilitate secular thinking. Religious practices are personal and spiritual and not political or social. Penetration of religion into the socio-political matters must be avoided. All these are effectively possible by education. Education should design programmes to make children tolerant and broadminded. Permanent solution to religious problems like fanaticism, riots, fundamentalism lies in the right type of education.

Education has a formal role in the secular development of society. School should function as a real model of secular society. School, which is a miniature of the society, may have students from all religions. Interaction between students with different religious beliefs formally and informally takes place in schools. They provide situations for such interactions. School itself is an agency of secular education. Children in school love each other, play together, act together, interact with their own emotional standards and share own outlooks and beliefs. Friendship will develop beyond religious limitations in schools. Peer groups and gangs are formed without religious barriers.

Education is to provide citizens with secular outlook. It has the potentiality of creating and developing secular values. Education has to develop values, which foster secularism in thought like love, toleration, mutual respect, consideration, renunciation, social respect, democratic outlook etc. through formal and informal ways.

Education creates tolerance and cooperation rather than conflict and competition. It is the instrument for the realization of secular ideas.

Curriculum and teaching method should also be able to develop secular outlook of individual and society as a whole. They should illuminate the cultural conditions, social reality and need of secularism. The conservation and transformation of secular values should become possible through curriculum. Every subject in the curriculum must be taught from the point of view of secular needs of the society. Hidden curriculum also is developed with the same interest. Curriculum should lay stress on emotional integration. This emotional integration is the platform for the development of nonreligious outlook and secular thinking. The secular policies taken by historical figures must be highlighted through out the curriculum.

A teacher must be secular in all aspects. He must get rid of all religious practices in school. No religious symbols in dressing or other codes must be highlighted. He should never speak in favour of a specific religion. A teacher should consider all students equally. Prompting a child's religious belief in classroom should be avoided. Any attempt to establish religious practices in school must be discouraged by the teacher. A secular teacher is a role model in the practices of secular values. He should be a person of nonreligious spirituality.

Education is a social function. It depends upon cooperation and sharing. School is the laboratory of the society. Of course, education is the best way to cultivate secularism in school.

## 4.2.4 Secularism in Schools or Classrooms

As D S Kothari said, the future of any society is being shaped in the classroom. The social values they preserve and practiced by individuals in future are received from schools. Only a secular classroom can develop secularism.

More specifically, a classroom can develop secular thought of pupils through the following attempts:

— In the school community religions must be considered as a personal matter and not as a social matter.

— Naming institution with a religion's name or religiously significant names must be discouraged.

— Teachers and other organizers of schools must be secular in all walks of life in school.

— School should organize programmes like elocution to develop secular values.

— Schools should celebrate programmes of all religions or get rid of the programmes of all religions.

— Admission to school must be open to all religions. Neighborhood school system should be encouraged

— Religious organizations should never be permitted to run public education centers.

— Schools must be free from fundamental religious thoughts.

— Forming religious organizations or clubs should be discouraged.

— Education in its framework and attitude must be nonreligious.

— A teacher is the best figure to transact non-religious outlook and secular practices in classrooms. He must be free from religious bias in schools. Only a secular teacher can develop secularism. Without him all attempts to foster a secular society will fail. A teacher has to be a 'pure secular' in all aspects; only then he can develop a secular attitude among children.

# Introduction to Philosophy and Educational Philosophy

Philosophy is the backbone of education. It is on the basement of philosophy that the edifice of education is constructed. An effective educational system is unthinkable without the support of a strong philosophy. The system of education that any state follows is the replication of the philosophy that the state possesses.

This chapter deals with the following areas

*Philosophy: Meaning and definitions*

- *Branches and problems of philosophy*
- *Relationships of philosophy and education*

*Schools of Philosophy or Thoughts*

*Epistemology, axiology and metaphysics of the thoughts given under:*

- *Idealism*
- *Naturalism*
  - *Concept of negative education*
- *Pragmatism*
- *Realism*

*The interpretation of each school on aspects of education such as aims, methods, role of teacher, curriculum and discipline*

- *Educational philosophy and its significance*

This chapter deals with philosophy, and its inter-relationship with education. It is the educational implications of philosophy and each thought, and not their philosophical explanations, that are focused.

There is saying that every individual in this world lives with a philosophy. Man has and needs philosophy. It makes a man a man. He can't live with bread and butter alone. Man needs something more for his conscious system of values and sense of beauty, his art, and his philosophy. The aesthetic sense of life is equally important like food and shelter to a civilized man. His aim of life, meaning of life and all other walks of life depend up on the philosophy, which he follows.

Philosophy and philosopher are terms with a long history. The word philosophy, though the meaning is well known, is still an abstract to a learner. The question 'What is philosophy' cannot be answered from a single source. We need a large explanation to answer this question. And answering this question itself needs a philosophical interpretation!

Education too is phenomenon to be explained from different sources. We need different platforms to interact with education. While we go deep into the concept of education and philosophy, we can see that they are vast and wide as we enter into them or the way to reach the end is as lengthy as we follow them. Both of them are interrelated and almost interdependent in performing their activities. Isolated explanation will not satisfy their grasping.

## 5.1 Philosophy: The Term

The term philosophy is derived from two Greek words 'philos' and 'sophia'. Philos means 'love' or 'fond of' and sophia means 'knowledge' or 'wisdom'. Thus, etymologically the word philosophy means 'love of wisdom' or 'love of knowledge'. No doubt, philosophy is a subject seeking knowledge and knowledge only!

> *A philosopher at a restaurant may order for chicken soup and mutton soup at the same time merely to know which one will come first.*
>
> **– A free interpretation**

Philosophers are the lovers and seekers of knowledge and truth. There is a saying that philosopher has a flame of freedom in his soul and light of science in his eyes.

### 5.1.1 Philosophy: Introduction

As a discipline, philosophy is the mother of all subjects. All subjects arise from philosophy. All subjects are anchored on philosophy. Questions from any area find their answers and life applications, and problems from any field find their solutions in philosophy. It is the ultimate source of knowledge. It is the mother subject. It is the study of nature and the meaning of existence. It is the final answer to what man is.

Philosophy deals not with mere information, but with higher type of knowledge, wisdom, values and reality. It is the comprehensive view of nature and universal explanation of nature, spirit, matter, things etc. and man's relation with all and each of them. It is logical reasoning.

Philosophy is not a subject like physics or chemistry and history or commerce. It is different from science or history. Science experiments and investigates the objects of senses. Philosophy seeks into the objects of thought. Philosophy does not bind up its area of study to restricted boundaries like physics, chemistry or history but discusses with all problems of life in-toto. Moreover it tries to answer the intricate questions of God, Godliness, Spirit, Soul, Moralities, Values, Reality, and so on.

As a subject philosophy is based on reason, logic, system and order. It aims at the acquisition of truth. By interpreting its method of knowledge acquisition, we can say that philosophy is dynamic. *Seek what is this and what is that, know them, then seek what is beyond this and beyond that. Know them, interpret them, interrogate them, reconstruct them, and again seek what is beyond the already known, again interpret, interrogate ….. Thus build knowledge and reach on truth is the method of philosophy.*

The system of philosophy we can read from the words of Socrates. He said, "one thing only I know and that is I know nothing." Man who feels I know nothing can only go on seeking truth.

*'When we double the known, we quadruple the unknown' is a philosophical saying. The more the facts are studied, the more difficult they become. The more we know the more unknowable the unknown become. More than we know always remain the 'unknown'. There is lot of things to know!*

The major tasks or functions of philosophy are:

a) speculation or meditation or thinking
b) description and analysis
c) prescription or give directions for.

## 5.1.2 Meaning and Definition

Philosophy originated from wonder and doubts – wonder and doubts of man towards this universe and its each and every aspect.

Generally, philosophy is beliefs and convictions or view-points and outlook. A philosopher is one who has un-quenching thirst for knowledge and who is never satisfied with the acquired knowledge.

To understand Indian philosophy, it is imperative to grasp the meaning of the word 'Darsan'. The connotation of Darsan applied to philosophy clearly denotes Indian attitude towards the highest knowledge. The word Darsan means that by which something is to be seen by external as well as internal eyes. From the practical point of view, the arguments given for and against the existence of physical or spiritual elements fall with in the purview of word Darsan. Philosophy is the realization of eternal truths in the background of time, culture, etc.

As a discipline, philosophy is the systematic inquiry about the ultimate realities in and of the world. It is both knowledge and realization of knowledge. It is the realization of reality too. Questioning arising out of curiosity is the important factor of philosophical thinking. It involves all types of experiences – religious, social, moral, spiritual, material etc. Philosophy is the critical science of universal values. It is concerned with everything as a universal science. Philosophy is a general theory of criticism. It is a comprehensive synthetic science.

John Dewey said that the problem of philosophy is not how we can come to know an external world, but how we can learn to control it and remake it. Philosophy is the synthesis and coordination of knowledge and desire.

Philosophy is a collection of sciences, such as theory of knowledge, logic, cosmology, ethics and aesthetics. Its method, problems and conclusions are philosophical in nature. It is the acquisition of knowledge through induction, deduction, analysis, synthesis and dialectical method. Philosophy consists of theories of insights arrived at as a result of systematic reflection.

We cannot have a perfect definition for philosophy, because it is not a concept that can be defined from a particular point of view. Generally it is defined, as "the science of all sciences."

Brightman E S defined: "Philosophy is essentially a spirit or method of approaching experience rather than a body of conclusions about experiences"

According to Clifford Barr "Philosophy is not the specific content of conclusions, but the spirit and method by which they are reached, which entitled them to be described as philosophical."

Based on educational view an accepted definition is: "Philosophy is the rational interpretation of the universe of our experiences". It also defined as "the interpretation in intellectual terms of man and nature and their relationship towards each other."

According to Spencer, "Philosophy is concerned with everything as a universal science." Lexical definition to philosophy is: "Philosophy is the study of nature, universe and the meaning of existence."

Philosophical issues and arguments are so deep and complex that when we begin to examine any one of them, we will soon find that it is near impossible to come to a settled conclusion without also examining others.

### 5.1.3 Major Branches (Problems or Issues) of Philosophy

The main branches of philosophy are epistemology, metaphysics and axiology. Epistemology is the science of knowledge. Metaphysics is the science of reality and Axiology is the science of values. Ontology can also be considered as a branch of philosophy though it s not considered independent problem of philosophy. Ontology is a part of metaphysics, which treats of the nature and essence of things.

**Epistemology**

Epistemology is the theory of knowledge. Major concerns of this problem or branch of philosophy are knowledge and truth. Truth is 'the true knowledge'. Knowledge is not information. It is something beyond. Information gathering through the process of rote learning cannot be considered as genuine knowledge by an epistemologist. Epistemology tries to answer and question 'what can we know beyond the information provided by our sense organs?' It deals with the knowledge of the nature of the subject, the object and the process of acquisition of knowledge. Acquisition of knowledge is not the completion of the task. It is only a stop to seek more knowledge.

To an epistemologist, process of acquisition of knowledge itself is life. Epistemology as a science of knowledge discusses the origin of knowledge, different types of knowledge, promotion of knowledge, and process of acquisition of knowledge etc. Areas of epistemology are the origin of knowledge, different types of knowledge, promotion of knowledge, process of acquisition of knowledge etc. It deals with the origin of different types of knowledge like intuitive knowledge, revealed knowledge, rational knowledge, bookish knowledge, authoritative knowledge and empirical knowledge.

**Axiology**

Axiology is the science of values. There are different types of values like spiritual values, natural values, intrinsic values, human values, eternal values, personal values, social values etc. Axiology targets to answer the questions on the origin of values, types of values, process of acquisition of values, source of values and imparting values in human life.

The most obvious or noticeable mode of thinking (assumption) in axiology is prescriptive. Axiology deals with the true values. It is also the theory of values – truth, beauty and goodness (Satyam, Sivam and Sundaram). It also deals with the consequences of improper ordering of values; the consequences like crises and problems – alienation, social crises, identity crises etc. Philosophically one's conception of the nature of values and their ordering depends upon one's total philosophy of life. As a science of values, axiology critically analyses the problems of values.

**Metaphysics**

It is the science of reality or theory of being. It seeks what is really real. Metaphysics is an attempt in speculation. It deals with spiritual reality and material reality. It is not a question of reality as such in physics or chemistry. For example, a question on reality "has man a soul apart from his body?" discusses the real existence of human being in the world in different way than that of science.

Is reality a concept as we conceived? Is it a belief? How does reality face the theory of hallucination? Is reality a reality? All these questions are discussed under the mode of metaphysical tasks. The reality may be different from conception.

Edward Feser says that there is the matter of casual relations existing between perceptual experiences of physical objects and the objects themselves. Reality here is a matter of hallucination. Hallucination can seem indistinguishable from the normal perceptual experience, which presents us with a reliable picture of the external world. The science of reality is a matter of seeking what is really real. Feser suggests an example. The light reaches our eyes virtually immediately, but in the case of looking at the sun, the light takes a full eight minutes to reach our eyes, meaning that what we are seeing now is the sun as it appeared eight minutes ago. The light from the star Alpha Centauri takes over four years to reach us, and light from other outer space objects takes much longer –in many cases, so long that some of the celestial objects we see in the night sky no longer exist! The philosophers' search for reality is a subject of difference. All the questions regarding reality fall under the branch, metaphysics.

## Branches of Philosophy and their Influence on Education

Epistemology, Axiology and Metaphysics have a direct role in education. These divisions of philosophy determine different schools of philosophy. The epistemological description and analysis, the metaphysical or ontological speculations and axiological prescriptions draw the mode of education.

More briefly we can state that epistemology largely influences the content, methods of education and teachers' role in instructional (teaching-learning) process. Axiology is the source of aims of education and metaphysics is the major determinant of the perspective of the curriculum. That means, epistemology determines methods, axiology determines aims, and metaphysics determines curriculum.

**Areas of Philosophy**

In the modern world philosophical theories have great influence on different areas. It has become an inevitable part of various scenarios. It has strong influence on all walks of life as man's life becomes more fast and mechanical. Educational philosophy, social philosophy, managerial philosophy and industrial philosophy are some of these areas of philosophy.

## 5.1.4 Philosophy: Interrelations with Education

Education is the dynamic side of philosophy, in the words of Adams. His analysis clarifies the strong relationship between education and philosophy.

Philosophy is a factor that influences different aspects of education. Education will fail to attain its end without philosophical supports. It has no identity without a philosophical background.

In real sense, education is nothing but the practice of philosophy. It determines the aspects of education such as aims, curriculum, and teacher's role, scope of textbook, content matter, discipline and method of teaching. Philosophy touches and brushes all segments of education. Education is the practical means of realizing the philosophical ideals of life. Separate from philosophy, education would become an aimless attempt. There is a saying that without education philosophy is fruitless and without philosophy education is rootless.

> *'The art of education will never attain complete cleanness without a philosophy'*
>
> **– JG Fichte**
>
> *Education and philosophy are two sides of the same coin; they represent different views of the same thing and one is implied in the other.*
>
> **– James Ross**

Philosophy is thought and education is action. Action and thought are interdependent. So we cannot segregate education from philosophy and vice versa. Philosophy stands for certain values and knowledge. Education supplies light to individuals to realize the values and knowledge. Thus philosophy is the end and education is the means.

Modern education is shaped by different philosophical thoughts. The education system of a country is being planned and executed according to the philosophy that the country follows. Education depends upon the prevailing philosophy. It is the basement on which the edifice of education built.

Education is the media to broadcast the programmes of philosophy. Philosophy preserves the thoughts and education transforms them. Both of them are conservators and transmit heritage. Philosophy and education are interrelated as well as identical.

## 5.2 Schools of Philosophy

A school of philosophy is a thought – a deviated philosophical thought.

How does a school of philosophy originate? What does a school of philosophy mean? How does a school or thought develop with distinguished identity? Answering these questions is not an easy job. It needs a big effort to answer them. An attempt is made here to answer them briefly.

A well-knit system of philosophy integrates metaphysics, axiology and epistemology. A philosophical ideology means the well-integrated ideological explanation on these three problems or branches of philosophy. For example, John Lock's philosophy means his concept and ideological explanation to epistemology, axiology and metaphysics. Many people may approve his conceptual notions and explanations. When different thinkers positively interpret this theoretical explanation, it paves the way for a new philosophical school.

More specifically, the concept of values is different for different schools of philosophy. Some schools believe that values are eternal and static, cannot be changed by man and are not applicable. Values are permanent and divine. There is scope to oppose these views. Some thinkers might oppose these views on values. They may say that values are applicable and manmade. Diversity on this like concept makes to way of thought. (It is believed that human species on this planet are the ancestors of Adam and his sibling. If we believe it, no doubt we have to admit that there happened sex intercourse between brother and sister – son and daughter. Such a relation was approved with values. But modern world will never consider such a sex relationship as socially valued one. The explanation to value concept is applicable).

Certain philosophers believe that knowledge (epistemological element) and values (axiological element) are made by God. Some others are of the view that all values and knowledge are manmade. Some others say that all these are neither manmade nor Godliness but created and developed by nature. There are three types of axiological, metaphysical and epistemological rationalization to the same element. We call these deviated and distinguished streams of thoughts schools. Hence, a school of philosophy is called a stream of thought. It is the stream of thought based on the epistemological, axiological and metaphysical rationalizations to the philosophical notions.

A philosophical thought is not a completely alienated one. It might not be an isolated thinking. One school can never segregate from the other completely. They are not watertight compartments but reciprocal in nature.

Usually a thought starts from dissatisfaction with the existing schools. The thinkers have knowledge and come out with deviated explanations suggesting changes to the existing concepts. These alternative speculations critically refine or replace the existing principles and prescribe a new order of thought. This new order of thought is the cradle in which the new school of philosophy lies. It does not mean that the new school of philosophy is a hybrid. It should be a pure birth.

There are several schools of philosophy – the isms:

Idealism, Naturalism, Pragmatism, Realism, Humanism, Existentialism and Materialism are some among them. Taoism, Confucianism, Budhism, Jainism, Marxism, Positivism, Socialism, Gandhism etc. are some others, generally called individual or social philosophies. Some of the schools of philosophies are too independent and as old as the discipline philosophy.

## 5.2.1 Idealism

Idealism is the oldest school of philosophy. It is as old as Plato in the West and Vedic Rishis in the East. It is so traditional and antique. In his book 'Republic', Plato says idealism 'is the science of ideas'. It is the ism of ideas to Plato. He synonymously used 'idea' with soul, spirit and mind. The term idealism is derived from idea –ism.

### Idealism: Conceptual Interpretation

Every thing in this world has an idea behind it. Idea is abstract, but permanent. Things made by idea are concrete, but not permanent. There are abstract ideas and concrete ideas. The theory of gravitation is an abstract idea. We can't show the idea, but it is a reality. It is a truth. Idea is first and matter is second. Mind is first and body is second. It is matter; body can be damaged, idea or mind can never be destroyed.

## Mind and matter in idealism

Idealism is a school of philosophy, which believes that mind or spirit is the only reality. Man exists out of his body! Mind determines the material existence of the world. George Berkley conceived of the physical world as mere appearance to the perceiving mind. It very much like the idea of hallucination or Maya of Material world in Indian thought.

*Take the case of famous scientist Stephen Hawkins; who is living with a workless body! He is unable to read and write; even to speak. But he contributes to the world with his mind.*
*Only the idea of spiritual existence of mind can serve explanation to his 'existence'. Human mind, not body, is the reality.*

The spirit or soul of man or any living organism is a part of the universal spirit. The individual soul comes from the universal soul and goes back to the same. The existence is a universal divine idea. There is nothing created out of this idea. It is like water in the earth. There is rain, but not even a drop of water produced in this planet is more than what quantity had been here at the time of creation. Human soul too is like that. It is only the part of universal soul, personifies from there, goes back, and comes again…..a process of revolving of spiritual soul with the same idea behind it. The personification may spoil, but the idea never! It said that 'as is the universal soul so is the individual soul'

The Indian concept is also the same. Lord Krishna in Bagavat Gita says that there are two types of existences – the substance and spirit, can be called body (deha) and mind. One can destroy the body – substance – only. Body is mortal, can be destroyed. Mind can't be destroyed; it is eternal, divine and immortal. According to Indian concept idea is perfect. Whatever we see is material result of the spiritual idea. Material appearance is mortal. Whatever came out of the perfect soul, the perfect soul will remain pure— "poornamatha, poornamitham, pornath poornamuthachyathe, pornasya poornamathaya poornamevavaseshaythe".

Idealism clearly states, whether in the West or in the East, that there are two elements – mind and body. Mind has separate existence without body as idea has its own existence without matter. Mind is beyond all destructions. Though the concrete material made by idea can be destroyed, the idea will exist. It is saying like 'one may destroy all motor cars in this world but can't destroy the idea behind it'.

*You can destroy entire schools, but can you destroy the idea of school? No! Idea has its own existence without any concrete evidence. The concept and theory of gravitation is an idea, in fact we cannot show a concrete thing or matter to point this is gravitation. Still the idea exists in all human minds. It is a reality.*

Idealism says mind is spiritual and idea is divine. God is the creator. God framed the idea of universal bed (Plato). Every thing in this world exists because of this universal creation. The idea is there without man's interpretation.

What we experience is our own perception only. 'To be is to be perceived'.

**Major Exponents of Idealism**

Socrates, Plato, Spinoza, Berkley, Kant, Hegel, Emerson, Vivekananda, Gandhi and Aurobindo were some of the idealists. Platonic idealism, Absolute idealism, and Subjective idealism are the major types of idealism.

**Epistemological Aspects of Idealism**

Idealism believes in the spiritual origin of knowledge. According to it, real knowledge is spiritual knowledge. The ultimate of knowledge is the knowledge on spirituality. In the eastern concept it is the knowledge on 'atman'.

Idealism says that spiritual knowledge is beyond man's ability to create knowledge and is out of man's interruption. It is created along with the idea behind the creation of knowledge. It is divine and intuitive to man. Idealists expect a type of holy life by education and to them real 'Jnana' is important. The summom bonum of all knowledge is spirituality. The moral and intellectual possessions are the conquests of one's own soul. Hence knowledge, which doesn't contribute moral and spiritual uplift of man, is not real knowledge. Man is a spiritual being.

In brief according to idealism knowledge is not the information of a concrete object but knowledge of the idea behind all subjects. Knowledge is not a means but an end.

### Axiological Aspects of Idealism

Idealists basically believe in absolute values. In the East it can be called *Sanathana Dharma.* The absolute values are permanent values. They are not manmade but heavenly created. Real values are spiritual values. Idealist values will not decay or degenerate. They are the eternal values or values forever.

Values are universal in character. The three basic absolute values are truth, beauty and goodness. They are Satyam, Sivam and Sundaram in the East. All values are blended upon them. Man cannot create values. Man can only practice them. His senses cannot grasp the real value. Values are assessed by the universal idea behind them. The value to man on any object is according to his perception. That is why it is said to be perceived. Only by virtue of man's rationality, he possesses the power to create values in the form of art and literature.

### Metaphysical Aspects of Idealism

George Berkeley conceived of the physical world as mere appearance to the perceiving mind. This is almost equal to the Indian concept of Maya. Physical world is hallucination. Idealism is monastic. It believes in ultimate reality. Idealism signifies spirit, God and the spiritual reality.

> *Earth is big in character. It is its physical character, not mental or idealistic character. This physical character, the size, is not real, but mental character is real and eternal. It is according to the universal divine idea behind it. Suppose the sun metamorphosed to a black hole; what will happen to earth? The unreal physical appearance of it will decay and the planet with its all objects will be absorbed by black hole! The universal divine idea of earth will exist but its physical appearance will go out.*

Idealists believe that mind or spirit is the only reality. A real substance is ideal or mental in character. Idealism emphasizes super-natural existence of realities rather than the reality of the physical object. The reality may be beyond man's sensibility. Man's mind is the real substance and body is not a real thing; it is beyond it physical appearance. It is hallucination. Reality of mind will exist even after the decay of the body.

Reality is rational in character and within the reach of human understanding. Reality also has absoluteness in character. Matter has no reality apart from the mind, which perceives it. Not the perceived material appearance, but the perceived idea behind the object is real. The explanation to the reality of world is possible only in terms of ideas. Reality is changeless and inherent in the form of pure mind. Idealistic reality is permanent, eternal and static. It is spiritual reality.

**Major Tenets of Idealism**

Other than the above discussions, the major tenets or principles of idealism are as follows:

a) The world has two forms; one is the spiritual and the other is material. Idealism gives importance to the spiritual form because it will never perish or degenerate. But the material side is supposed to decay. The material form is only hallucination.

b) Ideas are more significant than objects. Ideas behind objects are more permanent than the material appearance.

c) Man is a divine entity. Man is the supreme creation of God.

d) Mind is the only reality. Body is mortal. Mind has separate identity and existence without body.

e) Values are permanent. Truth, Beauty and Goodness (Satyam, Sivam and Sundaram) are the universal spiritual values.

> *Our classrooms are strongly based on the idealistic principles – believe in the practical side of* Aham brahmasmi, thathvamasi..
> *Our students stand up and show respect to a teacher at his/her entrance; this is a simple practice of idealistic spiritual principle.*

f) Idealism believes in the harmony of diversity. Every thing is 'one' beyond their physical diversities.

g) Reality is absolute and spiritual, not material.

h) The peak of all knowledge is spiritually revealed knowledge

i) Knowledge is intuitive. Knowledge of ultimate reality is not possible through method of experimentation, reasoning and observation. Ultimate knowledge is above the methods of science that observes the physical knowledge.

j) Physical world is destructible and changeable. The idea behind it cannot be distracted or changed.

## Idealism and Education

According to idealism man is the paragon of creations. This paragon of creation definitely needs education. Education is a spiritual necessity. Idealistic education is for realization. It is for the realization of the universal truth and divine idea, which is universal and eternal in character, behind every thing.

Education is not at all formed to create values or knowledge. It makes individual soul to realize the truth, beauty and goodness and other spiritual existence of value and knowledge. According to idealism the culturing of mind is a process of education. Education must be blended with the universal eternal reality and be idealistic in character. Only such education is effective and worthy. Education is for mind. Only mind can dig out the universal features of idea behind the material performance. Education, hence, is for the realization of the idea behind this material expression. It aims to develop sound mind in a sound body. Education in idealistic view stands for conversion of inborn nature to spiritual nature.

**Aims of Education**

Idealism gives more significance to aims of education than to the curriculum or method. The aims of education are fixed and static. The ultimate aim is self-realization. In East the aim of education is *Moksha* or liberation. As the saying goes *sa vidyaya vimukthaya.*

The specific aims of idealistic school of philosophy are:

— Spiritual development

— Conversion of inborn nature to spiritual nature

— Make individuals realize the relation with individual creature and universal soul behind it.

— Make individuals realize that everything is based upon the universal eternal idea. It means education is to understand the spiritual idea behind the universe

— Development of strong moral character

— Conservation or preservation and transformation of cultural heritage.

— Protection of eternal values and real spiritual knowledge.

— Preparation for a holy life

While going through these aims, we can come to a conclusion that the real idealistic aim of education is to help man

– man who possesses a spark of spiritual reality – in the expansion of his self and perfection of his spiritual personality.

**Idealism and Curriculum**

Idealism has specific determination in the designing of a curriculum, because it believes that a good curriculum is necessary to provide education in accordance with the spiritual idea behind the creation of everything in the world. Idealistic curriculum is both the way and vehicle to attain the ultimate aim of education – self-realization.

Experts should properly design curriculum with idealistic view before its transaction or practice. It should aim cognition and practice of eternal values – truth, beauty and goodness. Curriculum should provide development of aesthetic tastes and moral advancement. Idealistic curriculum is ideal centered rather than child-centered. There should be provisions in it for cleaning of child's mind and sharpening or shaping of mind.

Since idealists are spiritualists, they welcome those subjects and activities to their curriculum, which are suitable for the development of spirituality in child. These subjects and activities in curriculum should develop spiritual nature, intelligence, rationality, holy faith, cultural heritage, and preparation for recognition of universal spiritual idea, concept of unity in diversity and idea behind the creation of the universe.

Idealists want to develop thought, emotions, feelings and training of the mind. So they welcome subjects like history, civics, social science subjects, literature, language studies, music, philosophy, art, mathematics etc. into their curriculum. To them, mathematics is the greatest among all sciences. Since they stand for sound mind in a sound body by education, they welcome sports and gymnastics too.

Idealist curriculum is not so flexible. It is anchored upon universal values, eternal knowledge and eternal realities. Teachers are given more importance in idealist approach of curriculum transaction. Yet curriculum is rigid in values, it is flexible to a certain extent, so that content can be modified with the changes and achievements of cultural and social life.

*Idealism aims at the holistic progress of human mind by education, not the physical development. Suppose an individual spend years and years in chemistry laboratory for study and research to achieve highest degrees and joins the society with the smell of a chemistry lab in his mind and action. What is the use of education given to him and acquired by him? Degrees are only physical performances. Education would be worthy if there is holistic development of human mind.*

**Role of Teacher**

Teacher is an indispensable necessity in idealistic system of education. A teacher is a preceptor or guru. He is not a mere instructor. Guru is a spiritual representation.

A student can never have knowledge without guidance and advice of a teacher. A teacher is a mature person trying to change desirably an immature child. Pupils need teacher's assistance for their development. A teacher can recognize the spiritual ability of individual child and can nourish it effectively.

An idealistic teacher should be an idealist and a pure personality. Pure water in water tank delivers pure water in the water tapes. A good teacher only can provide good students. There is a saying that a good teacher is worth more than thousand priests.

A teacher has the key to open the idealistic education process. A teacher has supreme power. He is an apostle of peace and progress. An idealist teacher is a coworker with god in perfecting man. A teacher should be a continuous learner, always seeking realization of spirituality behind the world. He is not a mechanical instructor to instruct or teacher to teach. He trains the mind of the child and develops a link between the child and the spirit of the universe. He should guide children according to their abilities for spiritual realization.

A teacher should possess vast knowledge. He should be a philosopher and guide. He must be ideal and should win respect and love by his sincere work and commitment to truth. According to idealism a teacher is not a classroom teacher alone. He should be a guru – a spiritual teacher – in all walks of life. He is like a gardener. Teaching is not a classroom process. It is a divine transaction, taking place at all times.

**Idealism and Concept of Discipline**

Discipline of individual as a subject received wide attention in idealistic philosophy of education. According to Idealism, strict discipline is essential to both mind and body. Only a disciplined person can achieve realization. Body activities should be trained and channeled properly where the mind is to be dwelled.

Discipline is discipline from the self. Discipline from the self is a little bit different from the regular concept of self-discipline. A man who is disciplined in all aspects can only attain the spiritual reality. It is the duty of a teacher to develop discipline in child. Pupils should obey their teacher. They should be obedient towards all rules and regulations. They have to carry out literally and rigorously the behest of their preceptor. A teacher has major role to make them obedient. Disciplined child with better concentration is essential for effective teaching-learning process.

Discipline can be emancipated discipline, but should bind with the universal spirituality. Discipline by external forces is a must up to certain level and later it should come from within as a result of realization. Obedience, cooperation, cohesiveness, sympathy, empathy, loyalty, respect and other qualities should be cultivated among children. Development of these values leads the child to emerge disciplined from the self.

Idealism gives qualified freedom. It denies the concept of *as is so is* indiscipline. Freedom must be qualified freedom. It is not the license to do any thing. They have no freedom to reject the ideals and call of spiritual urge. Freedom is the freedom to choose the right.

## Idealism and Methods

The method of teaching in idealistic classroom is mainly telling and instruction. A method should invariably be suitable for learning. Concentration is very important. Schools have to adopt suitable methods for the moral and spiritual development of the child. Transaction strategies should be ideal-centered. They stress on logical type of teaching and Socratic method. Socratic Method is one of the best methods to know the individual himself. Idealist educators welcome lecture method, discussion, narration, dictation, story telling, seminar, and socialized simulations.

In the early period, idealistic method is teacher-centered rather than child-centered. Lecture method is considered the best method because a preceptor can use it to establish a direct relation with the child. They stress is on self-instruction too. Idealistic methods zeroed in on simple instruction and high thinking.

In short, idealism welcomes all those methods, which help individual learners to develop their spiritual mindedness and idealistic sense.

## Idealism in Classroom

Idealism is considered as the oldest philosophy. The philosophy is rooted in idealism. Most of the ancient Indian educators had the same view.

Our teacher-pupil relationship is strongly influenced by idealistic principles. High respect towards teachers, con-sidering the teacher as Guru, qualified freedom, strict discipline, spiritual ethos, prayer etc. are examples of the influence of idealistic principles.

*Guru Brahma,*
*Guru Vishnu*
*Gurudevo Maheswara*
*Guru Sakshat Parabrahma*
*Tasmai sri Gurave Namah*

The classroom student is a spiritual entity. A teacher must treat a student as an equally important fellow. Pupils should be respected and highly considered. The punishment may be necessary in an idealistic classroom to inculcate discipline in students and lead them to the spiritual goal. A teacher should be an idealist both in and out side the classroom. He should be free from the bondages of mundane needs. He should be free from envy, hatred, disgust; flattering etc. The class should ensure pupil participation.

Though teacher-centered, the class should be active. Spiritual atmosphere and self-discipline should be developed in an idealistic classroom.

### 5.2.2 Naturalism

The philosophical controversy on the dualism of matter and spirit – body and mind – is one of the major reasons for the development of different schools. Idealism considers mind or spirit as a reality and has its own existence without matter or body; while naturalism believes that mind itself is constituted of matter. According to naturalism, mind is nothing but the brain function. Someone said that naturalism is an attitude rather than a stream of thought.

*There is no man and nature. Man is only one of the aspects of nature, like others.*

The philosophical attitude of naturalism is nature-centric. Everything in the world has its base in the principles of nature. It has its own principles and realities. God or spirit is only a belief.

The term 'nature' is interpreted differently. In one sense it signifies the life according to nature. It means man is an offspring of nature and lives according to its principles.

In another sense nature means a leading a life according man's inborn tendencies and impulses. A man should live according to his own nature. Though these two inter-pretations are primarily deferent, both lead to the same clarification. The inborn nature is the naturo-centric attitude.

Naturalism also stands for perfect freedom and self-determination. Rousseau said that anything natural is good and anything civilized is evil. It means the purest things remain in the nature alone. It is saying that whatever is beautiful is natural and whatever is natural is beautiful. Man is pure and born free. He is corrupted by society and civilization. Man gets nothing spiritually or from divinity. Whatever he receives or experiences is only from nature. It is said that everything lives according to nature's principles; fittest will survive and weakest will be weeded out by natural selection.

Contemporary naturalism rejects the spiritual environment and spiritual values – the eternal existence of truth, beauty and goodness. Permanent spiritual existence of values and mind without matter are stupid thoughts. Naturalism demands scientific enquiry into the nature of things. Mechanical naturalists say that the whole world is a time machine – a big machine – and man is only a part of that machine.

Naturalists believe that some physical forces or natural forces control the whole world. It is controlled by natural laws or principles. Man is controlled and influenced under these forces. Man is a living organism with his own metabolism. Man is an offspring of the nature. Follow the nature is the slogan of naturalism.

Naturalism is the doctrine that believes all reality comes under 'the laws of nature'.

## Major Exponents of Naturalism and Kinds of Naturalism

Rousseau, Bacon, Thomas Hobbes, Herbert Spencer, Pestelozzi, Tagore, Montessori, and Froebel are considered naturalists in views. Watson, Thorndike, Skinner and McDougall are considered mechanical naturalists. Physical naturalism, Mechanical naturalism, Biological naturalism, Evolutionary naturalism, Romantic naturalism, Neo naturalism and Absolute naturalism are the major kinds of naturalism.

## Epistemological Aspects of Naturalism

Naturalism denies the divine origin of knowledge and the idea of eternal spiritual knowledge. Knowledge exists here, here in this nature only! The real knowledge is the knowledge of the mechanical reality of this nature. By acquired knowledge one can find all the characters of evolution in man's life. Man is not a social creature but an offspring of nature. Knowledge is not something that can be poured into the individual. A child can acquire knowledge from nature by his personal instincts. Knowledge is acquired through sense organs with the support of brain. It is acquired through individual's interaction with the nature. He can acquire knowledge himself, from nature and from others. The knowledge from others is to be filtered. But the knowledge from nature is pure and real. Nature is the ultimate source of all knowledge. Human brain is the instrument to reach and realize the knowledge in the nature. Knowledge is empirical and experimental. In epistemology, naturalists are empiricists.

## Axiological Aspects of Naturalism

Naturalism rejects the spiritual environment with its emphasis on the traditional trinity of values – truth, beauty and good-ness. There are no spiritual or eternal values. Values are mechanical, evolutional and applicable in character. Values are created by man as a result of his interaction and interpretation with the nature and its aspects. William McDougall had a view that all forms of values are evolved by the proper sublimation of individual's instincts and emotions. Value is not absolute, final and divine, but a product of environmental conditions. They are relative and provisional. Values are neither permanent nor eternal. They are changeable. Nature is the ultimate source of all values.

## Metaphysical Aspects of Naturalism

Naturalism believes in naturalistic reality. Nature is real and reality is naturo-centric. It is real both in its idea and appearance. Universe is not spiritual but material character. Evolution is another important phenomenon to explain the character of universe. Matters alone constitute the world. Man is not a spiritual component, but only the composition of matters – atom and other elements. God, spirit and even religion are not material in character; so naturalism will say 'no' to answer a question to seek whether they are real or not. Not our thought but our nature determines the reality. World is shaped not according to our thinking or perception. It is independent according to the principles of nature. As in the case of the knowledge and values, naturalism views that nature is the ultimate reality. Actually there is no man and his nature; man is only a part of this nature; one in the evolutionary constitution of nature.

## Mind and Matter

Naturalists deny the spiritual existence of mind. According to them mind has no separate identity apart from the body. Mind is not a spiritual reality and it doesn't have any spiritual explanations. Mind is nothing but the brain function. Matter is the only reality and anything that exists in this universe is a form of matter, not the idea.

That the concept like the final or spiritual truth can be known through the spiritual mind only is folly; it can be known through senses and brain. Divine inspiration of mind, spiritual strength of prayer, spiritual world other than material world, universal soul and individual soul; all these are illusory. Not the spiritual soul but the human brain is the source and analyzer of all knowledge. If there is a 'separate mind' as stated by idealism, that mind is built by matter. That means mind is composed of atoms and molecules.

**Notable Principles of Naturalism**

Major tenets of Naturalism can be summarized as follows:

a) Naturalism is naturo-centric. Naturalists believe there is no God, spirit or universal eternal idea.

b) Mind alone has no identity and existence. Mind is matter. It is the brain function.

c) Nature is the supreme source of knowledge and our senses are the instruments to grasp this knowledge.

d) Nature is the ultimate reality.

e) Nature is governed by its own laws, and not by any spiritual laws.

f) Man is not a social animal in instincts. He is the offspring of nature.

g) Values are not fixed or final or absolute. They are the products of environmental conditions.

h) Values are being created by man's interaction with the nature.

i) Nature is man's teacher, friend and guide. There is no other teacher better than nature.

j) Nature renders love, affection and unconditional considerations. It rears man as mother

k) Divine inspiration, supernatural strength of prayer, spirit, and soul are illusory.

l) Man has natural instincts. He interacts with the instincts and develops.

m) Individual is to be allowed to attain the fullest development of his original nature.

n) There is no divine knowledge. Knowledge is acquired through experience and experiments.

## Naturalism and Education

Man has infancy. This infancy is not a mere stage for future maturity. Infancy has several characteristics. Individual develops as a matured person through different stages of development like infancy, childhood, adolescence, etc. Naturalism demands separate stream of education at each stage of development of individual. Education should be suitable to the natural development of child. Romantic naturalists suggest negative education at early stages and formal education at a later stage only.

Education should prepare child for a complete living. Education is a natural necessity. It is the responsibility of education to make the child free for the fullest development of his original nature. In its educational philosophy, naturalism aims to reach the motto 'follow the nature'. Since senses and brain are the interactive sources of knowledge, sensory training or education to senses is a must. Child is the centre of education and he is the hero in the classroom. Education must be paedo-centric. It is said that a teacher must know John and Latin. Teacher is the person to deal with John–pupil –psychologically.

Naturalism is against rigid curriculum, strict classroom, traditional textbooks, rigid timetable and examination. It gives least important to chalk and talk method. Education must be for prosperous and natural development of child. There should be complete freedom of growth. It is against rigid formal education patterns.

In fact, education is not a process taking place in a school between a teacher and the learner. It is a highly informal process of naturalization of individual. Education must help an individual to adapt with the changing natural laws and physical environment. It should help one in the perfection of oneself. Education aims at conditioning of the reflection of thoughts and action. It should help an individual to struggle for existence and/or survival. McDougall says that education is to redirect and remold the personal instincts.

## Naturalism: Aims of Education

The aim of education is to prepare the child for complete living. Self-expression is the important aim of education. Education should aim at perfect utilization of natural resources and the use of organized energy and natural development of child. Education aims to make one fit to struggle successfully for survival. Education aims at individual's harmonious adjustment and adaptation with environment. Creative evolution and social progress is another aim of education. Naturalist education also aims at earning a living. Citizenship training and self-preservation are also aims of naturalistic education.

Education aims at the transformation, synthesis and sublimation of instincts.

## Naturalism: Curriculum

Naturalist curriculum is not rigid and teacher-centered. It is flexible and child-centered. It should follow the principles of curriculum construction such as child-centeredness, provisions for direct experience, learning by doing, experimentation and verification, individual differences, interests of child and activity-centeredness. There is less importance attached to educator, textbooks and formal lessons in curriculum for early stages. Scientific studies are better than humanities. A naturalistic curriculum gives importance to science subjects. It does not mean that there will be no place for humanities, arts and languages. Curriculum should be able to take child 'to the nature'.

Curriculum should have scope for scientific analysis and empirical teaching. Subjects and curricular activities are selected according to the stages of development and interest of the child. Personal instincts of each child must be considered at the time of construction and transaction of curriculum. Though naturalists arranged curriculum with science as it nucleus, much significance is laid upon modifying curriculum to suit the instincts, interests and needs of the individual for his natural development.

## Naturalism: Role of Teacher

Nature is the first and best teacher, always renders love, affection, consideration to all and teaches effectively. No teacher can teach the child in a better way than the nature can.

Naturalism opposes the idealist concept of supremacy of teacher, who is a preceptor, and leads students to desired directions. A naturalist teacher is a stage setter and facilitator for child's learning. His place is behind the curtain. He leads students not to spiritual entity but to experiences and interaction with environment. He need not be a man with supremacy in all knowledge. A teacher is one among the students. A teacher is a friend and guide and should recollect his own infancy and childhood in his interaction with children. He should provide freedom and free environment for unrestricted self-expression of child.

A child's development is not teachers' burden and a teacher has nothing to do other than providing atmosphere for his natural development. Child has his own ability and instincts for natural development. Teachers' burden is to provide opportunities, environment and experiences for the development of abilities and nourishment of instincts. A child grows himself and it is governed by natural laws.

A teacher should never impose his personality or ideas on the pupil. Naturalism warns teachers against unnecessary seriousness, authoritarian behaviour, physical punishment, nonfriendly atmosphere, transacting superstitious and illusory ideas etc. A teacher should carefully interact with pupils according to their stages of development. It is said that a teacher is a gardener, school is a garden and pupils are the plants and flowers.

**Naturalism: Discipline**

Discipline is not a formal concept in naturalism. Actually, the one and only discipline is the discipline through natural consequences.

A child needs freedom. Freedom is the pivot of discipline. Discipline is not to be imposed but to be naturally acquired. Participation in extracurricular and non-curricular activities is a useful channel to direct or redirect pupils' energy and that can overcome the disciplinary problems. Discipline should be paedio-centric. Best discipline is self-discipline.

> *Fit school to the child (to the nature of child) rather than make the child fit to the school.*

Freedom does not mean that freedom to invade others privacy. It is not the license to do all things. It is the freedom to interact with the environment without any restriction. Such interaction leads to enjoyable, rational, enthusiastic and emotionally developed life. Naturalism welcomes a child's discipline through his own interaction, self and natural consequences. It is nothing to be imposed. There is no scope of physical punishment to maintain discipline. A teacher has no right do so. Recognition of right and wrong is advised through the consequences of child's actions. There is a rhythm of nature, let the child to live according to that. He will be disciplined.

**Naturalism: Methods**

Naturalists believe that infancy and childhood are important periods in life. These periods need special ways of rearing and interaction methods. Naturalists stressed on play-way techniques of teaching and learning. They welcome all child-centered methods, especially learning by doing, deductive methods and play-way learning. They advise to leave the child free to learn from environment; so he can make use of personal instincts and natural abilities. The child is to teach himself by his spontaneous activities. By that the child gets opportunities to express or manifest his innate power.

All methods for early childhood have to be zeroed in on sensory training or training of the sense organs. Learning will be effective when it takes place by observations, experiment and direct experiences. In the classroom, naturalists give importance to learning aids, visual aids like working models and the concept of things before words. Such methods only provide direct experience and better learning. Naturalism gives less importance to textbooks and bookish learning. It stresses upon observation, scientific experimental, heuristic, laboratory, inductive and deductive methods and fieldtrips. They welcome any method, which provides free and integrated interaction with nature.

### 5.2.2.1 Concept of Negative Education

Negative Education is a concept developed by naturalists. It is focuses on education in infancy and childhood. Rousseau is the propagator of negative education. It is informal in character. It opposes all traditional and formal forms of teaching and learning.

Traditional teaching, Rousseau called it positive education, stresses on 'to right through right.' Learning may not be like that always. Mistakes, which are natural phenomena, may lead the child to reach right learning. To right through wrong is possible. This is the essence of negative education.

Education should not be so formal and should be in conformity with human nature, in a natural setting. Let the child by all means make errors and be corrected naturally. The real spirit behind negative education is free discipline. Negative education doesn't attempt to mould child's natural behaviour according to teacher's desire.

Other major characteristics of negative education can be grouped as follows:

a) Negative education is 'negative' towards formal systems.
b) It is focused on education of young children
c) Less scope for direct teaching and formal classrooms.
d) As far as possible textbooks and bookish learning are to be avoided.
e) Methods and classrooms are to be informal. Belief that there is no teaching only learning.
f) Mistakes are corrected naturally. No corporal punishments.

Negative education trains the children to use their sense organs, instincts and skills to acquire knowledge instead of filling their brain with information.

**Naturalism in Classrooms**

Our schools are idealistic in approach. But we use several advices of naturalistic approach in teaching and learning. Montessori Method is an example for naturalistic classroom. Maximum freedom in creative and sensible activities is given to children. Like the concept, "nature will not teach, but one can learn everything from nature", the classroom teacher should be free and flexible in all aspects of teaching –learning; from that the learner can absorb everything. A naturalist teacher never tries to 'teach' the learner. There will be no strict following of rigid timetable or formal time schedules. Enough facilities to play will be provided. Provision for learning by doing is the special character of naturalistic setup. Pupils in classroom will not be introduced with ideas, but only with matter. Pupils develop ideas with their own interpretations. A child is the hero and programmes will be child-centered. A teacher with dedication and democratic attitude can make naturalistic classrooms effective.

### 5.2.3 Pragmatism

Pragmatism is a distinctly American philosophical movement founded by Charles S Peirce (1839–1914) and expounded by William James (1842–1910) and John Dewey (1859–1952). This thought is known as the dominant American philosophy because characteristically it is an American product. Essentially, pragmatism asserts that truth is to be determined by its practical implications. In other words, as J Normandy said, if a certain proposition has practical meaning or produces practical results, then the proposition is determined to be true.

Social circumstances created by immigration, urbanization, and industrialization in the second half of the 19th century raised the philosophy of pragmatism. Associated with such thinkers as C.S. Peirce, William James, and John Dewey, pragmatism exerted a strong influence on the shape of education in the United States, and affected educational ideas and practices in Europe and all over the world.

More than a school of philosophy, pragmatism is a philosophical attitude. It is not a 'darsan' but an approach to life. It is a method of living rather than the meaning of life.

The word pragmatism has its etymological base on 'pragma' which means utility, use, action or work done. The word, almost with the same meaning, which is also considered the root of pragmatism, is 'pragmatigos'. Pragmatism is a philosophy, which is based on utility or activity. It is said that this ism is as old as mankind! The idea behind pragmatic thought is traditionally built upon the old Protogorus statement "Man is the measure of all things." Protogorus was a Greek philosopher. (Somebody has a view that 'man is the measure of all things' is the word of Pythagoras.)

Man determines the utility of the universe. He only determines values, spirituality, materialistic character and all. Knowledge is measured by him only. Man alone acquires and evaluates knowledge. He determines the reality too. Man develops values and knowledge for his practical life. 'Today's life is important, not the past or the future'. So pragmatism is known as down to earth philosophy.

Man is an organism, biological in character. He may have spiritual identity. But he is to interact with the environment constantly. He judges what is useful for him; what is useful is true, good and worthy. Pragmatism is a philosophical thought based on man's attitude towards utilitarian values of the entire products in this world and this universe as a whole. Ideals and ideas have meaning, only if they can be recognized in this world not as spiritual illusion but as constant material with utility. It should be useful for the practical life in the earth.

Pragmatism doesn't believe in absolutism. It stands midway between naturalism and idealism. John Locke expressed his pragmatic view in the words, 'our business is not to know all things, but those which concern our conduct.' Pragmatism agrees with Comte that 'universe is composed of laws and relations and not substance'.

**Major Exponents and Forms of Pragmatism**

Charles Sanders Peirce is known as the founder of pragmatic thought. S Scheller, William James, John Dewey, GH Mead, John Stuart Mill, John Lock and Kilpatrick are some of the major exponents of pragmatism.

Major forms of pragmatism are Humanistic pragmatism, Experimental pragmatism, Biological pragmatism and Nominal pragmatism. Pragmatism is also known as the Chicago school of philosophy or dynamic idealism.

## Certain Major Views of Pragmatic School

Pragmatism is based on the theories of practical utility. Man is what he makes of himself. Everything is valuable while it is utilized for mankind. Each and every thought and action should be channeled for the welfare of human being. Welfare is the better opportunity in this world not at the 'other' world – spiritual or divine world. The principles of experiments and verification are significant in life. Adaptation with changing environment is very important for the success of practical life.

Pragmatism believes in change. (In this aspect pragmatists are very close to Marxian philosophy.) Change is the key word. Change is the law of nature and life. Nothing is static in the universe, except the fact of 'change'. Even the height of mountains and depth of oceans does change. The law of nature is neither moral nor immoral but amoral. As change is the basic principle, how is it possible to think of fixed values, ideals, truth etc? Then there is no scope for eternal values, universal truth and spiritual knowledge. It can be said that there are no fixed values, no fixed objectives, no fixed attitudes or operations, no fixed reality and no fixed knowledge. Everything undergoes change.

*Suppose, when one drive his car, its wheel is punctured. The driver may be an expert in rubber farming, or rubber industry or may be able to talk for hours on A to Z of rubber products. But all these knowledge are unnecessary and unworthy at the moment. The real and useful knowledge he needs then is practical knowledge to repair puncture and pump up the wheel. That is the knowledge, which works and is worthy, is zeroed in on by pragmatists.*

## Epistemological Aspects of Pragmatism

Since pragmatism has faith in change they say there is no ultimate or spiritual knowledge. They welcome all types of knowledge, which are useful to individuals and society. Real knowledge is the knowledge that works. The knowledge that helps individuals for a better life in this world is the knowledge to be attained. Knowledge acquisition is not an end, but a means to an end. Utility and practicability of knowledge is must to recognize it as knowledge. Pragmatists mostly welcome experimental knowledge, rational knowledge, scientific knowledge, and authoritarian knowledge. Activity is the method to attain knowledge. Experience and experiments are the ways to acquire real knowledge. Knowledge is valuable while it is individually and socially worthy.

There is no finishing point in the race to attain knowledge. No knowledge is complete. It will change. Worth of knowledge is applicable. Man measures the worth of it. Knowledge is recognized so while it becomes utilitarian and practical, not divine or spiritual. Man creates, develops, and utilizes all knowledge. It is not nature created or spiritually created but man created.

## Axiological Principles of Pragmatism

Values are not permanent or eternal and are not with nature alone. "Values are in the making". Change is the cardinal principle of values too. Values are manmade. Pragmatists welcome intrinsic values, instrumental values and all these types of changing values. They are related with needs of man.

Values of past may not be values of today. Today's values may not be values of tomorrow. Values change according to different time and space. Human life is a laboratory in which values are created or developed through experiments and experience. Values, which have no practical utility or life applications, are not values at all. For the pragmatists, the only criterion and measure of value of anything is its utility. Worthless values like universal eternal values are not considered.

Man creates new values by modifying his environment. His experiments and experience with the environmental aspects are significant in determining values. Nothing is final or absolute. So, there is no single truth or values but many truths and values. Pragmatists are pluralists. All values are created by man and they are not static, but changing. There are no eternal and permanent values. Value is that which serves man's needs and purposes.

In brief, pragmatism has a different concept of values. Pragmatists believe in changing manmade and utilitarian values and not in eternal or spiritual values. Value is that which provides practical support to human being. In short, pragmatic values are not the value of past and future but values of present. They are not illusory. They change according to time, circumstances and situation. While needs change values are also changing.

## Metaphysical Explanations of Pragmatism

As in the case of knowledge and values, pragmatism doesn't believe in the permanent and ultimate reality. Reality is not static; it will change. Reality is always in the making. Reality is not one but many.

There is the pragmatic view that 'thought and action and individual and society are inseparable things.' Hence reality is made out of these connections. Pragmatic reality is based on pluralism. There is no unchanging single and ultimate reality or truth. Reality is that which is experienced by man. Once man's experience changes, reality also changes. As James said, "reality is in the making and still awaits a part of its completion from the future".

Man is a product of society and essentially he is social. So reality has social perspective too. Reality is changing according to the social utility and practical needs of individual. As it is in the case of values, every man is empirically developing his reality concept. Reality is a flux.

## Major Principles of Pragmatism

Major conceptual principles of pragmatism can be codified as follows:

a) The main principle of pragmatism is that 'the theories that work are true' – (HH Horne.)

b) Man is not a fixed entity. He is the measure of all things.

c) Society is an inevitable part for the development of human personality. Man is highly social in character.

d) Change is a universal phenomenon. The world is always in a state of change. If there is any ultimate reality, that is change only.

e) There are no eternal or absolute values, knowledge, truth or reality.

f) Man only judges what is useful for him. Value, knowledge and reality are based upon this judgment.

g) Experiences and experiments are very important in determining reality, knowledge and values. This world is a process, a flux.

h) Universe is composed of laws and relations. World is mechanical and physical in character. But there may be a spiritual order behind it.

i) Pragmatists are pluralists.

j) Utility and practical uses are important to determine the value of anything. It stands for novel, dynamic and practical ideals.

k) Pragmatism has strong faith in democracy

l) Man is the supreme creation in this world. Everything is for his utilization. He is to adjudicate everything.

m) Truth is formed by its result. Problems are the motives of the truth. That means man seeks truth to find solution to the problem he may experience. (Life is a laboratory and every individual is experimenting to find out the truth)

## Pragmatism and Education

Like other schools of philosophy pragmatism too has influenced education in all its aspects. There is no other philosophy that influenced modern education trends more than pragmatism. Pragmatic concept has specific determinations in framing aims, curriculum, teaching methods, discipline and teacher's role.

According to pragmatic thought, philosophy is the product of educational practice rather than education being the outcome of philosophy. Philosophy is an educational theory, which is an outcome of education. John Dewey was against to the opinion that education is the dynamic side of philosophy. He believed education is the 'producer' of philosophical thoughts. Educational practices take to the creation and development of knowledge, values and reality or truth.

Pragmatists give importance to school and schooling. They do not admit the value of gaining knowledge for knowledge sake. Knowledge acquisition is for better living. Education aims to enable pupils to create their own values. Occupation is important for a valuable life. Education is not for education sake, but for the sake of better living. Beyond man's practical need, education is purposeless and aimless.

Education should focus on democratic approach and on the idea of learning by doing. Socialized activities are must for social experiences. These experiences and interaction with the environment must be provided by education. It is envisaged by education that an individual can mould his environment according to his needs, interest, purpose and practical utility. These are being desirably directed by education. Education is indispensable for personal and social development.

The chief task of education is to make life worth living. Man's success is not the 'success in education'. His success is success in society where he lives.

Education must be interesting according to the developmental stages of educant. Educational practices need a child's active participation. Pragmatism stressed on individual's practical success in his future life. It should make the child able to adapt himself to the social environment. Education is a social necessity rather than an individual need. Pragmatic education is based upon practical utility, personality development and social development of individual and better and worthy living.

**Pragmatism: Aims of Education**

There is no singlc and permanent aim in pragmatic education. Aims are determined not by education but educant. So the aims of education will change according to the personal and social needs of the individual. The individual aim will change in different stages of life.

Education is a lifelong process; informal, non-formal and formal. All these three are education with different ends. As there are no fixed values and truth or reality there is no scope for fixed and ultimate aim. The destination of education is the development of spirit of cooperation, development of social values and democratic feeling.

Pragmatic education aims growth and progress of individual and society. Education functions to reach the end – that is 'development of individual's ability to create his own values.' Education aims well-knit adjustment of an individual with his environment. Another aim is that of solutions for day-to-day life problems. It also aims practical utility in life. The teachers, students, parent, management and state, who are some of the different segments of education, may have developed their own idea of aims of education. The aim of education depends upon the aim of life of an individual. That is the reason to say aim is to individual and not to education.

Pragmatic education is progressive education. Progressive education has no fixed and static aims. Aims are in the making according to the practical life needs and approaches of individual.

**Pragmatism: Curriculum**

The major principle of curriculum construction, according to pragmatic thought, is the practical utility. Curriculum should be utilitarian and purposely oriented to support life on this earth. Selection of subjects should be based upon an individual's everyday life needs. A child's interest in artistic expression, construction, activities, conversation or communication, tendency to discover and play should be satisfied by curriculum. There should be enough provisions for learning by doing.

Pragmatic curriculum is an integrated, diversified and activity-centered curriculum. Curriculum development is based on certain principles. They are the principles of actual experience, child's interest, learning by doing, individual differences, stages of development, subjects' integration, psychological bases, social needs, practical utility, child-centeredness and experiments and verification.

At the primary level pragmatists give importance to development of basic language skills, communication skills, arithmetic and basic science. It will provide certain activities to the child's tender muscles. Curriculum provides activities to develop the value of dignity of labour. It must help the child to develop the ability to make values from time to time. Pragmatists follow the principle of flexibility in curriculum development. Rigid curriculum is against the concept of democratic classroom. Learners can interpret the framework of curriculum according to their social needs and interests. The possibility of learner's interpretation in curriculum development is a special characteristic of pragmatic curriculum construction. Disciplines, which can't help a child's adaptation with environment, should not be included in the curriculum. There should be provisions for updated introduction of curricular subjects.

———

Pragmatism focuses on play-way, activities, observation and experiments as ways of curriculum transaction. It gives importance to science subjects. Social science, health and hygiene, language and physical training are also emphasized. There is no strict advice in selection of types of subjects. Any subject can be selected for the curriculum based on the utility, needs and significance to the learner.

**Pragmatism: Role of Teacher**

A pragmatic teacher must be a pragmatist in thought and action. A good teacher is a teacher technician – a techno guru! He must have the ability to locate the problems of students and to give proper guidance in solving problems.

A pragmatist teacher must have faith in activity-centeredness, learning by doing, democratic classroom, flexibility of curriculum and transaction, interest-based teaching, experience, observation, experimentation and verification. Ability of communication is an important quality of a teacher. A teacher should constitute programmes like school parliament, club activities, social service, self-government activities and so on with equal importance to classroom teaching.

The teacher has an important role in the teaching-learning process. But he is not a person to impart all knowledge to the pupils. In pragmatism, a teacher's place is not as significant as in idealism and not less significant as in naturalism. It is said, "neither does pragmatism treat teacher as an onlooker as desired by naturalists, nor is the teacher an indispensable necessity as idealists believe. In pragmatists philosophy a teacher occupies the middle role. He is a guide, friend, leader and an observer."

A teacher is not a static personality. He should not be rigid but flexible. He should welcome change in all aspects of teaching from time to time. He should be aware of modern trends and psychological developments in the learning process. He must adapt modern technological developments into the teaching-learning process. He should be able to run the classroom along with the technological advancements of the world. Keep the classroom live and active and scientifically tempered. Adapt all communication strategies with the help of technological devices.

A teacher should bother about the spirit of democratic attitude, cooperation and brotherhood. He must use the possibilities of collaborative learning, cooperative learning, socialized simulation and interactive teaching strategies. A teacher, better to call an educator, is the most important element in keeping school adaptable with social environment.

*Nobody will select a tailor, if he follows a stagnant single mode of fashion in stitching; no one may go to a haircutting saloon if the barber follows only one fashion of hairdressing. The tailor and the barber should change according to the trends and fashion that the time and person demands. Then why not a teacher? A teacher never stagnates in his approach; instead he should change in method, style of teaching, approach, interaction strategies and all other aspects of teaching according to the demands of time and leaner.*

**Pragmatism: Discipline**

Pragmatism orients child to self-discipline through cooperative and democratic work. The best form of discipline is auto-discipline or the discipline developed by self-experiences.

Pragmatists always welcome individual freedom, subject to social freedom. Individuality is highly acknowledged. At the same time freedom enjoyed by the individual should not harm the society. They welcome individual discipline, which leads to social discipline. Discipline is a primary factor to lead better social life.

While children engage in free, real and purposeful activities, automatically discipline will emerge. Development of discipline is an activity-centered process. Through interested, cooperative and creative works they can develop inner discipline. A school should provide opportunities to experience such situations. Corporal punishments are to be avoided. Negative reinforcement is suggested as an alternative of punishment and as a device against indiscipline problems.

Development of discipline in pragmatic system is a voluntary attempt. It is based on self-experience and activities. A child should inculcate a sense of discipline in accordance with the creation of values. A free atmosphere with provisions to engage in cooperative works and democratic interaction shall provide children real experiences and through these experiences a sense of discipline will emerge.

## Pragmatism: Methods

An individual learns by doing rather than thinking. A child has innate interest for activity and creative construction. Pragmatic methods zeroed in on the development of these capabilities of child. Pragmatists welcome any suitable method, which provides realistic situations for experiencing the problems of learning. They aim at preparing a child for practical life.

Pragmatists welcome experimental method, trial and error learning, discussion method, socialized simulation skills and techniques, team teaching and all other activity-based methods.

**Project method**: Pragmatists describe project method as the best method to provide learning based on real and practical life problems to the learner. According to Stevenson 'project is a problematic act, carried to completion in its natural setting.' Thomas and Lang commented, "Project is a voluntary undertaking which involves constructive effort or thought and eventuates in objective results." Project method is a process-oriented method. The teacher is a guide and supervisor in this method. He has to interact and involve in the whole activities or processes while the pupil undertakes a project. Project has processes like,

Problem identification

Planning, execution

Data collection

Analysis, and

Documentation.

"A project is a wholehearted purposeful activity proceeding in a social environment" is the opinion of Kilpatrick. Pragmatists say that purposeful teaching, practical experience, social and psychological environment, social interaction, integration of qualities and all related aspects are there in the project method. This method is founded and developed by Kilpatrick and John Dewey. Among the applications of pragmatic principles in education, project method stands at the top.

While adopting a method of teaching, the teacher has to bear in mind certain principles like principle of interest, principle of individual difference, experience activity centeredness, child-centeredness, practical utility and principle of learning by doing. Pragmatists agree with any method of teaching based on these principles. Experience from activity is the basis of the entire learning process. (Child learns more through activities than thinking) So any method selected by a teacher should be introduced with activities. Effective learning is learning by learner's own effort. Teachers' responsibility is to provide opportunities to pupils to learn by their own effort; i.e. atmosphere for self-learning. The method regards the teaching-learning process as natural, purposeful, utilitarian, highly motivating, interesting and need-based. It should be democratic and child-centered in all aspects.

**Pragmatism in Practice**

Pragmatic thoughts highly influenced contemporary classrooms. It is believed that rather than a distinguished school of philosophy pragmatism is an attitude. It has no well-defined dogma, no doctrines, and no deep explanations for eternal values, knowledge, truth and reality. It gives a few notions on spiritual and divine world. Pragmatism is oriented towards utility and practical life. Pragmatic attitude is very effective in regular school system. Synthesis of pragmatic principles with other thoughts is more effective in classroom.

Pragmatists believe that values are creates by individuals. The value creation and development is the result of school experience. Their attitude is against the traditional classroom practices, teaching learning strategies and evaluation systems. They focused not on 'content learning' but on creative expression of students.

In the classroom pragmatism doesn't aim at spiritual goals or naturalization. It focuses on personal and social development of individuals to lead better life in this world. School is a center to educate learners. Its organization should be better with infrastructure, technological devices and all other supports. Teachers must be given sufficient training and refreshment or in-service courses to keep them up-to-date with modern advancements.

Most of the pupils seek education to serve a purpose –Job. They aim at a profession by education and not liberation or spiritual development. Hence education is better if it is job-oriented. Vocationalization of education is a notable suggestion of pragmatism.

Pragmatism is practical in approach. Pragmatic educationists plan education for this world. Hence all aspects of education must focus on practical utility. It might be properly planned. Utilitarian concept of education is a pragmatic contribution.

Pragmatists give importance to project method, socialized simulations, cooperative learning strategies. Vast use of technological devices and audio-visual aids are advised. They gave importance to communicability of teacher. Communicability of educator is equally important as qualification and thorough knowledge in content.

Pragmatic educational thoughts do not argue on dogmatic principles but demand practical utility to individual to live in this world as a better human being. Classroom is nothing more than a classroom. It must be used as an effective center for learning. It is not a spiritual environment. It is a place for learning; makes it purposeful and activity-centered for better learning and better social life.

John Dewey's Laboratory School is considered as an outcome of pragmatic principles. This school is founded by Dewey at Chicago in University of Chicago. There he practiced his own philosophical thoughts. There followed the principles of living in social setting, closer relationship with social units, everyday experiences based instruction and attention to individual needs and interests.

The use of technological developments and psychological practices in classroom is the notable reflection of this philosophy. Project method, which is a contribution of pragmatic thought, is adopted all over the world. In short, pragmatism as a philosophical thought highly influenced the modern educational practices in almost all aspects.

### 5.2.4 Realism

"Realism in general is the doctrine which holds that objects have an existence of their own, i.e. existence independent of their being. Object's relation to the subject in knowledge is only an external relation." – J. Normandy. In epistemology realism is the doctrine that the external world exists independently of perception, and substantially as perceived by us; in logic, the doctrine that universal ideas have objective realities corresponding to them.

Realism is the philosophical theory that states existence of object is real. It is not spiritual but material. Quality of an object is independent of subject. The independent qualities determine reality of object, not the perceived qualities. Object exists irrespective of our knowledge. A flower has its own qualities, beauty, fragrance, etc. These qualities are there with flowers whether they are enjoyed or not (perceived or not perceived) by a man. The qualities of flowers are independent of man's perception.

Realism is a metaphysical philosophy. It gives importance to material reality. 'Object and qualities are independent of and uninfluenced by the knower and the process of knowledge.' Perception and experience do not frame reality. A piece of tube in the water is perceived as broken. But it is not the real fact. A coin under the water seems bigger than the actual size. But it is not big, as we perceived. Oasis and Horizon are not reality as we see or perceive them. Material appearance of object with all qualities is the reality. To be is not as perceived. It is not the idea that determines the object's existence. Objects have existence without any idea behind them.

Realism is a philosophy of objective reality. World of idea, illusion, abstraction, spiritual reality, and absolutism are not there in the dictionary of realism.

Realism is concerned with the real world. Real world is the material world. Reality of this material world is outside the mind of man. The human mind does not determine material reality. The material world around is the real world and not a world of fantasy. The spiritual idea and ideas like universal soul and individual soul are unwanted beliefs. These are human interpretations. Man can interpret. But the features of anything will remain with it irrespective of man's interpretation. Qualities of Potassium Cyanide can be interpreted and explained by one as a precious element, nutritious and tasty to eat. Whatever is the interpretation and perception, potassium cyanide has its own features. Man will die by it because it is toxic. That feature is its reality above interpretation and perception. That 'quality' exists with it above our knowledge of it. It is the reality, which is material. It is said by C V Good that 'reality is the doctrine that objective reality or the material universe exists independently of conscious mind, its nature and perception are being affected by being known.' Aristotle viewed that 'man doesn't infer the existence of external objects from representative images or 'ideas' in conscious, but perceives them directly in some form through a presentation of the objects themselves in sense perception level.'

## Major Thoughts in Realism

Realism has been divided into different groups. Some of them are critical realism, neo realism, naïve realism, scientific realism, Platonic realism, humanistic realism, sense realism, social realism and objectivism (objectivism considered as a synonym to realism).

Aristotle (383–322 BC) is generally considered as the father of realism. John Locke, Kant, John Frederick Herbert, George Santayana, John Hopkins, Montague, Barton Perry, Francis Bacon and Cominius are some of the propagators of realistic philosophy.

## Mind and Matter in Realism

Realism emerged as revert against extreme idealistic views. This revert can be understood from the views against idealistic concept of mind and matter. Realists do not deny the existence of mind. To them mind is a material reality. Realism gives equal status to both mind and matter. A man can't live without body and mind. It is the reality. Both mind and body are equally needed for acquisition of knowledge and practice of values. John Locke said that mind is a "tabula rasa", which means a clean blank slate. There is nothing inside the mind at first. Mind receives knowledge, values and truth slowly through interpretation with physical environment. Acquisition of material reality is the function of mind. Mind has no spiritual existence without body. It is almost material and is the constitution of brain function.

**Epistemological Principles of Realism**

Real knowledge exists with the object and not with the subject. The knowledge about object is beyond subject's perception. Whether they are known or not they exist independently with the object. Knowledge acquired by a subject may change. But the knowledge, which persists with object, is unchangeable. Persisting qualities of object are static and realistic.

All knowledge whatever we perceive exists with object. Knowledge is object-based and not subject-based. Acquisition of knowledge is possible through scientific methods like observation, experiment, and inductive and deductive method. Knowledge is material and realistic, not spiritual. Knowledge of object is direct and perceptual. Perceived knowledge does not affect the object. Different individuals may have different knowledge of identical objects. What object really has is really trustable. It has existence apart from ideas.

*Suppose one person touches you. It doesn't mean that he touches your one cell or a limb or a part. He touches you as a whole.*
*It is the realistic experience. A friend talking to you means he talks to you, and not to your sense organ and receives reply from another sense organ.*

**Axiological Principles of Realism**

Realism believes in object-centeredness of values. Axiological concept of realism is against the heavenly created values and ideal values. Realists do not believe in spiritual values and permanent values. They are favorable towards aesthetic values and naturalistic values. Values can't be created or developed without man's effort. As in the case of knowledge realism believes values known by subject may vary. Object has its values irrespective of knowledge about it.

Value is materialistic and matter in motion. Values exist and function in the social life of human beings. Realism approves mechanical explanation to value and its scientific analysis. Values are not absolute or fixed. They are relative. An individual develops values according to circumstances, needs, situation and purpose. Realists welcome all values as practical and needful. Man develops values to face realities of life in this material world. They are the supporting factor to lead life practically.

**Metaphysical Principles of Realism**

Philosophically, realistic reality is an image beyond imagination! It is the query, what is really real. According to this school reality is objective reality. Entire world has mechanical order and physical existence. Human beings are part of this mechanical order.

Reality is independent of mind. This can be understood from the words of John Locke, "mind is a tabula rasa, and reality is outside the mind". It is the matter and material characteristics make mind colorful.

*A white dot on blackboard is perceived as 'white on blackboard'. But the reality may be different. It may be a white board, painted black all over except the white dot!*

*Suppose fifty men are killed in a train accident. The immediate perception is that fifty men lost life. But there is another reality; only fifty are killed, a lot of people are saved from the accident.*

Objects possess their own truth. A thing can exist with its qualities without being humanly known. Jasmine, the flower, has fragrance. Whether the man recognizes it or not it possesses the fragrance. Things – objects – are there whether human mind knows or recognizes or experience or not.

Reality is based on cause and effect relation of the material existence. Everything has cause and effect relationship behind it. It is the real fact applicable to matter and mechanical order. It is said that realism believes in 'satysya satyam' – the truth of the truth.

## Major Principles of Realism

Though major tenets of realism are discussed under the above titles, a glance through them will help to get more specific acquaintance with realism. The major principles are listed below:

a) Realism is a practical philosophy.

b) Realism gives equal status to both mind and matter. They consider both as material and mechanical in character.

c) Knowledge and reality of an object are independent. Knowledge of the subject doesn't affect the object or its qualities.

d) World is not an illusion or hallucination. It is real in all aspects.

e) There is cause and effect relationship behind everything in this universe.

f) Realists reject the existence of spirit, God, spiritual existence of mind, nonmaterial idea of world and telelogical creation of universe.

g) They consider religion is manmade.

h) Scientific inquiry, observation and factual analysis are important in knowledge acquisition, and knowing values and truth.

i) Scientific method is the realistic approach to know the reality.

j) Material world is the real world.

k) There is a natural or physical law and mechanical design to govern this world.

l) Realism believes in scientific knowledge and approach based on observation and experimentation. To a certain extent realism is a philosophy of experience too.

**Realism and Education**

Realistic education emphasized on present life. Education is to make man realistic to live in this material world. Man should be able to face the realities of life and should get awareness about the problems of life by education. The education, which makes man able to live in this world with realistic approach, is the education proposed by realism. Realists advise education should be done in free environment.

Education is being approached not as a spiritual entity but as a scientific necessity. Education is a social process. Education of an individual is the responsibility of society, by and large responsibility of state. It is the preparation of life. Education is to develop individual as a master of his environment. Economic self-sufficiency and job assurance are considered realistic ends of education. Realists do not stand with such concept of education, which is explained spiritually. Realism propagates a fact that life is not a bed of roses. It has pebbles and thorns too. As there are conveniences there are struggles. An individual should be able to face both of them with realistic feeling. Education must function as a device to serve these purposes.

Realistic education is science-based. This philosophy puts forward certain basic interpretations regarding education. Some of them are:

— Education should not be a complex task. Entire method of education should be as simple as possible.

— Classroom learning is the important aspect of education. Teaching learning processes must focus on vast use of learning aids, scientific equipments, communication instruments and all psychological devices for better classroom teaching learning.

— Stressed vast use of technological devices.

— The purpose of reading materials, supportive items and devices must be designed according to the need of students.

— Only scientific and useful knowledge are to be given to children.

— Teaching should make use of effective and modern methods. Teachers should be aware of psychological applications in teaching and learning. In-service training programmes to teachers must be effectively planned and executed.

— Maxims of teaching, principles of teaching, motivation, and psychological consideration of child age, interest of teaching learning process and relevance of subject matter are considered important.

— Education must provide social security to individuals.

Realistic education is not a concept of vagueness. It is practical and scientific. As it is a practical philosophy, there are practical explanations and interpretations to educational problems than ambiguity of explanations. It strongly propagates that philosophical principles alone will not work in education; what we need is psychological, technological and need-based and scientific development.

Human life is a metamorphosis from biological existence and heritage to social existence and heritage. It is a change from a biological animal to social animal; education accelerates this process. Education is a cultural and social necessity. It is said that education is not to perceive or enjoy Rome, but to live in Rome.

## Realism: Aims of Education

Happiness is the real goal we aim in our life. Education should aim to fulfill needs and desires of an individual to make an individual happy. Education aims to acquire knowledge and skills to meet with the needs of life. Education is for complete living. Aims of education are not a static idea. Aims vary from time to time. There are no spiritual or eternal aims to be achieved by education. Aim of education differs from person to person.

The major aims stated by Herbert Spencer are:

a) Self-preservation

b) Earn a living

c) Education for upbringing children (this is a naturalistic aim too. Pupils should be taught the basic principles of family life and how to nurture children because there is a social reality everybody should face – reproduction. Education should aim at making good parents in future.)

d) Citizenship training

e) Utilization of leisure – education aims at proper utilization of free time in happy recreational activities and needs of activities

Other major aims are self-determination, self-realization and self-integration. (Dr. Broudy). Self-determination helps an individual to understand his own strength and limitations. Self-realization is not the transcendental or spiritual perfection as is said by idealism. Here it means the realization of one's own potentialities. Self-realization is recognition of self-estimation. Realism also aims at character development and moral development of an individual. Development of scientific attitude and scientific temper are also aimed at by realistic education.

Actually, by education realism aims deviated ends. We can see that different sections of society are developed by different aims of education. Here it has almost the same attitude as that of pragmatism. Parent, teacher, student, state and administrators have aimed different ends by educational processes. We can't assign the same aims according to their intentions. It is difficult to point out a specific aim suited to all. There is no common and universal aim. If there is a common aim to realism, then that is 'preparation for good life.' All other aims are subordinate to the major aim, which is social reality.

However certain common aims normally suggested by education are:

— Create good individuals with character, mores and attitude.

— Development of vocationally efficient pupils

— Create good society

— Create good citizens with effective citizenship training.

— Development of good state or nation.

Realistic education also aims at development of willpower and ability for decision-making.

The major individual aims of education suggested by realism are:

— Preparation of the individual for happy and successful life

— Development of physical and mental powers of child.

— Development of ability of senses.

— Improvement of vocational efficiency

— Child's adaptation with nature and social environment

— Development of problem-solving ability, reasoning and intelligence.

**Realism: Curriculum**

Realistic curriculum includes the areas, which propose the following:

— Primary place to the consideration of real situations, science, vocational practice and subjects for character development and moral development.

— Secondary place to arts, literature and linguistic studies.

Mother tongue is the medium of instruction for curriculum transaction. Realism advocates free selection of subjects from the given subjects by learners according to their needs and interests. Curriculum is the means to form desirable learning habits. Possibilities to achieve mastery of subject matter by learners must be considered while framing the curriculum. It should be framed according to the principles like simple to complex, general to specific, easy to difficult etc. Curriculum should consider developmental stages of the child. It must provide opportunities for physical training, sensory training, intellectual training and moral education.

Integration of subject and social relevance of content matter are significant in the selection of subjects. Curriculum is not for knowledge sake, but for life's sake. It should develop scientific attitude and temper of the child. Curriculum must be fact-centered. It should be concrete and never abstract in approach.

Realistic education prefers general curriculum for early stages and specialization at the later stages.

## Realism: Role of Teacher

The role of teacher is fairly important. He has a significant role to perform behind curtain and on the stage.

A teacher must be a scholar. He should try to develop scientific attitude among pupils. A teacher must be a scholar. He should try to develop scientific attitude among pupils. A teacher should possess thorough knowledge of subject. He should be informed of modern trends in educational practices, changing methods, developments in educational psychology, technology and philosophy and needs of society. A teacher should be ready to make use of any techniques till the learner achieves satisfactory learning. He should think from students' side. A teacher is responsible to make the pupils realize about the realities of life they may face in the society.

A good teacher is a good scholar and a continuous learner. He should recognize that idea alone would not work. He should be practical. Concrete, scientific and factual processes in teaching and learning are the approaches of realistic teacher.

A teacher must be facilitated with simple, scientific and innovative methods and vast use of audiovisual aids. As audiovisual aids are concrete, factual and possess the principle of concrete to abstract, their use is important in classroom communication.

A teacher is not an isolated personality. He should have day-to-day contacts with the society. He must be knowledgeable of the current socio-political affairs. Then only he can lead students to a life of social consequences.

**Realism: Freedom and Discipline**

According to realistic concept, discipline is not a rigid concept. Discipline is for the convenience of students. Concept of freedom and discipline varies from person to person and society to society. It is object-centered. Discipline emerges as social discipline. It is to be developed along with other activities. Social interactions and opportunities to interact with social consequences or realistic situations shall make an individual disciplined.

School atmosphere is an important factor in the development of child's discipline and proper direction of freedom. Realistic discipline is the smooth adjustment of child with his environment. Through the interaction self-discipline shall be developed. Emergence of discipline is an automatic development. It is not to be imposed. Discipline is to be realized and practiced by the child himself. The socialization process itself is a process of acquiring discipline. A child has to become a part of the society. Moral development and character development are mainly associated with the socialization process. A child acquires moral development from his family and society. It is said that school should be like the lap of mother, full of affection, love and sympathy. 'Make the school fit to the child rather than making child fit to the school' is the realistic view.

Self-discipline is considered as the best discipline. Realists welcome discipline through social consequences. They welcome emancipated form of discipline. Pupils must be given freedom to plan and decide their activities and to execute them. Teacher-pupil interaction, institutional climate, teaching morale, ethos, classroom atmosphere etc. are important in the development of discipline in a child. Discipline is not a destination or an end. It is the means. It is a process (a continuous or lifelong process) that helps an individual adjust with his environment. Determination of the discipline is to be developed by the individual himself.

**Realism: Methods**

Realism gives less importance to bookish knowledge and textbook method. Methods of teaching adopted should be effective and interesting to both learner and teacher. A method should be adopted primarily from the learner's side and it should keep direct and real experience in the teaching learning process. Teaching is a reciprocal contact. Like naturalism, realism also gives importance to training to senses. Gaining knowledge through senses in accordance with the natural ability and capacity of the child and method of experiments and observation are also signified by realism.

The methods should be innovative and relevant. Vast use of audiovisual aids is advised. Motivation in learning is very important. Scholastic lectures, discussions, Socratic method, problem-solving method, case study approach, inductive and deductive method, experimental method, project method, seminars and symposium are the major methods advised by realism. A method of teaching should develop scientific attitude and provide realistic experience to the learner.

More specifically, we can explain the adoptable methods with the help of Spencer's idea of method of teaching, which is based on the common maxims of teaching. Major maxims of teaching are:

a) Easy to difficult

b) Known to unknown

c) Concrete to abstract

d) Definite to indefinite

e) Specific to general

f) Inductive to deductive

g) Analysis to synthesis

h) Experimental to rational

Based on all these maxims, a teacher can make classroom teaching more effective.

J F Herbert advocated scientific method to teach any subject. The method of teaching should follow five steps.

a) Preparation

b) Presentation

c) Comparison

d) Generalization

e) Application

To conclude, realism doesn't argue on the method, which is selected by the teacher but the mode of making use of the selected method. The administration of method should focus on its scientific and realistic use.

## Realism: Concept of Learning

Realism has different and realistic views on learning. Learning is an individual and social necessity. It is a psychological notion. Realism says that learning will be effective if it takes place in a realistic experience. Motivation, need of learning, interest in content matter, readiness to learn and prerequisite or previous knowledge play a significant role in effective learning.

Senses also have an important role in making learning effective. Classroom atmosphere is equally significant. Hearing, seeing and doing are the three ways of learning. Learning by doing is more effective.

The teacher has a major role in the learning process of a child. He should make use of innovative strategies and be able to use the AV aids and realistic experiences in classroom. Learning is object-centered behaviour. Each individual learns in different ways. Learning strategies, learning tasks and meta-cognitive awareness differ from individual to individual. Learning to learn is the habit to be developed. Individual differences in learning should be well considered by the teacher. Principles like things before words, sensory learning, practice at each stage of learning, learning through realistic experiences and prohibition of rote learning are important in effective learning.

## Realism in Classroom

To realism, education is a social necessity. Realists do not spend their time to discuss much on spiritual attainment and nature centrism. Classroom teaching is for knowledge development and skill development of the learner. School is to satisfy the livelihood of both educators and learners.

It is not the philosophy but culture and society that determine the role of teacher in the classroom. A classroom should not be static. It should change according to social change, cultural change, and social development, technological and psychological development.

Realistic classroom is zeroed in on effective teaching and learning. Education is for earning a living. School should prepare student for his future life in the society. Hence, realistic classroom should make use of methods and strategies to develop a child's ability to face realities in future life and social consequences. A realistic classroom is a miniature of the real society.

Education is for sociological, economic, psychological, intellectual and cultural uplifting of individual and society. It aims at an individual's upward social mobility. Education itself should function as an asset.

## An Epilogue on Schools of Philosophy

There are several deviated thoughts in philosophy. Idealism, naturalism, pragmatism and realism are discussed here. They are the typical schools of philosophy that influenced education scenario to great extent. A quick run through their tenets and principles will help in clear-cut understanding of their application in education.

Idealism is considered the oldest philosophy. It influenced education from its very origin. Educational contributions of Plato are based on idealism. It is a philosophy that speaks about spiritual world and considers education as a means to reach spirituality. Education for 'Moksha' is their concept. Education is that which emancipate us.

Idealism is criticized as a rigid, dogmatic and abstract thought. It believed idea is the reality behind this world. Every thing in this universe is the material appearance of spiritual idea behind it. Matter can exist only with this idea. They are spiritual knowledge and spiritual reality; both are eternal. The spiritual values ascertain this universe as truth, beauty and goodness. No other philosophy can stand prominent like idealism as this thought connects education with spirituality.

Naturalism believes in the infinite influence of nature. Nature is the supreme source of values, knowledge and reality. The ultimate reality is the nature. There are no values outside the nature. Man acquires and creates knowledge and values by his interaction with the nature. He learns everything from the nature.

Man is not a social animal but an offspring of nature. Education is not a process with spiritual end. It is nature centric and aims at better synthesis with nature.

Pragmatism is a down to earth philosophy. It is not philosophically fit to explain various issues like spirituality, universal soul, etc. It is focused on practical utility and better life of man in this world. Man is the measure of all things. Everything in this world is made for human being. Man is the supreme creation in this world. Pragmatism gives importance to human experience to value any thing; knowledge is that which works. Practical utility is the value of knowledge. Reality is always in the making. Education is a social necessity. It is for better life, not for another spiritual world.

Realism is objectivism. Knowledge, value and reality are object-centered. It is not the subject that determines the quality of object. Education also has the same character. Educational values are determined by teachers, administrators, organizers and pupils independently. Education is socio-cultural necessity. It is scientific and intends development of scientific attitude in the child.

In education, idealism considers ideals of life, naturalism is concerned with child's nature, pragmatism deals with practical utility of educational process and realism, which is more materialistic, considers realities of life and social consequences.

An educated man to idealism is a man who realized the spiritual idea behind the universe and its elements. Education is not the degrees an individual attains. He is not '*vocationalist*' but a spiritually cultivated human being.

To naturalism, an educated one is nature centric in his thoughts, feelings, ideals and actions. He is a nature-nurtured individual. No habits or character can be developed in an individual by education. They are naturally acquired. Nature is the asset of man, which functions not according to cosmic principle, but according to the laws of nature. Educated man is one who identifies self-abilities and expresses his capabilities and creativity.

As a humanistic 'down to earth philosophy' pragmatism considers educated human being as a well-knit person, who will be utilitarian, practical and able to live a more practical life. Its educational concept is anthropo-centric. It is not a static but dynamic and pluralistic philosophy in educational practices. So an educated man is not static in his ideology. He welcomes all changes. Change is the only unchangeable fact.

The typical realism says education a socio-cultural necessity. An educated man is 'fit' to earn his livelihood and to lead a better life by facing realities of day-to-day social consequences. An individual is educated not for another world, but for this world. Moral development, character development, development of scientific attitude, etc are the aims of education.

On a general analysis we can find several similar opinions regarding philosophy of education and aspects of education in the principles of major schools of philosophy discussed here. It means these thoughts are not a watertight compartment, but share the ideals among them. They all influence the philosophy of education and do reciprocal contacts to nourish the education scenario.

## 5.3 Educational Philosophy

### 5.3.1 Meaning and Importance

Educational philosophy is the application of philosophical thoughts and theories in the field of education. It is the area in which philosophy discusses the matters and issues of education. It has the greatest importance in the scenario of educational practices. Along with the development of formal education system the development of educational philosophy emerged as a subject of discussion. No state can plan a system of education without the help of educational philosophy. No educationist can contribute to the discipline of education without considering the educational philosophy.

Philosophy is the contemplative side of life and education is the dynamic side. It is education that makes life a success. But its way is planned by philosophy. Hence educational philosophy has significant importance in the educational development of an individual and society.

Educational philosophy carries the ideals of education. Philosophy lays down principles, which are carried into effect in education. Educational philosophy links the process of formation of doctrine, which is a function of philosophy, and the practice of the doctrine by education. It carries the whole principles and ideologies to be practiced by education. The success of educational philosophy is determined by the practice of these principles by education.

Educational philosophy discusses the arising effects of philosophical problems or issues in education scenario. It is the basic thought of how epistemology, axiology and metaphysics contribute to the development of education. It also seeks how these problems or branches of philosophy interact with a single aspect or the whole aspects of education for the fruitful end of education as a discipline.

Educational philosophy is an area of discipline that deals with different features of education in depth. It influences the facets of education such as planning, administration, school atmosphere, school morale, curriculum, textbooks, teaching methods, strategies, discipline, teacher-pupil relationship and even evaluation.

There are different values that can be achieved by the study of educational philosophy for educational practitioners like administers, organizers, governing bodies, policymakers, head of institutions, teachers, students, researchers and counselors.

Study of educational philosophy provides a comprehensive approach to educational practitioners on the meaning of education and place of education in the social life. It philosophizes the education. Philosophy of the educational system will help to develop positive, progressive, and critical attitude towards life. It also develops critical thinking.

Smooth running of educational system and its effectiveness are directly influenced by educational philosophy. Seeking solutions to educational problems without the support of a sound philosophy will be a fruitless attempt.

# Three Other Schools – Existentialism, Humanism and Eclecticism

The fusion of all well to do principles of all thoughts is better than a single philosophical thought' is the idea behind the coming out of eclecticism. The philosophical views of are the core of explanations in this chapter. Content of this chapter explains the tenets of each of these thoughts of philosophy and their influence on different aspects of education.

*Existentialism,*
*Humanism* and
*Eclecticism*

Like the former this, chapter also zeroed in on the educational implications not the doctrinal explanation.

**There** have several schools of philosophy. As human beings have differences in thought and as they have differences in their interpretations and approaches towards every thing, there will arise different streams of philosophy. Some of these major philosophical schools are existentialism, humanism, materialism, rationalism, dialectic materialism, essentialism and eclecticism. This list is not complete.

Here, we are going to discuss three out of them – Existentialism, Humanism and Eclecticism.

## 6.1 Existentialism

Existentialism is emerged as a philosophical school in nineteenth century. Soren Kierkegard (1813–1855) and Friedrich

Nietzsche (1844–1900) were the earlier exponents of this thought. Jean Paul Sartre (1905–1980) is adorning top in the list of its modern thinkers. Though genesis is old, existentialism emerged as a perfect philosophy after the Second World War. Threat against human existence and the quest like why man lives in this universe, were paved the way for its emergence.

Existentialism is subjective in its approach. Objectivity is not a major trait. As it is subjective, it is difficult to find an 'all accepted' definition to existentialism. Existentialism is a philosophy believes on human essence. It seeks answer to 'how man exists rather than why man exists'. We can see notable contradictions in the views of famous existentialists. Even, some of them are theists and some others are atheists. But these contradictions do not harm the perfection of existentialism.

> *Treat every man as an end never as means. Manmakes himself. An individual is nothing else but his own or her own conscious existence.*
>
> – Existentialist view
>
> *There are two questions – how man came in to existence? And, why man exists in this universe? Existentialism is given importance to the second question. It seeks the purpose of individual existence.*

## Basic Philosophical Principles and Themes of Existentialism

There are six major basic themes and principles to understand existentialism.

*First principle*: The basic existentialist stand point is that 'existence precedes essence'. Man is a conscious subject, rather than a 'thing' to be predicted or interpreted or manipulated. Man exists as a conscious being.

The *second principle* is that of anxiety or the sense of anguish, a fear or dread which is not directed to any specific object, a generalized uneasiness of human existence. Anguish is the underlying, a felt everywhere and universal conditional of human existence. (This theme is highly criticized by some existentialists themselves)

The *third theme* is that of absurdity – unreasonability. An individual has his own existence but that existence is absurd or uncertain. To exist as a human being is wholly absurd. Life is incongruous, illogical and dependent on chance.

The *fourth theme* is that of nothingness. It is the principle of the void. Existentialists reject all philosophical ideologies which fail to define man's existence as conscious being. Individual has his own existence but that existence is nothingness.

*Fifth principle* is the theme of death. It is the final nothingness hang over the man like the sword of Democles at each moment of life. The whole of individual's being seems to drift away in to nothing at the moment of death (Some existentialists are against to this view. The feel death is as absurd as birth. It is not ultimate authentic moment of life).

The *sixth theme* is the principle of alienation. It is the estrange-ment, a type of separation. There is alienation between objects and individual's own consciousness. He tries to alienate from his own self and from the society. It may be at the time of the arousal of quests against his essence of existence.

## Metaphysics, Epistemology and Axiology: View of Existentialism

In its philosophical approach existentialism is subjective. According to most of the existentialists, ultimate reality can not be defined objectively. (Actually there is only one ultimate reality that is 'death' which is common to all). An individual is an existent. The individual reach to a personal inference of ultimate reality according to his own unique experience with the factors affect his existence: i.e. time and space. What is the purpose of one's existence? Why an existent does exist? Individual has a self awareness that he is an existent in a complex, changing and infinite world. He always struggle with purposes, hopes, fears, anxieties, beliefs, attitudes, aptitudes and desires. At the end of this struggle he anchors himself on a need to find a purpose for his existence. Then he realizes what is really real to him.

Reality is 'being' or existence of an individual. Existentialists stress man's concrete existence, his contingent nature, his personal freedom and consequent responsibility. They wish to restore the status of man which he has lost in the mechanized society. Existentialists considered mind as the source and substance of all knowledge. They welcome rational knowledge as the important knowledge. Knowledge has subjectivity. Each individual acquires and preserve knowledge in own way. Ways of processing and transforming are unique. In his existence man is alone; hence he is to learn by his own effort, activity and insight.

Each human being has his/her own uniqueness. He is one with deviated identity in the crowd. He is alone. He has he is own free will and thought. Each human being is presented with innumerable amount of choices. To define this aspect Sartre used the phrase 'existence precedes essence'. It means that the human essence is not fixed according to some abstract concepts. An abstract concept can not define what man is. The human essence is formed by the existent through own free will and choices.

Modern existentialism concerned with the problem of becoming rather the problem of being. Not the reflection but the life itself is important. Individual is the pivot of the universe. Man makes the society. Man develops **values** from his own insight and personal uniqueness. Values are developed not by man's social life or life in this nature, but by his own unique personal insight.

> The essence of philosophy is not the possession of truth but the search for truth.
> *The important concern of a Christian, if he is an existentialist is not the acquisition of knowledge of Christianity but how can become a good Christian.*

Man is the source of all values. Individual is the person to decide his values. Man is alone and is the person to lead himself.

Existentialists do not believe in absolute values. There are no universal values and common values. Individual has the freedom to choose the values that cherish and follow. Freedom is the source of all values.

### Existentialism and Education

Existentialistic education is an individual's necessity. The question 'Why my existence' can clearly be answered only by proper education. Education is not process of knowledge acquisition of something but an inquiry of how to become an existent with all the essence one individual has. Education is for 'life in this universe.' Existentialistic education makes individual able to face the one and only ultimate reality; i.e., death. It should bestow the idea 'live and let live'.

Sense of responsibility and duty are to be developed by individual. Recognition and practice of both of them are necessary for life. Sense of correctives and insight to own existence is also to be developed by education. Recognition of problems and ability of problem solving is to be cultivated by education.

Ideological dilemma is not a major problem of the world. Problems of practical existence are the major questions. We can not get rid of the practical problems. Human existence needs practical solutions and efforts to face the problems. Man needs sense of responsibility and freedom of choice.

Education is not the application of philosophical slogans. Philosophical ideologies will not work; for man's existence, man should work. Philosophical slogans are not the solutions to survive threat against human existence. Education is need based and aim oriented process. For example, if we aim national integration, international understanding and world peace, we should educate man orient to these needs. All these are to be developed in the mind of individual. Philosophical talk on secularism will not create a secular society. The process of education should practice its essence. Secular principles must be cultivated in each and every individual by education. Then only it becomes practical.

Education is realization of the individuality. Education is the tool to make individual realize his consciousness. Man is alone in his whole life. He has many problems to face – personal, social, psychological etc. individual has to be trained to over come all these problems by educational process. It should make him free from conflict and dilemma. Based on this concept, to a certain extent, religious education and moral education are welcomed by existentialists.

Existentialistic education stands for uncompromising affirmation to authentic freedom and individual uniqueness. Each individual is unique, independent and alone. He can never compare with another one. This is the most important message of existentialism to modern education.

Authentic freedom is the key word in educational process of existentialism. Authenticity can be explained in three ways:

a) One must have awareness on one's own self or existence. That is the awareness of one's own role.

b) One's own self is the basic of one's own judgment.

c) There must be congruence between word, thought and action.

All these three aspects of authenticity and authentic freedom and will are to be assimilated by education. it is possible by education only. According to existentialist view, education is a practical tool to use measure man's essence of existence.

## Aims of Education in Existentialism

Education in existentialism aims self-realization – realization of the reason of existence of human being. Education aims to promote the possibilities of liberating the mind from prejudices. Development of the spirit of 'live and let live' is also an aim of education. Acquisition of authenticity in the will of freedom and total development of personality are also aimed by existentialists.

Education is not simply a process for knowledge acquisition and skill development, but for over all development of individual. Personal qualities, personality traits and individual uniqueness are to be treated properly by education.

Existentialism aims realization of value of human personality through education. Another general aims are realization of inner truth and essence of human existence. It should aim realization of subjective consciousness and self confidence. Education must develop will power. Education is a process aimed emergence of practical personality.

## Curriculum and Methods

Existentialists say that teacher and taught are more important than curriculum in its designing, transaction, implementation and practice. They determine what to learn and how to learn. A predetermined and well defined curriculum with rigid principles will not satisfy the aims of educational process. Such a curriculum is not a must. From a platform of discipline or area of subjects, teacher and taught shall emerge curricular frame work. Methods also have the same behaviour. From a blend of methods they can select apt one. 'This is to this content' is not better suggestion in selection of methods.

The outlook of curricular frame work should be progressive, prosperous and optimistic. Mere science education and scientific methods shall not give progressive and humanistic outlook. Such an approach on curriculum and methods may fail to develop insight to the self. It will be a failure in inner realization and development of peace in individual mind. Science education should possess a humanist or existent outlook in its content and method. Curriculum should stress on social science, languages, philosophy and all humanity subjects equally or more with science subjects.

*Subjects, especially sciences have got many ramifications or upshots. Modern science subjects face 'specializations and super specializations'. Such specialization may make child narrower and narrower. Subjects should possess humanistic outlook and transact the spirit of the essence of human existence. Humanity subjects and humanitarian methods are necessary to develop existential attitude in child, to make his mind broaden and to develop insight to self.*

Education is an act of discovery. But the term discovery doesn't mean observation and experiments which leads to invention are the best methods. Best methods are the methods which provide insightful learning. Socratic Method is welcomed by existentialists because it helps individual to treat in teaching. Question and discussion in this method will continue until the problem being solved. Existentialists welcome any method with innovative approach if they save the ideal of existentialistic teaching.

## Role of Teacher

An existentialist teacher must be an existentialist. He has to act the role (in Socratic sense) of a midwife in classroom. Midwifery role of teacher helps the pupil to be a new baby! Teacher should have to work in the imagination of the child. He must find time to think and act according to the imaginary level of child. By teacher's involvement and interaction child should become able to image beyond teacher's imagination! Teacher is to create tissues of humanitarian attitude in the canvass of child's mind.

A teacher is a facilitator more than a tutor. Authenticity in attitude and performance is important. He should not let pupils to imprint knowledge unimaginably to their senses from second hand.

Certain specific advises to an existentialist teacher are:

— an existentialist teacher should possess thorough knowledge with authenticity.

— A teacher must be frank and open minded

— Should lead students to new images.

— Should have faith in freedom and will to choose.

— Should realize the uniqueness of individuality

— Should be active, polite, loving and affectionate

— Should be competent and conscious

— Must be co operative with others and never act as aloofer personality.

**Freedom and Discipline**

Real discipline is the discipline from insight. A child will develop discipline while he recognizes uniqueness of his individuality and purposes of existence. Hence, self realization is essential for discipline and qualified freedom. Freedom is the pivot of human life. But it must be qualified. It does not mean license to harm others. Freedom in classroom is essential. Students should be free to interpret with teacher, to ask questions, to encage in free discussions and to criticize teacher and school. Freedom is the 'life gas' of a child.

Existentialists stand for qualified self discipline. Recognition of the purpose of existence and uniqueness of individuality must lead an individual to acquisition of qualified self discipline. Disciplined individual will be able to remove all conflicts and to develop subjective consciousness. He only can ensure self development.

**Existentialism in Classroom**

In classroom existentialism has open minded policies. It is more practical. It accepts divinity and dignity of teacher and spirituality of classroom.

Freedom in classroom is stressed. A teacher should be democratic in approach and be free in class to be interpreted by children. Freedom of child must be ensured. Teacher must render individual attention. Individuality of child must be recognized and respected. The policy of 'give respect and take respect' must be followed.

Classroom must have provisions for self development of child. Sufficient opportunities for free interaction with others only provide provisions for recognition of individuality of one's own and others. Existentialists practically stand for supply of free learning materials, feeding and other support to students. Schooling and learning must not be a burden to pupils.

Teacher in classroom have to create situations in which the student may establish contact with his own self. There should have various opportunities in which the student must avail opportunities for various performances. Classrooms are not for teacher centered content transactions alone, it is a center provides basements for individual's all round development. Teacher must have subjective attitude. Teacher should realize the ills of modern over objective attitude. Children should relax from confusions, tension, anxiety, conflicts and corruption. School atmosphere must be oriented towards this aim. Humanitarian approach in attitude, interpretation and teaching methods must be followed. A classroom is a moral atmosphere to make a man "a man" and not to make a man an 'educated'. "A man should be a sincere man and not merely a consistent thinker" is the existentialist concept.

## 6.2 Humanism

Humanism is based up on a thought that man is a sensitive being, a creative soul. It is a philosophy of man-ism or human being-ism. It is concept of world humanity. The world is one family! We can see the rout in Indian thought *Vasudaiva kudumbakam*.

'It is a philosophy of joyous service for the greater good to all humanity in this natural world and according to the methods of reason and democracy' is the definition given by Lamon. It considers man is the measure of all things. 'Humanism is a faith in people, in all humanity and science as a means of attaining truth. It is also a quest for the ethical and spiritual values of life through philosophy, science, art and literature. It is a philosophy where is the centre and sanction. It stands for the **reasonable** balance of life. It is philosophy stand for the unity in diversity of world humanity. Humanism tries to liberate the minds of men from the blind compartments of religious principles. It has identified humanity with the divinity of the world. Milton, William Blake, Words Worth, Schiller F.C.S, Feltre, John Colet Erasmus, Lamon and Percy Nunn are some of the humanists. Gandhiji, Tagore, Dayanandha Saraswathy, Vivekanandha and Aurobindo are also humanists in certain aspects.

### Metaphysical Aspects of Humanism

Reality is not a static one to humanistic thought. Like Pragmatists, Humanists believe mundane world and its aspects are real. This world is a reality. Man is a social reality! He ha no other place to for happiness or fulfillment of life ambitions. Live now or not at all is the real concept. Humanists consider nature as a totality of being. Man is the evolutionary product of this great nature. He is the highest product in the universe with nothing above or beyond him but his own aspirations, principles and ideals. Man by himself can do little. It is only in the association with others that he can express his individuality in perfection. They believe that man is the master of his own destiny.

As far as the mind is concerned humanists believe it is a natural function of living organism and a product of evolution. Reason is the main instrument of mind. Mind is a device for effective social. It gives him identity in this mundane world.

**Epistemology**

Humanists believe in casual and evolutionary nature of the knowledge. Knowledge is cumulative. Man gets knowledge from experience. The real knowledge is that which function for the welfare of humanity. Scientific approach is necessary to generate knowledge. Reasoning is a universal ability to adjudicate knowledge. Humanists believe that rationality is inevitable in the process of knowledge acquisition. Rationality is the product of intellectualism.

**Axiology**

Humanists do not believe in eternal values or permanent values. Values are measured by man. Man is the rationale element to assess a value. The ethical and aesthetic values are determined by man for his life in this mundane world. They stress on democratic values like co operation toleration, cohesiveness and etc. they believe in humanistic and personal values like truth, beauty, goodness, (not in a spiritual sense but in humanitarian sense) love, sympathy, empathy, peace and nonviolence. Humanism considers liberty, equality and fraternity as the worthy values. Individual freedom is essential to achieve all values. It is also said that freedom is an instrument to create and develop social values.

**Humanism and Education**

Humanism in education has a vital role. Humanistic education is an attempt to liberate man from his bondages. It focuses on the future of humanity. The outlook of humanistic education is progressive, optimistic and evolutionary. The validity of education is assessed on the basis of human welfare. Humanism advocates human approach to educational theory and practice. Humanists believe in universalisation of education. Each and every individual in this world has right to avail education. Education is a fundamental right. Free and compulsory education and equality of educational opportunities are to be ensured. Man in this world has the right to get education irrespective of all discriminations like regional, cast, religious, communal and etc. education for exceptional children, financial support like loans, scholarships and special education are the responsibility of state's education system. They stand for democratic approach in education. To them, education is a social and cultural necessity. Education itself is a preparation of life.

## Aims of Education

Education, according to humanism, aims at man making. Education is for the development of rationality, scientific temper, secularism, democracy and personal and social values and for the welfare of humanity. It enables man to solve problems in individual life and social life. Education aims the progressive development and integration of human mind, body and soul. It is the integration of man, nature and God. Education must aim the fostering of toleration, co-operation and other democratic values in human mind. Major aims of humanistic education are human perfection and human excellence. It should help individual to reach at the highest degree of development of which he is capable.

Development of free moral personality, rationality and intellect is other aim. Self perfection of human personality is being considered as the supreme aim of humanistic education.

## Curriculum

Curriculum should lead pupils to rationality and creativity. A curriculum must be dynamic. The maximum expression of child's ability should be possible by curriculum. It should consider child psychology and stages of development. Strong philosophical, psychological and technological supporting is a must. A god curriculum is one which transform creative child hood to creative adult hood. According to humanism education should be liberal. It should develop free thought and action. So, curriculum should provide provisions for free interpretations and free transactions.

Humanists advocate study of classics, languages, science subjects, geography, history, human right education, sex education, physical education, domestic subjects, physiology, handicrafts and related subjects. They consider language as a gate way to human civilization and science subjects, natural science in particular as human construct to control the world. Physical education is a must to train body, mind and observation power. Man should possess all such abilities. The curriculum should be child centered and activity – activities to develop rational thinking – centered. There must have provisions to develop the concept of universal humanity, equality and liberty and brother hood in a curriculum. Extra curricular activities are to be considered with equal importance.

**Methods of Teaching**

Methods should consider child psychology, stages of development and child's inborn abilities, interests, attitude, aptitude and peculiarities. There should have separate instructional techniques or methods to different types of children like gifted, slow learners and others. Mother tongue is the best medium for instruction. Teaching and learning in mother tongue will help to develop creativity. Communication should be emphasized. Child should be treated as the hero in the teaching process. Method should be child centered and never be a teacher dominated one.

Classroom atmosphere is equally important as the selection of method. There should have an atmosphere of equality, fraternity and liberty in class room. Democracy in class room is a must. Freedom and individual differences have to be given consideration. Teacher should encourage co operative attempts in class room. Teacher should be aware of the rights of child as a human being. The humanists protest against all rigid methods or mechanism of teaching where there is good teaching and poor learning. They given importance to project methods, co operative and collaborative methods, play way methods discussion methods and etc.

**Freedom and Discipline**

Humanism neither believes in laissez faire (license to all) attitude or dogmatic rigidity. Pupils are supposed to respect essential aspects of social norms and social traditions. Humanists plead for individual freedom. Freedom is not the absolute freedom, it is limited. It is not a license to interfere others rights. They believe that social approval of good behaviour leads to individual discipline. Discipline is to be emerged through individual's social life. Recognition of universal humanity will create discipline in all aspects. Child can develop discipline through co curricular activities, co operative learning and play. Democratic approach and atmosphere are must to develop qualified discipline in individual. Qualified discipline is the most acceptable discipline.

**Role of Teacher**

Teacher has given importance in a humanist classroom. A teacher should consider individual differences. He should be aware of the developments in educational psychology, developments in methods, strategies and other aspects. Building of a democratic class room atmosphere is a teacher's responsibility. Not teaching, but learning is to be emphasized. A teacher is not a supreme personality, but a team leader in the class room. He is the person to lead students to democracy, equality and other social values. Development of individual abilities should be focused by he teacher. A teacher must be a humanitarian in all aspects.

**Humanism in Modern Education**

In many aspects humanism and realism are complimentary to each other. Hence, humanists possess a realistic approach in education. The concepts like free and compulsory education, education for all, equality of educational opportunities and areas like human right education, value education, population education, sex education, environmental education are being stamped by the influence of humanist philosophy. Education for exceptional children and special children and amenities like scholar ships, stipends, loans to education and special considerations to the deserving segments are the contributions of humanists. Creative classroom, democratic approach, ideal class room atmosphere, methods like socialized recitation, simulation, programmed learning, problem solving, discussion, seminar and relate techniques are encouraged by humanists' interpretation.

## 6.3 Eclecticism

Eclecticism is a philosophical thought with differences. Other than a different school of philosophy it is a tendency or an approach. A philosophical parasite! In simple sense, eclecticism means the harmonious blend of good aspects of different philosophical thoughts. Instead of being rigid to a particular ideology, we can select good and worthy principles and practices of all living philosophies. It is the fusion of different philosophies. It is the compound of different philosophies. Eclecticism follows the principle that no thought is completely perfect, but there are perfect views in all thoughts. It is the sum and substance of all these perfect views from all schools.

No thinker is completely idealist or naturalist or pragmatist. They are to a greater or lesser degree eclectic. One philosophy alone can't give valuable direction in all fields, especially in education. No school of thought is able to meet all the requirements of man. So there is adopted the tendency of accepting theories and principles from different thoughts and fuse them together. When the summum bonum of all thoughts is harmoniously blended to one stream, there is the origin of a new philosophical school that is 'eclecticism'.

The term eclectic lexically means select or pick up. Ideas, principles and concepts from and picked up and blended together to frame a new philosophy. Thus, eclecticism is a philosophy of purposeful selection or choice. Embracing only one thought for all type of philosophical solutions is almost impractical and harmful in this modern era. The world needs flexible approach, innovative outlook and divergent interpretation. The philosophical approach should be dynamic too. No philosophy is complete by itself. No philosophy is full-fledged to answer all queries on epistemology, axiology and metaphysics. A finalization of thoughts is necessary to assimilate the unity in diversity of this universe. Hence, eclecticism is the need of the hour.

*Eclecticism is nothing but fusion of principles, ideas and knowledge from all thoughts. It is the highest good from all philosophies. It is blend of all philosophical thoughts.*

## Eclecticism in Education

No man or man made system on this earth can stay completely self dependent or isolated in-toto. What we say 'own' is actually not 'own' but a contribution of others too. Nothing can depart completely from other. If needed to be effective it should accept from others.

Education as a system needs contributions from all schools of philosophies. Modern education is based on eclectic tendency.

Education may determine its aims according to idealism and may design its curriculum according to pragmatism. The methods may be from realism and idea on teacher and discipline may be from naturalism. Yet the education will possess a strong philosophical basis. This strong base is the eclecticism. Education designed according to the different educational philosophies and principles. It determines individual aims of education, social aims of education, methods of teaching and etc in an independent format depending up on all philosophies of education. Eclecticism in education never denies the contributions of different educational philosophies, instead it elect worthy from all of them and constitute a new stream for aspects of education. Eclecticism is the actual philosophy of the modern world education.

Education can be made worthy and effective by accepting inspirations and supporting from all sources. Eclectic tendency in education has a base on Rig Vedic sermon 'let all noble thoughts come form all sides'.

# Chapter 7

# Plato

"If you wish to know what is meant by public education, read Plato's Republic", said Rousseau. Plato is the greatest among the philosophers and educationists of all time. His deep sensations can stagger the learner even in this most modern period.

This chapter is an attempt to generate educative interactions between the reader and Plato's philosophy and education. Content narrates the –

*Life of Plato*
- *His works*

*Significance of the Republic and Academy*

*Plato's Philosophical Ideals*

*Concept of Platonic Realism*
- *Allegory of the Cave and Divided Line*
- *Plato's Concept of State*
  - *Ideal Society*

*Plato's Philosophy of Education*

*Educational Philosophy*
- *Education to Classes, and*
- *Plato's Views on Aspects of Education*

**Plato** – the term in Greek means "wide, broad-shouldered'. He was an immensely influential ancient Greek philosopher, writer of philosophical dialogues, and founder of the Academy in

Athens. The most famous of Socrates' disciples was this aristocratic young man. After the death of Socrates, Plato carried on much of his former teacher's work and eventually founded his own school, the Academy, in 385 BC. The Academy would become in its time the most famous school in the classical world, and its most famous pupil was Aristotle.

## 7.1 A Brief Life Sketch

**Birth**: 427 \ 428 BC (his birth date is not exactly known, majority of thinkers believe that he was born in May, 428 BC and some others believe in December 427 BC)

**Death**: 347 BC

**Family**: He was born and brought up in a moderately well-to-do aristocratic family. His father was named Ariston and his mother Perictione. (His family claimed descent from the ancient Athenian kings, and he was related – though there is disagreement as to exactly how – to the prominent politician Critias)

**Works**: Plato's famous work is the great dialogue called The Republic. His other major works (dialogues) consist of twenty-eight *Dialogues.* Symposium, The Laws, The Statesman, Apology and the Phaedrus are important among them. (Plato's *Dialogues* cover a wide range of subjects: duty, courage, virtue, justice, love, beauty, science, nature, rhetoric and the harmony of words with Being and with Ideas; the nature of humankind, wisdom, kingship, legislation, etc.)

Socrates is the main character in Plato's great dialogues. How much of the content and argument of any given dialogue is Socrates' point of view, and how much of it is Plato's, is disputed, since Socrates himself did not write anything.

There are also thirteen ***Letters***, which are generally recognized as written by Plato.

## The Republic

The most famous of Plato's dialogues is an enormous dialogue called *The Republic*. The Republic is one of the single most influential works in Western philosophy. It deals with the central problem of how to live a good life. This inquiry is shaped into the parallel questions (a) what is justice in the State, or what would an ideal State be like, and (b) what is a just individual. How the citizens of a state should be educated, what education means, what kinds of arts should be encouraged, what form its government should take, who should do the governing and for what rewards, what is the nature of the soul, and finally what (if any) divine sanctions and afterlife should be thought to exist. It also discusses what the nature of justice is; the nature of an ideal republic; and the allegory of the cave and the divided line, both of which explain Plato's theory of forms. The Republic covers just about every aspect of Plato's thought.

**Thought or School** The school or tradition is known as Platonism. Major idea is Platonic realism.

## Plato's Life

As a child, Plato received the education that was commonly given to boys of his age. He attended a private school in Athens (there were no public schools at that time). There he studied reading, writing and arithmetic, following which he committed to memory a considerable part of Greek poetry, above all the works of Homer. Plato also attended the gymnasium, for physical training.

Plato seems to have traveled extensively in Italy, Sicily, Egypt, and Cyrene in a quest for knowledge. Said to have returned to Athens at the age of forty, Plato founded a school, one of the earliest known organized schools in Western civilization, on a plot of land in the Grove of Academe. It is believed by somebody that Plato became a pupil of Socrates at the age of forty. Some others say that in 407 BC he became a pupil and friend of Socrates. In Academy he taught until his death.

*The Academy was "a large enclosure of ground which was once the property of a citizen at Athens named Academues..." Some, however, say that it received its name from an ancient hero. For some 40 years Plato was the motivating force and principal teacher of this intellectual centre of ancient Greece. The Academy remained open until 529 AD, that is, for almost 900 years after Plato's death. It was closed by Justinian I of Byzantium, who saw it as a threat to the propagation of Christianity. Many intellectuals were schooled in the Academy, the most prominent one being Aristotle.*

Plato was destined to witness the decline of Athens to which he was so dearly attached. As a young man he endured, probably as a soldier, the defeat of his city in the Peloponnesian War and experienced the ensuing decline of the Athenian democracy.

## 7.2 Plato's Philosophy

To understand the depths of Plato's thought one must keep closely in mind the fact that his philosophy is not in any sense a doctrine. Plato did not set up a philosophical system, which independently stretch out in the manner of a deviated ideology – for example Hegel's philosophical ideology. The distinguishing feature of Plato's philosophy is the progression or process by which his ideas are formed. His philosophy does not involve solitary preaching, hence is not unilateral or reflection, but is rather a collective exercise by which friends or opponents move forward in argument. Moreover, Plato's *Dialogues*, often dealing with the clarification of a concept – such as beauty, duty, love, justice or pleasure – do not usually come to a final conclusion on the subject or end on universal agreement. They are participants on vision-like emergence of knowledge.

**Plato's thoughts:** Plato was insistent in his analysis of the conditions and limitations to the acquisition of knowledge imposed by a world that was indefinable. He believed the world as indefinable because it was in constant movement. He also believed that all human beings, with the exception of true philosophers, lived in a world of appearances.

On the one hand, he explored the human condition as it related to the supreme values of beauty, truth and goodness. He looked to 'permanence' as the sole guarantor of absolute values. On the other hand, may be he was troubled by his experience of the decline of Athens, convinced that all change carried within itself the seeds of corruption or disintegration. He considered that he had discovered the concept of 'Ideas'.

Plato's thought is centered on the human being. More particularly, his thought is focused on the ethical problems the human being has to face. The questions of right, justice and the individual's place in society, that is in the *polis* (the Greek city-state), are the ethical questions that concern him to the highest degree. Plato considered the human being a political animal.

It is only through a proper education and through the pursuit of philosophy that human beings can free themselves from the chains of their senses, desires, ambitions (such as wealth and power) and passions. By education and pursuit of philosophy they can accede progressively from one level of enlightenment to the next, to true knowledge and, ultimately, to the vision of the Final Good.

The fundamental aspect of Plato's thought is the theory of "ideas" or "forms." Plato, like so many other Greek philosophers, was obstructed by the question of change in the physical world. They believed there is nothing certain or stable in the physical world except the fact that things change and the philosophers claimed that all change, motion, and time was an illusion

In the course of his assessment of the human being, Plato developed a new 'science' of the soul. Socrates states that 'all good and evil, whether in the body or in the whole man, originates in the soul'. The care of the soul is essential for a person's future. With his theses concerning the immortality of the soul, Plato also approached the area of religion.

**Metaphysics:** Platonism has traditionally been interpreted as a form of metaphysical dualism – sometimes referred to as Platonic realism. According to this reading (dualism), Plato's metaphysics divides the world into two distinct aspects: the intelligible world of "forms" or ideas, and the perceptual world we see around us. The perceptual world consists of imperfect copies of the intelligible forms or ideas. These forms are unchangeable and perfect (a part of universal bed), and are only comprehensible by the use of the intellect or understanding. This intellect is a capacity of the mind that does not include sense-perception or imagination. In the perceptual world, the particular objects we see around us bear only a dim resemblance to the more ultimately real forms of Plato's intelligible world. It is as if we are seeing shadows of cut-out shapes on the walls of a cave, (it is the essence of the well-known allegory of the cave of Platonic realism) which are mere representations of the reality outside the cave, illuminated by the sun.

Plato regarded the rational soul as immortal, and he believed in a universal soul, the creator of the physical world. He argued for the independent reality of Ideas, or Forms. This real divine idea or form is the unchallengeable archetype of all worldly phenomena and the only guarantee of ethical standards and of scientific knowledge.

**Epistemology:** Plato's concept of the nature of knowledge and learning which is discussed in the dialogue the *Meno,* began with the question whether virtue can be taught. His idea proceeded to expound the concepts of recollection of knowledge as virtue. Plato described learning as the discovery of pre-existing knowledge and right opinion, opinions which are correct but have no clear justification. Plato stated that knowledge is essentially justified true belief. Plato argued that belief is to be distinguished from knowledge on account of justification. He associates knowledge with the knowledge of the physical matter and knowledge of the Forms.

A philosopher has the moderate love for wisdom and the courage to act according to wisdom. Wisdom is knowledge about the 'Good' or the right relations between all that exists.

Plato says about three types of knowledge:

a) Knowledge attained through senses. The knowledge attained through senses is not true. It is only a false account of universe.

b) Knowledge derived from the opinion regarding things. This type of knowledge is also not true knowledge.

c) Knowledge in mind or reason. This is innate and true knowledge. This is philosophical and universal knowledge.

**Axiology:** Plato believed in a world soul – the universal soul – and the creator of the physical world, which is immortal. Virtue consists in the harmony of the human soul with the universal soul, universe of Ideas. Harmony of universal soul with human soul assures order, intelligence, and pattern to a world in constant flux. He argued for that harmony for the eternal existence of truth beauty and goodness. They are eternal values and ultimate reality. Supreme among the values is the Idea of the 'Good.' The values are not man created. They determine the forms. If there are manmade values, they are mortal, will change. Values from Universal Good are immortal.

## 7.3 Platonic Realism

### 7.3.1 Idea of the Allegory of the Cave and Divided Line

Plato used several metaphors to describe his concept of reality and axiology. 'The allegory of cave' and 'divided line' is important among them. There is a saying that the most influential passage in Western philosophy ever written is Plato's discussion of the prisoners of the cave and his abstract presentation of the divided line. For Plato, human beings live in a world of visible and intelligible things. The visible world is what surrounds us: what we see, what we hear and what we experience. This visible world is a world of change and uncertainty. The intelligible world is made up of the un-changing products of human reason. It is the world of idea or form that man cannot experience. Anything arising from reason alone makes up this intelligible world, which is the world of reality.

The intelligible world contains the eternal "Forms" (*idea*) of things. The visible world is the imperfect and changing manifestation of these unchanging forms or ideas. Material world is the reflection of the universal world of forms or ideas. This form is the 'idea' behind every thing. For example, the "Form" or "Idea" of an elephant is intelligible, abstract, and applies to all elephants. This 'Form' or 'idea' never changes, even though elephants vary wildly among themselves. The Form of an elephant would never change even if every elephant in the world were to vanish. An individual elephant is a physical, changing object and the Form of an elephant or "idea of elephant" never changes. As a physical object an elephant only makes sense in that it can be referred to the "Form" or "Idea" of 'elephantness'. It proves that idea behind the object is real and immortal. At the same time the physical elephant is mortal and not a final reality. This view satisfies that Plato was an idealist in his philosophical thought.

The metaphors try to define the illusion may experience while one observes and experiences the cutout shapes of animals inside the cave. The 'reality' inside the cave may not be as it is sensible to the man. The shadows of the objects on the walls of cave seem to make the real picture of animals inside it. But the shadow, made by sun rays, is an illusion and the animal outside is the reality. The actual reality is the achieved knowledge of the observer about the idea behind the cave animals. It is as if we are seeing shadows of cutout shapes on the walls of a cave which are mere representations of the reality outside the cave, illuminated by the sun.

Plato imagines these two worlds, the sensible world and the intelligible world, as existing on a line that can be divided in the middle: the lower part of the line consists of the visible world and the upper part of the line makes up the intelligible world. Each half of the line relates to a certain type of knowledge. We can have knowledge of the visible world. We can only have opinion of the intelligible world; we achieve "knowledge".

Each of these divisions can also be divided into two. The visible or changing world can be divided into a lower region, "illusion," which is made up of shadows, reflections, paintings, poetry, etc., and an upper region, "belief," which refers to any kind of knowledge of things that change, such as individual elephant. "Belief" may be true some or most of the time but occasionally is wrong (since things in the visible world change). Belief is practical and may serve as a relatively reliable guide to life but doesn't really involve thinking things out to the point of certainty. The upper region can be divided into, on the lower end, "reason," which is knowledge of things like mathematics but which require that some claims be accepted without question, and "intelligence," which is the knowledge of the highest and most abstract categories of things, an understanding of the ultimate good.

### 7.3.2 Plato's Concept of State

Plato's philosophical and educational views are strongly anchored up on his concept of state or polis. Plato stands for a theocratic state and theocratic government, and for philosophical rulers. State has certain ethical ends. It has to perform divine functions. State should function as an agency of 'universal good'.

He believed that religion is to be the centre of the state. Deviation is to be strictly punished. The governors of the State should be theologically trained leaders. What the State needs for its harmony with universal good is the leaders with philosophy.

*"Until philosophers rule as kings or those who are now called kings and leading men genuinely and adequately philosophize, that is, until political power and philosophy entirely coincide, while the many natures who at present pursue either one exclusively are forcibly prevented from doing so, cities will have no rest from evils,... nor, I think, will the human race."* Plato *in* Republic. *Plato describes these "philosopher kings" as "those who love the sight of truth".*

He considered individuals as the tools of state. Each individual is to be trained as the tool in order to defend the state. They are also to be trained as administrators of state affaires. Here comes the significance of education.

Plato considered state as an organism. It is like a 'person' with personality, having all aspects and faculties, traits and attributes found in an individual. He was of an opinion that state consists of three classes of people:

a) Vast body of people – the general public. They are the industrial or artisan class.

b) The auxiliaries – army, military.

c) The ruling class. (the Guardian class).

(Somebody interpreted the military or army group as guardian class.)

Plato suggested education in accordance with this classification of citizens in the state.

He advocated that state should function in a healthy and well knit manner. The best interests of individuals and State would not be experienced any conflict. If the State's function is healthy and well-knit the individual will be in the same manner. Education is an instrument to develop this harmony between individual and State. Education is State's responsibility.

Plato's polis (State) is essentially an educational community. It is created by education. It can survive only on condition that all its citizens receive an education that enables them to make rational political decisions. It is up to education to preserve the State unbroken and to defend it against all harmful innovations. The aim of education is not personal growth but service of the State, which is the guarantor of the happiness of its citizens for as long as they allow it to be the embodiment of justice.

### 7.3.2.1 Plato's Ideal Society in Republic (Ideal State)

Plato asserts that societies have a three-tier class structure corresponding to the appetite/spirit/reason structure of the individual soul. Like the individual soul, society also possesses this division based on appetite, spirit and reason. These divisions are:

**Productive** (workers): the labourers, carpenters, plumbers, masons, merchants, farmers, ranchers, etc. These correspond to the "appetite" part of the soul.

**Auxiliaries** (warriors or protective): those who are adventurous, strong and brave; in the armed forces. These correspond to the "spirit" part of the soul.

**Guardians** (Rulers or governing group): those who are intelligent, rational, self-controlled, in love with wisdom, well suited to make decisions for the community. These correspond to the "reason" part of the soul and are very few.

Control on three aspects of soul occurs when the emotions are ruled over by the intellect, and the bodily appetites are ruled over by the emotions and especially the intellect. An individual may be said to be just when the bodily appetites and emotions are not only ruled over by the intellect, but do so willingly and without force.

Plato divides human beings based on their innate intelligence, strength, and courage. Those who are not overly bright, or strong, or brave, are suited to various productive professions: farming, building, carpenter, mason, etc. Those who are somewhat bright, strong, and especially courageous suited to defensive and military professions. Those who are extraordinarily intelligent, virtuous, and brave, are suited to run the state itself. They are the rulers. Plato's ideal state is an aristocracy, a Greek word which means "rule by the best." The majority of human society in a state consists of the 'producers.' (They are called so, since they are most suited for productive work). The middle sections of society, a smaller but still large number of people who make up the army are called 'Auxiliaries.' The best and the brightest, a very small and rarefied group, are those who are in complete control of the State permanently. Plato calls this group 'Guardians.'

In the ideal state, "courage" characterizes the Auxiliaries; "wisdom" displays itself in the lives and government of the Guardians. A State may be said to have 'temperance' if the Auxiliaries obey the Guardians in all things and the Producers obey the Auxiliaries and Guardians in all things (a hierarchy of obedience). A state may be said to be 'intemperate' if any of the lower groups do not obey one of the higher groups. A state may be said to be Just (State with justice) if the Auxiliaries *do not simply obey* the Guardians, *but enjoy doing so*. It means, they don't complain about the authority being exercised over them; a Just State would require that the Producers not only obey the Auxiliaries and Guardians, but that they do so willingly.

## 7.4 Plato: Philosophy of Education

According to Plato education is "the first and most fair thing that the best of men can ever have". He gave greatest importance to the subject education with idealistic and intellectualistic view. Education is a process of moral training. He emphasized the necessity of sound interaction between body and mind as the basis of education. Education is a divine necessity, an essential function of cosmic order. Only educated persons can integrate the beauty and goodness of universal soul in to his own existence. He can only realize the faculties of soul—the appetite, spirit and reason.

> *Only slaves in the State were to be permitted to lead an unrestricted family life. Marriage of others should be regulated by the state.*
>
> – A Plato opinion!
>
> *Plato is silent on education to the slaves. There is no notable suggestion of education for artisan class in Plato's Republic. This group was denied the profits of citizenship. This is regarded as the defect of his ideal State education.*

Plato considered State as a divine agency and he proposed education as a State responsibility. There are three groups or classes in the society, the artisan or industrial class, the military class and the governing class. Plato spoke more on education to soldier class and ruler class. He suggested almost general form of preliminary education to these classes.

Mental education is to head physical education. Training in music and gymnastic is advised. Music is proposed for the training of soul and gymnastics for body. But both are aimed at the improvement of soul.

Education is to develop the discrimination power-ability to distinguish good and evil. Nothing must be accepted in education if it does not contribute to the promotion of virtue. Children need good and simple environment. Such an environment is necessary for imitation and assimilation of virtues. The assimilation of virtues is necessary to perform as the best tools of state. Children are the future guardians – the military and the ruler.

Plato was against the compelled learning. Learning has to take place in free atmosphere. He believed that 'the gymnastic –

bodily exercise – when compulsory does no harm to the body, but knowledge which is acquired under compulsion obtains no hold on mind.' While learning is introduced compulsorily it will be ineffective learning. Plato's opinion was very innovative, ".... does not use compulsion, but let early education be a sort of amusement." He maintained the concept that education to all should be compulsory, but method or learning strategies should be free in character. It means compulsion for education only, not for learning.

Plato also introduced play-way learning as a guiding principle of learning. He emphasized the positive significance of play in teaching-learning. A child's interest in play is natural. Hence it is to be made use of in education.

Higher education is not a programme for knowledge acquisition. It is the programme of integration of universal good to the individual existence. Higher Education is the education to make philosophers or rulers.

> *Education is the process of drawing and guiding children towards that principle which is pronounced right by the laws and confirmed as truly right by the experience of the oldest.* – Plato

One of the important aspects of education is right training at right time. Throughout education, a child should be guided by love. Love, affection and consideration should function as guiding principles. Plato's education programme is based on the concepts like wisdom, virtue, service and leadership. Education is a moral effort on the side of the older generation to pass to younger generation all the good habits, wisdom and virtues.

He considered education as the best device to demolish individualism and establish supremacy of State. Every individual must think above his personal interest for the sake of the State.

## Specific Functions of Education

We can consider the following points as the specific functions of education:

a) Determine harmony between universal 'good' and individual soul.

b) Ensure citizenship training and develop civic efficiency. Plato considered civic efficiency a great virtue.

c) Develop the rule of reason. Education should aim at the development of philosophized rulers.

d) Develop love towards universal eternal values such as truth, beauty and goodness in the child.

e) Development of self-governing individuals

f) Harmony of mind and body of an individual.

g) Develop harmony of individual's interest and State's interest.

h) Ensure temperance in State by employing enjoyment in obeying the higher class by the lower class. Education has to develop this temperance and State with justice.

## 7.4.1 Education to Classes

Plato's educational programme does not envisage uniform education to all. Education is different to each class.

Plato suggested primary education to all. The period of primary education is from the age seven to twenty. After the proposed common education a group of tests will be administered (students will have undergone many contests and examinations of all sorts). The fellows who pass the tests can be sent to military education. Those who fail the tests will remain in the working group. They will have no right in the military and administration of the State. Military education along with other education to the selected group will continue for some years. After this, some other tests will be administered. Those who fail the tests will remain in the military class (auxiliary class). Successful students will be sent for higher education. This group is selected for the rulers' class (guardians). They are to join the government administrative service. Regarding the aim of higher education to this class, Plato said, 'not a mere extension of knowledge, but the conversion of a soul from study of the sensible world to contemplation of real existence'. Hence, higher education is for the realization of universal soul and the ultimate reality behind the universe.

**Curriculum and Frame of Study**

Plato's curriculum has put forwarded several psychological and philosophical principles. He suggested a scheme of education based on gymnastics and music for early stage. Curriculum is divided into three parts:

a) Curricula for bodily development

b) Discipline for mental training

c) Training in music.

For the fist ten years of education, a child should be taught arithmetic, geometry, music and astronomy. This teaching should focus on child's understanding of universal relations underlying them.

In the second stage Plato proposed subjects and methods to develop abstract thinking. Teaching of poetry, music, theoretical arithmetic, formal gymnastics, military training and religion are to be taught at the second stage. Together with this literary and musical education students of the Platonic State engage in all sorts of sports, including horse-riding and weapons training. The balance between culture and gymnastics should be maintained as perfectly as possible

Higher education has two phases. One is scientific phase and another is philosophic phase. The scientific phase has about ten year's duration from twenty or more years of age to thirty or more. Arithmetic, geometry, music, poetry and astronomy can be the subjects at this stage along with formal military training.

**The Socratic Method as Way of Teaching**: The Socratic Method is not a teacher-centered method. It is strictly based on give and take of knowledge between the learner and teacher. The Socratic Method is to be distinguished from the traditional method of teaching. In traditional approaches teachers seek to transmit their knowledge to their pupils, who are expected to assimilate it on the whole passively. The Socratic Method is an interactive method in which the teacher and pupil cooperate in the pursuit of knowledge through dialogue. A series of questions and answers involve the two parties in the same cognitive search. 'There will be a question on content, seeks answer, from answer go to the next question, accepts answer, go to next question .....' is the way of activating this method. Plato's Socratic Method argues that 'there is no teaching, only recollection of knowledge '

## Role of Teacher

Plato has given great importance to the teacher in the educational process. The teacher is considered as a torch-bearer in the darkness. He is the person to lead the child into learning good habits and avoid bad ones. He has to develop the attitude towards the eternal values – truth, beauty and goodness. A teacher should be an idealistic person. He is the person to make the children realize the 'good' of the universe and the harmony between universal soul and individual soul. He has to realize the universal relation underlying every thing. The Socratic method of teaching has often been characterized as an affectionate method, or one in which the teacher assumes the role of a midwife. Teachers should play the role of midwife in order to deliver to the pupils the knowledge they unconsciously possess. The teacher has to inform the children the reality that the sensible human nature is only a mortal-earthly-identity in the immortal universal bed.

**Certain Notable Characteristics of Plato's Education.** Some of the major characteristics of Plato's educational ideology can be listed as follows:

a) Education is a State responsibility. It is the primary duty of a state.

b) "Education must be a substitute for State regimentation and innumerable laws"

c) The centre of education (school) should function as the greatest humanizing and socializing agency.

d) Education has two faces – education for practical affairs and education for State service.

e) Education has class-wise segregation. (Common education for all, after the common education a test will be administered and the failed will be considered the artisan group. The successful will be selected for military education. After military education another test will be there. The failures will be retained as the military group (auxiliary class) and the successful will be selected to rulers' class and they will be provided higher education.)

f) Plato's education was silent on education to slaves and gave less importance to education of artisan group in the society. (Plato has very little to say about the education of crafts workers and merchants, which consists of no more than a simple apprenticeship, and slaves received no mention at all)

g) Education to develop moral attitudes and good habits.

h) Civic efficiency by education is considered a social value with greatest importance.

i) Education is compulsory to all, compulsion in learning is denied. Learning must be in free atmosphere.

j) Education, higher education in particular, is for the realization of the harmony between universal soul and individual soul.

k) Education should not be considered a manmade function. It should be dealt as a divine function.

l) Deviated educational functions for the early periods, nursery, elementary stage, later stage, higher education etc.

m) Education divided in to two parts – gymnastics and music (i.e. culture).

n) Importance to formal and informal gymnastics, military training and music.

o) Regarded women education as must for the performance of State.

The above points are only some of the major peculiarities of Plato's education. We can understand that this man made his concepts on education with a deviated view. While adjudicating them with an awareness of Plato's period, we can reach a conclusion that Plato's contribution to education is immensely rich in its ideological performance and great and unique in its characteristic features.

# Jean Jacques Rousseau

Love childhood, treat and encourage its sports, its pleasure, and its delightful instinct. Why deprive these innocents of the joys which pass so quickly............. Childhood has ways of seeing, thinking and feeling, peculiar to itself, nothing can be more foolish than to substitute our (adults') ways for them": Rousseau.

Rousseau tried to emancipate the child from tramples of society and medieval self-possession. Rousseau was a vagabond without family ties or social attachments. It is reasonably strange that a man who failed to look after his own children and sent them to the care of a child-orphanage had written marvelously about the nurture, care and education of children!

This chapter is an attempt to examine the contributions of Rousseau to education. It covers:

*Rousseau's Life*

*Rousseau's Philosophy*

- *Concept of natural human state*
- *Concept of general will*

*Rousseau's Educational Philosophy*

- *Concept of education for stages*
- *Ideals of women education, and*
- *Ideals of negative education*

**Jean** Jacques Rousseau is one of the most influential thinkers during the Enlightenment in eighteenth century Europe. Rousseau was born in Geneva but became famous as a 'French' political philosopher and educationalist. His first major philosophical work, *A Discourse on the Sciences and Arts*, was the winning response to an essay contest conducted by the Academy of Dijon in 1750. In this work, Rousseau argues that the progression of the sciences and arts has caused the corruption of virtue and morality. This discourse won Rousseau fame and recognition. Rousseau greatly influenced Immanuel Kant's work on ethics. His novel *Julie or the New Heloise* impacted the late eighteenth century's Romantic Naturalism movement, and his political ideals were championed by leaders of the French Revolution. Rousseau's most celebrated theory was that of the "natural man." He maintained that human beings were essentially good and equal in the state of nature but were corrupted by the introduction of property, agriculture, science, and commerce. People entered into a 'social contract among' themselves, establishing governments and educational systems to correct the inequalities brought about by the rise of civilization.

## 8.1 Rousseau's Life Sketch

**Birth**: June 28, 1712

**Death**: He died on July 3, 1778

**Family**: Jean-Jacques Rousseau was born to Isaac Rousseau and Suzanne Bernard in Geneva. His father Isaac was a clockmaker.

**Works**: In 1750 he published the '*Discourse on the Arts and Sciences*' (It was an essay prepared in response to the Academy of Dijon's essay contest on the question, "Has the restoration of the sciences and arts tended to purify morals?")

In 1753 Rousseau published *'Discourse on the Origin of Inequality among Men'*. (It was an entry to another essay contest announced by the Academy of Dijon. This time, the question posed was, "What is the origin of inequality among men, and is it authorized by the natural law?")

His opera is Le *Devin du Village* (The Village Seer)

In 1761, he published a novel, '*Julie or the New Heloise*'.

In 1762, April '*The Social Contract*' (a perfect work on political philosophy).

In 1762, May "*Emile*" – Émile or Concerning Education – (a book detailing his views on education)

In 1770s, he wrote '*Rousseau: Judge of Jean-Jacques*' and the '*Reveries of the Solitary Walker*'

Rousseau wrote the *Confessions* (biography) late in his career, and it was not published until after his death. (The "Reveries of the Solitary Walker" and "Rousseau Judge of Jean Jacques" are also autobiographical.)

**Thought or School**: Naturalism, Romantic Naturalism

## Rousseau's Life

Rousseau's life is a journey of experiences. His life itself is an explanation to his philosophical contributions. He was a wanderer and a man of conflict. What can such a man offer educators? His life answers this question. He was a vagabond without family bonds or social recognition. He had a little schooling and no teaching experience.

Jean-Jacques Rousseau was born in Geneva. His mother died only a few days later, and his only sibling, an older brother, ran away from home when Rousseau was still a child. He was brought up mainly by his father, a clockmaker. With his father at an early age he read ancient Greek and Roman literature. He had an unusual childhood with no formal education. His father, due to a quarrel with a French captain, left Geneva for the rest of his life. Rousseau stayed behind and was taken care of by an uncle who

> *'Rousseau was artificiality from head to foot, a jack dog of his own life, a supreme paradox, and a creature of caprice'.*
>
> – Voltaire
>
> *But Napoleon remarked that without Rousseau the French revolution would not have been possible.*

sent him along with his cousin to study in the village of Bosey. His formal education was started at a later age. Rousseau was apprenticed to an engraver at the age of 12 and began to learn the trade. He left Geneva in 1728, at the age of 16 and fled to Annecy. Here he met Louise de Warens, who was influential in his conversion to Catholicism, which forced him to forfeit his Genevan citizenship. Rousseau's relationship with Warens lasted for several years and eventually became romantic. Twelve years his senior she was in turns a mother figure, a friend and a lover. During this period he encaged with teaching, music and secretarial jobs.

In 1741 or 1742 Rousseau went to Paris. He met Voltaire at Paris. This meeting and Voltaire's suggestions led him to a systematic life. He married Therese Levasseur, a 40 year old lady, in 1768. They had five children together, all of whom were left at the Paris orphanage. (It is said that they were to stay together, never officially married, until he died) It is ironical that Rousseau the educationist who spoke greatly of education for children from the bounties of nature sent his own offspring into the boundary of an orphanage. Rousseau had argued the children would get a better upbringing in such an institution than he could offer! They would not have to put up with the artfulness of 'high society'.

In 1750 he published the *Discourse on the Arts and Sciences.* This discourse made Rousseau famous as it won the Academy's prize. The work was widely read and was controversial. Rousseau attempted to live a modest life despite his fame, and after the success of his opera, The Village Astrologer (Soothsayer), he promptly gave up music composing.

He settled in Switzerland for two years. After encountering difficulties with Swiss authorities, he spent time in Berlin and Paris, and eventually moved to England at the invitation of David Hume. However, due to quarrels with Hume, his stay in England lasted only a year, and in 1767 he returned to the southeast of France anonymously. After spending three years in the southeast, Rousseau returned to Paris in 1770 and copied music for a living. He died in 1778.

His life was filled with conflict, first when he was apprenticed, later in academic circles with other Enlightenment thinkers like Diderot and Voltaire, with Parisian and Swiss authorities and even with David Hume.

*Rousseau claimed he lacked money to bring his up children properly. There was also the question of his and Tharese's capacity to cope with childrearing. Last, there is also some question as to whether all or any of the children were his. For example, Tharese had an affair with James Boswell whilst he stayed with Rousseau. What we do know is that in later life Rousseau sought to justify his actions concerning the children declaring his sorrow about the way he had acted.*

*He was a poor teacher. It seems that unable to bring up his own children, he sent them to orphanages.*

As a brilliant, undisciplined, and unconventional thinker, Jean-Jacques Rousseau spent most of his life being driven by controversy back and forth between Paris and his native Geneva. Orphaned at an early age, he left home at sixteen, working as a tutor and musician before undertaking a literary career while in his forties. Rousseau sired but refused to support several illegitimate children and frequently initiated bitter quarrels with even the most supportive of his colleagues. Rousseau's mental health was a matter of some concern. There were significant periods when he found it difficult to be in the company of others, when he believed himself to be the focus of hostility and duplicity.

He frequently acted 'oddly' with sudden changes of mood. These peculiarities led to situations where he falsely accused others and behaved with limited respect for the humanity.

## 8.2 Rousseau's Philosophy

Rousseau's major works extents the mid to late eighteenth century. So it is appropriate to consider Rousseau, at least chronologically, as an Enlightenment thinker. The major goal of Enlightenment thinkers was to give a foundation to philosophy that was independent of any particular tradition, culture, or religion: one that any rational person would accept. His philosophical contributions are in this scenario. At the same time he is considered as a "counter-Enlightenment" thinker. Rousseau was influenced by the modern natural law tradition, which has a systematic approach to human nature that emphasized self-interest. In philosophical views, Rousseau was a naturalist.

To the question, "Has the restoration of the sciences and arts tended to purify morals?" Rousseau answered an emphatic "no." He believed that science and socially illustrated arts and virtues make a man impure. Man is pure at his birth. It is the society that makes him corrupt. Rousseau argues that the progress of science and arts create a false sense of need for luxury, so that science becomes simply a means for making our lives easier and more pleasurable, but not morally better. Man's natural development is being prevented by them. Rousseau argued that men are inherently good, but become corrupted by the evils of society. We are born good and that is our natural state.

He was a lover of nature. He tried to inculcate a view that "everything is good as it comes from the hands of man".

### 8.2.1 Rousseau's Concept of 'Humans in the State of Nature' (Natural Human State)

Rousseau described human beings in the pure state of nature, uncorrupted by civilization and the socialization process.

Rousseau's picture of "man in his natural state," is radically different from others. He describes natural man as isolated, timid, peaceful, mute, and without the foresight to worry about what the future well bring. Man is an offspring of the nature. This is in severe contrast to the classical view which claims that the state of civil society is the natural human state and man is a social animal.

Rousseau's praise of humans in the state of nature is perhaps one of the most misunderstood ideas in his philosophy. Although the human being is naturally good and the "noble savage" (life according to nature order) is free from the vices that plague humans in civil society, Rousseau is not simply saying that humans in nature are good and humans in civil society are bad. Human beings in the state of nature are amoral creatures, neither virtuous nor vicious. After humans leave the state of nature, they can enjoy a higher form of goodness. This goodness can be called moral goodness.

## 8.2.2 Rousseau's Concept of General Will

As philosophical thought, the political thought of Rousseau is equally important. Rousseau describes his political views in Social Contract. His views in this regard are highly influenced by Plato's concept of ideal republic.

The major concept he defines is the idea of 'general will'. General will is the collective will of the individuals in the state. There is individual will and collective will. This can be understood in terms of an analogy. A political society is like a human body. A body is a unified entity though it has various parts that have particular functions. And just as the body has a will that looks after the well-being of the whole, a political state also has a will which looks to its general well-being. The major conflict in political philosophy occurs when the general will is in disagreement with one or more of the individual wills of its citizens.

Rousseau articulates three maxims which supply the basis for a politically virtuous state: 1) Follow the general will in every action; 2) Ensure that every particular will is in accordance with the general will; and 3) Public needs must be satisfied. This way of living, he argued, can promote liberty and equality – and it arises out of, and fosters, a spirit of fraternity. The cry of 'liberty, equality and fraternity' is familiar to us today through the French Revolution (1789–1799).

Rousseau claims that when laws are in accordance with the general will, good citizens will respect and love both the state and their fellow citizens. Therefore, citizens will see the intrinsic value in the law, even in cases in which it may conflict with their individual wills. Rousseau argues that following the general will allows for individual diversity and freedom.

This general will is supposed to represent the common good or public interest – and it is something that each individual has a hand in making. All citizens should participate – and should be committed to the general good – even if it means acting against their private or personal interests.

*Chapter one of* Social Contract *begins with one of Rousseau's most famous quotes, which echoes the claims of his philosophy: "Man was/is born free; and everywhere he is in chains." (*Social Contract, *Vol. IV, p. 131).*

## 8.3 Educational Philosophy of Rousseau

Rousseau's views on educational philosophy are revealed in Emile (Emile or On Education). The *Emile* is written as part novel and part philosophical treatise. The book is written in first person, with the narrator as the tutor, and describes his education of a pupil, Emile, from birth to adulthood. It carries a clear narration on principles of 'natural education'. The basic philosophy of education that Rousseau advocates in the *Emile* is rooted in the notion that human beings are good by nature. His educational concept based on naturalism is generally termed as 'pedagogic romance'.

The *Emile* is a large work, which is divided into five books. Book One opens with Rousseau's claim that the goal of education should be to cultivate man's natural tendencies. Rousseau is very clear that a return to the state of nature once human beings have become civilized is not possible. So man should not be a prey of social evil through the civilizing process. It does not mean that men should seek 'noble savages' in the literal sense; a life with no language, no social ties, and an underdeveloped faculty of reason. Rather, Rousseau says, someone who has been properly educated will be engaged in society, but relate to his or her fellow citizens in a natural way.

Rousseau calls the two forms of self-love: *amour-propre* and *amour de soi*. *Amour de soi* is a natural form of self-love in that it does not depend on others. Rousseau claims that by our nature, each of us has this natural feeling of love toward ourselves. By contrast, *amour-propre* is an unnatural self-love and is a negative product of the socialization process. Unlike *amour de soi*, *amour-propre* is a love of self that depends on comparing oneself with others. Essentially it consists in some-one basing his or her self-worth on a perceived superiority to another. It breeds contempt, dislike, hostility, and frivolous competition. Education should be a device against this.

Rousseau's philosophy of education is not geared simply at particular techniques that ensure the pupil will absorb information and concepts. It is better understood as a way of ensuring that the pupil's character be developed in such a way as to have a healthy sense of self-worth and morality. It is a way of negative education. This will allow the pupil to be virtuous even in the unnatural and imperfect society in which he lives. The character of Emile begins learning important moral lessons from his infancy, through childhood, and into early adulthood. His education relies on the tutor's constant supervision. The tutor must even manipulate the environment in order to teach sometimes difficult moral lessons about humility, chastity and honesty.

Rousseau had the idea that it was possible to preserve the 'original perfect nature' of the child, 'by means of the careful control of his education and environment, based on an analysis of the different physical and psychological stages through which he passed from birth to maturity.' Rousseau argued that the drive for learning was provided by the growth of the person and that what the educator needed to do was to facilitate opportunities for learning.

Some of the key elements of Rousseau's educational philosophy can be listed as follows:

— Children are very different to adults – as innocent, vulnerable, slow to mature – and entitled to freedom and happiness. Children are naturally good.

— Freedom is the pivot of learning process.

— People develop through various stages – and different forms of education may be appropriate to each.

— There is a guiding principle that what is to be learned should be determined by an understanding of the person's nature at each stage of their development.

— Education should not be organized with adult's point of view. It should conform to the needs of the child at each stage.

— Individuals vary within stages – and education must be individualized. 'Every mind has its own form'

— Each and every child has some fundamental urge to activity. Restlessness may be replaced by curiosity, mental activity being a direct development of bodily activity.

- The more the learners and educators were able to control the environment and its power as a determining factor the more effective would be the education.
- The child should remain in complete ignorance of those ideas which are beyond his/her grasping.
- Emphasized direct experience in learning. 'Things before words and objects before symbols, was his suggestion.
- It is possible to preserve the original nature of the child by careful control of his education and environment
- Concern for both individual and public education.
- Learners must be encouraged to reason their way through their own conclusions – they should not rely completely on the authority of the teacher. Instead of being taught other people's ideas, learner is encouraged to draw his own conclusions from his own experience. (E.g. 'discovery learning')
- Freedom is the pivot of human life. Child should be given freedom to maximum extent.
- No physical punishments! Punishments should be through natural consequences.
- The process of education should focus on unfolding of individual's innate capacities.
- Emphasis on physical education.
- Rousseau's educational concept can be called negative education.

### 8.3.1 Education for Stages

Education has three faculties:

a) nature b) human beings c) physical objects or things.

Education comes from nature, from men or from things. The inner growth of our organs and faculties is the education of nature; the use we learn to make of our growth is the education of men; what we gain by our experience of our surroundings is the education of things.

Education has three sources. We are each taught by three masters—by ourselves, by nature and by others. Education from others includes the circumstances too.

Men need strength, men need aid and men need reason. All those we lack at birth, all those we need when we come to man's state. What we lack at birth and what we need later is the gift of education. Effective education of an individual is based on an analysis of the different physical and psychological stages through which he passed from birth to maturity. In Émile, Rousseau divides educational development into five stages. The four stages described in the first four segments (books) of Emile are associated with males. In the fifth segment of Emile, Rousseau examines the education of Sophie that is women education. Here he sets out what he sees as the essential differences that flow from sex.

**Stage 1: Infancy (birth to two years):** The first stage is infancy, from birth to about two years. (Describes in Book I of Emile). Infancy finishes with the weaning of the child. He sets a number of maxims, the spirıt of which is to give children more real liberty and less power. It also lets them do more for themselves and demand less of others. By teaching them from the first to confine their wishes within the limits of their powers they will scarcely feel the want of whatever is not in their power. Child has ultimate pleasure in this period. The pleasure child experiences at this stage can never come to the child again.

Parents should love their children unconditionally. Let the children play and share play things with other children. Encage them in activities which ensure the physical development. A child should not be retard by tight clothes. Let the child experience cold, hot, sun, hunger etc. He has to grow with fitness.

Rousseau comments, "for weaker the body, the more it commands, the stronger it is, the better it obeys." So let the child harden their bodies through their own movements. A child learns in this period by touching things, lifting them and comparing them with one another.

**Stage 2: 'The age of Nature' (two to 12).** The second stage, from two to ten or twelve, is 'the age of Nature'(describes in book 2 of Emile). During this time, the child receives only 'negative education'. There should be no moral instruction, no verbal learning. Rousseau says the most important rule of education at this stage: *'Do not save time, but lose it... The mind should be left undisturbed till its faculties have developed'.* The purpose of education at this stage is to develop physical qualities and senses, but not mind. Rousseau denies artificial education at this stage.

The child should be allowed to face all difficulties and cruelties of nature. Education at this stage should aim to harness the body and the energy of the child. Give suitable exercises for the development of sense organs. Bookish learning is denied at this stage. The child should be allowed to learn only by exercise of his sense organs, according to his interests and tastes.

**Stage 3: Pre-adolescence (12–15).** Education at this stage is like a noble savage'. 'About twelve or thirteen the child's strength increases far more rapidly than his needs'. The urge for activity now takes a mental form; there is greater capacity for sustained attention. The educator has to respond accordingly. Learning through formal ways can be started at this stage.

*The only book Emile – the student – is allowed is Robinson Crusoe, an expression of the solitary, self-sufficient man that Rousseau seeks to form. Rousseau denies textbooks to small children.*

**Stage 4: Puberty (15–20).** During this period **the** child's reasoning will be well developed, and he will be able to deal with what he sees as the dangerous emotions of adolescence, and with moral issues and religion. The child still wants to reject societal pressures and influences. It is necessary for the natural preference of the person to emerge without undue corruption. The gradual entry into community life and moral development starts. It is called the stage of social education, general education and to a certain extent, positive education. The period of moral and social development starts at this stage.

This is the period of the emergence of sex. The boy began to develop virtues like sympathy, generosity, gratitude, friendship, equality and justice in this period.

**Stage 5: Adulthood (20–25).** In this stage the adult Emile is introduced to his ideal partner, Sophie. He learns about love, and is ready to return to society after such a lengthy preparation, against its corrupting influences. The final task of the tutor is to 'instruct the young couple in their marital rights and duties'. This stage is the period of education through social experiences.

Above are the five stages of education. These five stages are zeroed in on education of male pupils. Emile is the male character in the book Emile. The five stages are described in five parts in the book Emile. These parts are called book 1, 2, 3, 4 and book 5. The 5th is the part dealing with education of individual at adulthood. This part also discusses Rousseau's concept of women education. Sophie is the female character in the book. She is to be married to Emile. Rousseau reveals his idea on women education in the book 5.

### 8.3.2 Concept of Women Education

As Emile's is a moral education, Rousseau discusses in detail how the young pupil is to be brought up to regard women and sexuality. (Moral education here is not the direct moral lesson. Rousseau was against direct moral lessons. The moral development of child, he assured through negative education.

The child will be morally educated by ensuring his natural development)

He introduces the character of Sophie, a girl, and explains how her education differs from Emile's. Girl's education is not focused on theoretical matters. Men's minds are more suited to that type of thinking. Rousseau's view was that men are stronger and therefore more independent. They depend on women only because they desire them. By contrast, women both need and desire men. Sophie is educated in such a way that she will fill what Rousseau takes to be her natural role as a wife. She is to be obedient to Emile. And although Rousseau advocates these very specific gender roles, it would be a mistake to take the view that Rousseau regards men as simply superior to women. Women have particular talents that men do not; Rousseau says that women are cleverer than men, and that they excel more in matters of practical reason.

As men and women have different vocations and responsibilities, their education must be different. Rousseau advocated separate type of education for men and women instead of common education. Women education should protect womanhood of the female. Education for womanhood up to the age of ten involves physical training for loveliness and style. The other educational functions during this time are the dressing of dolls leading to drawing, writing, counting and reading; and the prevention of idleness and indocility. After the age of ten there is a concern with adornment and the arts of pleasing; religion; and the training of reason. 'She has been trained to be careful rather than strict, and her taste has been followed rather than thwarted', Rousseau says. A girl should learn the religion when young and it should be thorough. Her religion is to make her husband happy and be obedient to him.

To a certain extent, Rousseau's view on women and women education is unconventional. He was strictly against higher education for women. He even said that a higher educated woman (woman of culture) is the plague of her husband, her children, her family, her servants, society and to everybody! According to him a woman is meant to look after the home and hence she should be an ideal housewife. Women education should be framed with this point of view. She should be taught stitching, embroidery, dance, music and such other arts. She needs lessons in domestic science. This will be useful to make her husband and family happy. Philosophy, science and higher arts to woman will be of little use!

A woman is made to please man! Rousseau did not believe in freedom to women; instead he suggested strict control and discipline. He considered self-sacrifice, tolerance and patience as the symbols of womanhood. Education of women should be related to men. To please man, to be useful to him, to make himself loved, and honored by him, to educate him when young, to care him when grown and to make life agreeable and sweet to him – these are the duties of women at all times. Her true place is inside the house.

Though these are the ideas of Rousseau revealed in Emily, at first he strongly pleaded for high consideration to women. In his first Discourse he said that 'men will be what women choose to make them. He also believed that 'the hand that rocks the cradle rules the world'.

Rousseau shows emotional imbalances and contradictions in his opinions about women and women education. His views on women and their education are sometimes harshly eccentric. They are appalling and sound like whims of an unbalanced mind. But these freakish ideas could be out of Rousseau's own experiences. He was against his contemporary social life and family setup. He believed that the strong and stable social setup should need improvement in family life. Men and women have separate functions in life and harmony of the home depends upon their discharging of responsibilities properly. Rousseau probably believed that sophistication and fashions would ruin women.

**Concept of Curriculum**

Rousseau expected a system of education to follow the nature. Nature is the ultimate source of all knowledge. So his views clearly state the interest that curriculum should be 'naturo' centric.

Curriculum should be developed according to the stages of development. Each stage needs a different type of educational pattern, content and method. Elementary curriculum before 12 should not encage anything of traditional or conventional character. Subjects like history and geography are discouraged at this stage. There is no need of any formal lesson, formal classroom and formal teaching. 'Break the walls, demolish the formal schools, destroy the textbooks and throw the child into the bounties of nature' was the essence of his advice.

All matters in the curriculum cannot be introduced at all times. Principles of child's growth and development and characteristics and needs of child at different stages are to be kept in mind while designing the curriculum. According to Rousseau's suggestion, bookish knowledge is less important than the knowledge derived from the nature itself. Nature is the source of all knowledge.

Play and sports are included in the course of study. Such areas are necessary to build a healthy body. Agriculture is considered the most honorable job of man, hence it is considered as a subject to be practiced by child. A formally designed curriculum is suggested from the age of reason only. Curriculum during adulthood must include knowledge of human nature and social order. Psychology, social science and ethics are also a must. Modern and ancient literature was also suggested by Rousseau in this period.

Rousseau has distinguished views in the case of discipline also. He denied any type of physical punishment to young children. Punishment, he suggested, only through natural consequences. Repressing method of discipline is never to be used in education because repression hinders natural growth. A child should be given sufficient freedom to everything in this nature. Discipline revolves around freedom. Play is a natural instinct of child. So he should be given sufficient freedom to play. Discipline is not to be achieved through corporal punishment, but through naturo-centric approaches only, which are based on principles nature and psychological principles.

### 8.3.3 Concept of Negative Education

Rousseau considered two types education – positive education and negative education. It is his educational philosophy. The educational principles developed by Rousseau were very much against the educational system prevalent to his times. The widespread system, which was focused on intellectual development, was called 'positive education' by Rousseau. The contemporary education of Rousseau was a system which sacrificed the beauty of present for an uncertain future, which chained the child in every sort of life and began by making the child miserable. Rousseau requested all people to act against it. As against the positive format of educational practices, Rousseau's education has been called Negative Education. It is the concept zeroed in on early childhood, not on education for adulthood. It is not a separate stream of education, but the essence of Rousseau's educational philosophy. (Not Rousseau, but others called this idea negative education.)

Negative education was negative in its approach towards all of the traditional way of education. According to the idea of his negative education, education should begin with a psychological insight into the capacities and innate tendencies of the child. The individuality of each child has great value and so it has to be respected in all circumstances. It is the education not for the uncertain future. The child should enjoy the pleasure of present. Education should not be a burdensome process and an activity by making child miserable. Education should ensure maximum freedom. No corporal punishments.

Negative education is against treating child as a little man preparing for adult life. A child is a separate identity and not a miniature of the adult.

Other characteristics of negative education are:

- — Negative education is imparted in accordance with child's natural tendencies and faculties.
- — Training to sense organs is emphasized.
- — No direct moral lessons, but safeguards child from evils
- — No teaching virtues or truths but shields child from vices.
- — No significance to textbooks and formal classrooms. The child has to learn from the sources of nature
- — Ensuring the child opportunity to play in the open air.
- — Advised simple diet and light clothes.
- — Discouraged verbal lesson and bookish learning
- — Achieving moral aims through child's direct activities
- — Discipline through natural consequences

## A Specific Interpretation on Rousseau's Concept of Education

Some of the major aims of education, according to Rousseau, are:

a) Securing the necessity of life (preparation for the struggle for existence)

b) Self-expression

c) Natural development of individuality

d) Develop harmony with nature.

Rousseau' educational concepts are called pedagogy of romance. He was a true naturalist. Though he failed to love his own children, whatever he wrote shows his immense love towards children. A child is considered the purest offspring of the nature. It is the society and process of civilization that makes this purest child corrupted, was a revolutionary view. He saw in the nature an entrancing beauty and harmony. But in the world of man – the so-called civilized society – there are only evils, conflicts, envy, ugliness, selfishness etc. The child should be protected from this evil of 'civilized' society. Let the child live according to the order of nature, not with the social order. Education is the instrument to protect the child from the 'civilization'. To Rousseau, a reform of human nature could be possible only by going back to the nature. Go back to nature for a blissful life. Education is to go on with an order based on equality, fraternity, and liberty. Though criticized a lot by many, Rousseau's views on education still have a dominant place in the scenario of education without substitution.

# John Dewey

Dewey is considered as the most influential educationist of the 20th Century. You may reach this fact by grasping the following appreciations:

'.............In the view of Progressivism's most influential theorist, the American philosopher John Dewey, the classroom is to be a democracy in microcosm.'

'Children have to be encouraged toward experimentation and independent thinking.'

'Knowledge is not a fixed apprehension of something but a process of acting .....'

'.......And he believed school is not a preparation of life; it is life!'

This chapter studies one of the leading figures in the field of education, John Dewey. The chapter covers

*Dewey's Life*

*Works*

*Dewey's Philosophy*

- *Concept of thought and knowledge*

*Educational Philosophy*

- *Concept of democracy*
- *Ideals of laboratory school*
- *Concept of thinking as a mental process*

*Dewey's Ideals of Methods of Teaching and Learning*

More than a pragmatist Dewey was an instrumentalist. Instrumentalism is the doctrine that ideas are instruments of responses and adaptation, and that their truth is to be judged in terms of their effectiveness.

**John** Dewey may be placed at the top in the list of twentieth century educationists. Dewey, American philosopher and educator, was one of the founders of the philosophical school of pragmatism, and a pioneer in functional psychology. He was a leader of the progressive movement in education in the United States. Dewey's philosophy of education is widely known and thoroughly implemented. His creative ideas fit the realms of logic, ethics, politics, aesthetics, and religion, which constitute the intellectual environment of many of the leaders of his time. "Instrumentalism" is a philosophical thought with which his name is closely associated. He rejected authoritarian teaching methods. Regarding education in a democracy he suggested that education should function as a tool to enable the citizen to integrate his or her culture and vocation usefully. To accomplish those aims, both pedagogical methods and curricula needed radical reform. Dewey's view of democracy as a primary ethical value permeated his educational theories. He had a profound impact on progressive education and was regarded as the foremost educator of his day.

He was an educationist who tied theory with practice. The union between theory and application reached its zenith with John Dewey's development of 'laboratory school' at the University of Chicago in 1896 and the publication of his key-stone article, "The Reflex Arc Concept in Psychology" (1896). He attacked the philosophy of atomism and the concept of elementary behaviour modification, including the behavioral theory of stimulus and response. Dewey, whose writings and lectures influenced educators throughout the world, laid the foundations of a new philosophy that continues to affect the whole structure of education, particularly at the elementary level.

## 9.1 Life Sketch

John Dewey was born on October 20, 1859, the third of four sons born to Archibald Sprague Dewey and Lucina Artemesia Rich of Burlington, Vermont, USA. He died on June 2, 1952, at the age of ninety-three.

Dewey attended the public school and the University of Vermont in Burlington. While at the University of Vermont, Dewey was exposed to evolutionary theory through the teaching of G.H. Perkins and *Lessons in Elementary Physiology,* a text by T.H. Huxley, the famous English evolutionist. The theory of natural selection made a lifelong impact upon Dewey's thought. This impact moved him to focus on the interaction between the human organism and its environment when considering questions of psychology and the theory of knowledge.

After graduation in 1879, Dewey taught high school for two years, during which the idea of pursuing a career in philosophy took hold. Later he enrolled as a graduate student at Johns Hopkins University. George Sylvester Morris, a German-trained Hegelian philosopher and G. Stanley Hall, one of the most prominent American experimental psychologists at the time were his teachers at John Hopkins University. Dewey received PhD from John Hopkins University in 1884. He was a teacher at University of Michigan and University of Chicago. He founded Laboratory School at Chicago University to experiment his philosophical thought. Disagreements with the administration over the status of the Laboratory School led to Dewey's resignation from his post at Chicago in 1904. Later he worked in Colombia University and worked there for three decades. Though Dewey retired from active teaching in 1930, he kept his activities as a public figure or productive philosopher.

**School or thought**: Hegelian idealism and Instrumentalism. He was a philosopher of pragmatism.

**Works:** His first two books are Psychology (1887), and Leibniz's New Essays Concerning the Human Understanding (1888). (Both works expressed Dewey's early commitment to Hegelian idealism). The major works came out while he was working at Michigan, Chicago and Colombia and also at Minnesota, where he worked for a short period. He was restless in writing after retirement also.

The School and Society (1899), which he wrote taking his experience with laboratory school, is considered as first major work on education.

The Child and the Curriculum (1902)

Dewey wrote Ethics (1908; revised ed. 1932) with James Hayden and Tufts.

Dewey based on his experience at a teacher's college wrote an application of his theory of knowledge to education How We Think (1910; revised ed. 1933)

*Collection of essays published later:* The Influence of Darwin on Philosophy and Other Essays in Contemporary Thought (1910) and Essays in Experimental Logic (1916)

Democracy and Education (1916) perhaps his most important work in the field of education. It is considered one of the greatest works of all period in education.

Reconstruction in Philosophy (1920), Human Nature and Conduct (1922), Experience and Nature (1925), The Public and it's Problems (1927), and The Quest for Certainty (1929) are the collection of lectures.

Other works include Logic: The Theory of Inquiry (1938), Art as Experience (1934), A Common Faith (1934), Freedom and Culture (1939), and Theory of Valuation (1939)

Knowing and the Known (1949) was the last coauthored with Arthur F. Bentley.

## 9.2 Philosophy of John Dewey

The central focus of Dewey's philosophical interests was mostly in "epistemology," or the "theory of knowledge." However he expressly rejected the term epistemology,' preferring the "theory of inquiry" or "experimental logic" as more representative of his own approach.

### 9.2.1 Thought, Knowledge and World

In Dewey's view, traditional epistemologies had drawn too harsh a distinction between thought, the domain of knowledge, and the world of fact to which thought supposedly referred. Traditionally, thought was believed to exist apart from the world, either as the object of immediate awareness or as the unique aspect of the self. The doubt accompanies the view. If thought constitutes a domain that stands apart from the world, how can its accuracy as an account of the world ever be established? For Dewey a new model, rejecting traditional presumptions, was wanting. In his early writings on these issues Dewey offered a solution to epistemological issues (mainly along the lines of his early acceptance of Hegelian idealism): the world of fact does not stand apart from thought, but is itself defined within thought as its objective manifestation. But during the succeeding decade Dewey gradually came to reject this solution as confused and inadequate. It was because of his realization that Hegelian idealism was not advantageous to accommodating the methodologies and results of experimental science.

Unlike traditional approaches in the theory of knowledge, Dewey's approach understood thought genetically, as the product of the interaction between organism and environment. His approach signifies knowledge as having practical instrumentality in the guidance and control of that interaction. (Dewey adopted the term "instrumentalism" as a descriptive term for his new approach in pragmatism.)

Dewey came to believe that a productive and naturalistic approach to the theory of knowledge must begin with a consideration of the development of knowledge as an adaptive human response to environmental conditions. That should be aimed at an active restructuring of these environmental conditions.

How does an individual interact with the surroundings? The organism interacts with the world through self-guided activity that coordinates and integrates sensory and motor responses. The implication for the theory of knowledge was clear: the world is not passively perceived and thereby known; active manipulation of the environment is involved integrally in the process of learning from the start.

Knowledge is a product of an activity directed at the fulfillment of human purposes.

Dewey distinguished three phases of the knowledge acquisition process. It begins with the problematic situation (a situation where instinctive or habitual responses of the human organism to the environment are inadequate for the continuation of ongoing activity in search of the fulfillment of needs and desires). The second phase of the process involves the isolation of the data or subject matter which defines the parameters within which the reconstruction of the initiating situation must be addressed. It is the collection of data or information of subject matter. The third is the reflective phase of the process, the cognitive elements of inquiry (ideas, suppositions, theories, etc.)

John Dewey directly challenged the idea that knowledge is primarily theoretical. He argued experience consists of an interaction between a living being and his environment. Knowledge is not a fixed comprehension of something but a process of acting and interactive result with environment.

In the case of reality Dewey asserts that things experienced empirically "are what they are experienced as." Dewey uses as an example a noise heard in a darkened room that is initially experienced as fearsome. Subsequent inquiry (e.g., turning on the lights and looking about) reveals that the noise was caused by a shade tapping against a window, and thus harmless. But the subsequent inquiry, Dewey argues, does not change the initial status of the noise: it was experienced as fearsome, and in fact was fearsome. Our experience of the world is constituted by our interrelationship with it, a relationship that is imbued with practical import. While one walks through a street at night, some insect bites on his calf. He fears a snake bite on leg. He cried aloud and is nearly unconscious. Some wayfarers recognize it is not snake but just an insect; the truth is revealed. The victim comes out of the problematic situation. This recognition does not change the initial status; the fear of gnaw. It was experienced as frightening, and really it was frightening. Experience is the reality; made out of our experience with the environment.

The subsequent inquiry does not uncover a reality underlying a mere appearance. But by settling the demands of the situation, it effects a change in the appearance of the organism-environment relationship of the initial situation – a change in reality is possible. Second, the fact that the meanings we attribute to natural events might change in any particular situation in the future. Renewed inquiries lead to more adequate understanding of natural events. But it does not mean that our experience of the world at any given time as a whole be delinquent.

Dewey begins with the observation that the world as we experience it both individually and collectively is an admixture of the uncertain, the momentary and contingent aspect of things, and the stable, the patterned regularity of natural processes that allows for prediction and human intervention. The reality description must take into account both of these elements of experience.

Dewey maintained that an idea agrees with reality, and is therefore true, if and only if it is successfully employed in human action in pursuit of human goals and interests. It means idea is real if it leads to the resolution of a problematic situation.

In Axiology, Dewey formulated a distinction between instrumental and intrinsic value – between what is good as a means and what is good as an end. He presented a pragmatic interpretation and tried to break down this distinction between means and ends. Values are coming out of man's assertive effort to control the environment.

Instrumentalism is a philosophy advanced by John Dewey holding that what is most important in a thing or idea is its value as an instrument of action and that the truth of an idea lies in its usefulness. (Dewey favoured these terms over the term pragmatism to label the philosophy on which his views of education rested).

In his interpretation of mind, rather than understanding the mind as a primitive and individual human endowment, and a precondition of conscious and intentional action, Dewey offers a genetic analysis of mind as an emerging aspect of cooperative activity mediated by linguistic communication. Consciousness, in turn, is not to be understood as a domain of private awareness. It is considered as the pivot point of the organism's readjustment to the challenge of novel conditions where the meanings and attitudes that formulate habitual behavioral responses to the environment fail to be adequate. Dewey's claim that the mind has a social origin expresses the basic contention, that the human individual is a social being from the start, and that individual satisfaction and achievement can be realized only within the context of social habits and institutions that promote it.

In his views regarding social existence of human life, Dewey raises the following points:

a) A living being is one that defeats and controls for its own continued activity the energies that it would otherwise use up.
b) Life is a self-renewing process through action upon the environment.
c) Continuity of the life process is not dependent upon the prolongation of the existence of any one individual.
d) Society exists through a process of transmission quite as much as biological life.

## 9.3 Educational Philosophy of John Dewey

Dewey was a great humanist and educationist. Dewey's thoughts as an educational thinker and reformer were accepted widely all over the world. His writings and lectures influenced educators throughout the world, laid the foundations of a new philosophy that continues to affect the whole structure of education, particularly at the elementary level. Dewey believed that route of all educative process lies in the instinctive and spontaneous attitude of the child. Philosophy determines the desirable social values. Education is the instrument to promote the social values. Education is considered the laboratory of philosophical experiments.

Education based on activity programmes is the right education. Life activities are more important than any pre-planned course of study which take place in classroom. Even learning in reading, writing and arithmetic grew out of child's activities.

A child always reconstructs his experience. The reconstruction of experiences and active learning happen through activity, play, interaction, self-expression, contact with nature, etc. Even the spirit of the school is renewed through the activities of the child. Activities ensure cooperation among children rather than competition. Cooperation makes them socially efficient.

Dewey suggested that school should function as a center of social life and so it must be a social institution. Education is a social process.

He tried to inculcate his views by defining education as a process of reconstruction of social experiences. Education is a continuous organization and reorganization of experiences and adjustment with the environment. Environment means all aspects of social life.

A child's education is life itself. He grows from one experience leading to another. The process of education is a continuous adjustment and unending attempt to control the environment. It is based on both psychological factors and sociological factors.

Man is a part of the society. He cannot be isolated from social life. So, education as a social process must provide basic activities found in society. It is a planned process to develop social efficiency and social relationship.

### 9.3.1 Dewey's Concept of Democracy

According to John Dewey, democracy is the most desirable form of government because it alone provides the kinds of freedom necessary for an individual's self-development and growth – including the freedom to exchange ideas and opinions with others, the freedom to form associations with others to pursue common goals, and the freedom to determine and pursue one's own interests and attitude. He suggests that freedom is the pivot of education process. Free engagements in life-oriented activities are possible only in democratic situation. It is the basic factor for development of social efficiency. There is a saying that Dewey's classroom is a microcosm of democracy. Freedom to free learning, self-development and all other wills can be ensured and exchanged in democratic atmosphere in school.

Dewey suggests provisions for construction and reconstruction of experiences in the curriculum, and children were encouraged toward experimentation and independent thinking. The classroom as a democracy in microcosm ensures the equality of opportunity and freedom to will. The content, method, strategies and management must smell the spirit of democracy in all aspects.

Democratic approach in education stands for progressive educational outline. Progressive education should be progressive in approach and in the curriculum, and children were encouraged toward experimentation and independent thinking.

### 9.3.2 Dewey's Laboratory School

Laboratory school at university of Chicago was the pioneer school in the progressive education movement in the United States. The original University Elementary School was founded in Chicago in 1896 by John Dewey as a research and demonstration centre for the Department of Pedagogy at the University of Chicago. The school was designed to exhibit, test, and conduct research in educational methods centering on the child. Dewey founded and directed laboratory school at Chicago intended to afford an opportunity to apply directly his developing ideas on pedagogical method. It was a 'laboratory' to experiment Dewey's philosophical ideologies. Laboratory school was a wonderful assembling of theory with practice. This experience provided the material for his first major work on education, The School and Society (1899).

Dewey made his philosophical and pedagogical experiments at the Laboratory School in order to create 'the school of tomorrow'. The ideal of his school was to train pupils for complete living in society. To him schooling was not a content-oriented teaching learning process. School, to Dewey, was just like an enlarged form of community. The curriculum must be progressive. It must possess positive values of social life.

It should be relevant to the child's need. Everyday experiences must be considered in the use of instruction strategies.

Like Gandhian concept of basic education, Dewey's school gave importance to basic needs and interests of pupils. The departments of shop work with woods and tools, cooking, training in some sort of crafts, weaving and other work with textiles were made in the school. Students from both sexes were trained in all these three departments. Dewey divided the school life of pupils into three stages; the play period for age group 4 to 8, period of spontaneous attention to 8 to 12 age group and the period of reflective attention from the age 12 onwards. The school was a remarkable success to protect his philosophical principles and progressive education.

### 9.3.3 Mind and Mental Process (Thinking)

Dewey had a philosophical and scientific view on the evolution of mind and evolution of intelligence. They are almost identical and developing in a natural way.

Mind and intellect are the instruments to solve varied practical and social problems. Mind is the effective tool to solve problems. Mind and intellect make man a superior creature.

Mind is active in three aspects – thinking, feeling and willing. An individual always tries to control his environment in order to avoid pain or to obtain satisfaction. For this process of controlling, the individual develops ideas by the activities of mind. This is the core of Dewey's instrumental theory of mind.

Thinking is never the result of pure contemplation. Thinking is the active process associated with activity. Thinking does not originate from sensation or meditation.

Thinking does not take place in a vacuum. There will be one or more causes that stimulate thinking. The causes arise from the individual's attempt to control the environment. If there is no obstruction (hindrances) to individual's activities, there will be no thinking.

John Dewey suggested that directed thinking proceeds by "implicit trial-and-error." That is to say, it resembles the process whereby laboratory animals confronted with a novel problem situation try out one response after another until they sooner or later hit upon a response that leads to success.

The cause or problem that stimulates thinking may be a question to be answered or a haziness to be resolved. On such time, whole ideas and activities of mind propound to a definite channel to frame thinking process. Thinking is then a process to find an answer to the question that needs to be answered or uncertainty to be resolved. Thinking is a function of activity.

The process of thinking, Dewey says, involves five logical steps. They are:

a) The feeling of a doubt, feeling of difficulty or feeling, hesitation or problem.
b) Analyzing elements of situation or problem and locating the 'heart' of it
c) Making of suggestions as possible solutions
d) Taking most possible solution to experimentation.
e) Experiment and observe in order to accept or reject the solution.

These five steps are followed by every normal mind to find solutions to any problem. This mental activity of finding solution to feeling or problem is nothing but 'thinking processes. (This idea on normal course of mental activity – thinking and learning – is the base of project method envisaged by Dewey and other progressive educationists).

## 9.4 Methods of Teaching and Learning Project Method

Dewey emphasized direct experience both in teaching and learning. Learning by doing is the best way. A child should be provided sufficient situations, which can be called environment, in which he can do something. He can engage with activities in this situation. As activity is the basic of learning, the opportunities to perform activity are to be designed. Genuine interest in what he is doing is a major factor. Effective learning is possible through the activities in which an individual has genuine interest. Interest and effort are complementary.

For effective learning a genuine problem should develop within a situation as stimulus to think. There should be opportunities to possess the information and to make observations needed to deal with the problem that stimulates thinking. Suggested solutions which are responsible for resolving the uncertainty are developing in an orderly way. The child has to provide opportunity to test ideas and suggestions. He himself identifies the validity of suggestions and ideas. The acceptance of valuable suggestions to solve the problem is the basic of learning process.

Dewey's concept of teaching and learning focused on the aspects like freedom, democratic atmosphere and interpretation, activity, experience, socialization, creative expression, recognition of individuality and cooperation.

A child has some basic interests. These basic interests lead them to learning. Interests and feelings must be genuine. According to Dewey there are four fundamental interests which lead to effective learning. They are:

a) interest for communication and conversation

b) interest for inquiry and finding out things

c) interest for making things and construction

d) interest for artistic expression

Every normal child has these interests. A child's learning activities, experiences and effective learning are based on these interests.

Child activity, experiences, feeling of problem or doubt and genuine interests are the basic factors of teaching-learning process. The method of teaching should focus on these aspects. The method of teaching, according to Dewey, is to be developed on the basis of five steps. They are the basic principles of project method:

a) *Activity* Activity is aroused by motivation and interest of child on task.

b) *Problem* Problem is an aroused difficulty. Child considers the learning issue a problem. It may be a question to be answered, an issue to be analyzed or a problem to be solved.

c) *Data* Learner collects maximum information on data regarding the various aspects of the problem he faces.

d) *Hypotheses* Formation of hypotheses based on the data leads individual learner to reach the framing of solutions to the problem.

e) *Testing* Formed suggestions may be tested by the child to identify whether they are successful or a failure.

A method is effective while it based on child activity, genuine interest and motivation. Availability of opportunities to involve in learning is a must to the child. Dewey' approach of method was a process-oriented method. Child activity which is natural and base of all learning and thinking is to be projected by the teacher while making use the method.

Dewey rejected religious and spiritual interpretation of knowledge and learning. Scientific knowledge is the only real knowledge. He gave importance to scientific methods and approaches for learning.

John Dewey was the greatest educationist of 20th century. He was a great philosopher, democrat and humanist. His contributions to education and related scenarios are considered paragon and immensely valuable all over the world. He rejected the religious and spiritual beliefs completely. He had given very little note to aesthetic sides of human life. He completely ignored the supernatural explanations to human life. The prominence given to scientific knowledge and approach also gathered criticism from several sides.

Chapter 10

# Paulo Freire

Go through this episode: Coconut oil was the 'life blood' of kitchens of Kerala! But as a part of an international trade offer, as the palm oil came into the cooking vessels on ovens to take the positions of coconut oil, coconut oil faced the decline of golden era. The Keralites who ate tapioca with the chutney made out of coconut, onion and coconut oil as a major food item and lived the life up to 70 or more years without much health problems were advised by the biggest multinational companies that tapioca is starch and coconut oil carries cholesterol and hence give up that food! They advised the new oil as a substitute. People believed without further 'dialogue' and changed to palm oil and new generation food. They failed to recognize that it was a cultural invasion. Consequences were horrible. The backbone of Kerala's agri-culture, coconut, began to face a threat! The new practices of food brought cardiac problems and other diseases. At the time of introduction, the palm oil was supplied by multinational companies at a lower price. But as palm oil became the inevitable edible oil, the companies began to hike the price! The people were compelled to pay for the menu designed by multinational companies. A surprise was that the scenario of education failed to discuss this matter and the hidden agenda behind this attempt of changing the food culture of a people.

There was an educationist who warned the world against this type of cultural invasion on the poor people. He tried to alert the world against the active framework of the oppressors! The educationist was Paulo Freire.

The incident shows a fact; 'dialogue' is necessary between the policymakers and those who experience the consequences of policies. Education should enable the people to engage in dialogical cultural action with others.

'Education is a designed programme to protect the political mobilization of the oppressed. Education is for 'liberation' of the oppressed'.

*'Education must be an agenda of the oppressed and never be that of oppressor.'*

Paulo Freire who was a Brazilian, spoke a lot on the education and pedagogy for the oppressed and this is the content matter of this chapter.

The chapter covers:

*Paulo Freire's Life and Works*

*Freire's Educational Theory*

- *Concept of teacher student dichotomy*
- *Freire's view against banking concept of education*
- *Concept of problem posing methods*
- *Concept of dialogical cultural action and praxis*
- *Ideals of learning*

**Paulo** Freire (1921–1997), the Brazilian educationalist, has left a significant mark on thinking about progressive practice in acquisition of knowledge, learning and in education. Perhaps the most influential thinker about education in the late twentieth century; Paulo Freire has been particularly popular with informal educators with his emphasis on dialogue and his concern for the oppressed, and educational programmes for adult education and literacy. He is a true educationist of the contemporary era. His innovative ideas and theories created and are creating a lot of sound discussion in the education scenario.

## 10.1 A Brief Life Sketch

**Birth**: September 19, 1921

**Death**: He died on May 2, 1997

**Name in full**: Paulo Regulus Neves Freire

**Family**: His father was Joaquim Temistocles Freire. Joaquim was an officer of the Pernambuco (a province of Brazil) military police. His mother was Edeltrudis Neves Snows. They were a middle class family. He was born in Recife, Brazil.

> *"The future isn't something hidden in a corner. The future is something we build in the present."*
>
> – Paulo Freire

**Works**: Education as the Practice of Freedom (1967)

Pedagogy of the Oppressed (1970) – it was published in Brazil only in 1974 due to political disputes.

The Politics of Education: Culture, Power and Liberation (1985)

Pedagogy of Hope: Reliving Pedagogy of the Oppressed (1995)

Education for Critical Consciousness (1993)

Letters to Cristina: Reflections on my Life and Work (1996)

Above are his major works. Some others are, Present Day Education in Brazil – Ph.D. thesis – (1959), Pedagogy in Process: The Letters to Guinea-Bisseau. (1978), Pedagogy of the City. (1993), Pedagogy of the Heart. (1997).

He also wrote several articles and some books along with other writers.

### Freire's Life

Paulo Freire was born to middle class parents. He experienced poverty and hunger during the 1929 Great

Depression. Due to economic problems, the Freire family was forced to leave Recife, settling in nearby Jaboatao where Paulo spent part of his child-hood and adolescence. His father died when he was at thirteen.

> *"In Jaboatao, when I was ten, I began to think that there were a lot of things in the world that were not going well".*
>
> – Paulo Freire

Freire entered the University of Recife in 1943, enrolling in the Faculty of Law, but also studying philosophy and the psychology of language. Though he entered the legal bar, he never actually practiced law. He worked as a teacher in secondary schools teaching Portuguese. In 1944, he married Elza Maia Costa de Oliveira, a fellow teacher. The two worked together for the rest of their life. They had five children.

In 1946, Freire was appointed Director of the Depart-ment of Education and Culture of the Social Service in the State of Pernambuco, the Brazilian state of which Recife is the capital.

In 1961, he was appointed Director of the Department of Cultural Extension of Recife University. There, through the formation of cultural circles, he made an attempt to introduce literacy programmes. It was a success. Freire quickly gained international recognition for his experiences in literacy training in Northeastern Brazil. Following the military coup of 1964, he was jailed by the new government and eventually forced into a political exile that lasted fifteen-years.

Later, Freire worked in Chile for five years for the Christian Democratic Agrarian Reform Movement and the Food and Agriculture Organization of the U N. His first book came out in 1967. The book was well received, and Freire was offered a visiting professorship at Harvard University.

Freire went back to Brazil in 1980. He joined the Workers' Party in the city of Sao Paulo, and acted as a supervisor for its adult literacy project from 1980 to 1986. When the Party prevailed in the municipal elections in 1988, Freire was appointed Secretary of Education for Sao Paulo.

In 1986, his wife Elza died and Freire married Maria Araujo.

In 1991, the Paulo Freire Institute was established in Sao Paulo to extend and elaborate his theories of popular education. Freire died of heart failure in 1997.

For his contributions and achievements he was awarded several prizes including UNESCO 1986 Prize for Education for Peace.

## 10.2 Paulo Freire's Educational Theory

What is education? Who developed the agenda of education in the world? For whom is the education? Questions raised by Freire to be answered himself were many. Education, according to Freire was **progressive education**. He was of the opinion that people belong to two strata. One is the oppressor and another is the oppressed. Oppressor is the developer of the agenda of the educational process and programmes. Actually education is to be developed and practiced from the oppressed side. There should be dialogues between the two. Speaking between oppressed and oppressor is necessary. 'Dialogue' is the panacea for the eradication of the 'silence of culture'.

He put forward his concept of educational programmes through the theoretical views as follows. His ideas on education can be easily achieved by going through these theoretical views.

### 1. Theory of Value

Education is aimed to orient social values. Only through the social experiences an individual can learn. Freire tried to answer the questions like: what knowledge and skills are worthwhile learning? What are the goals of education? Thus he developed his ideas on value.

Education should raise the awareness of the students so that they become subjects, rather than objects, of the teaching-learning process. This is done by teaching students to think democratically. This is done by teaching students to continually question and make meaning from (critically view) everything they learn.

The learners should be respected by the educators. The educators should be aware of the concrete conditions of the learner's world, the conditions that shape them. There should be dialogues between learners and educators. The speaking in its effective sense will develop the values of learning.

There are no themes or values of which one cannot speak. Teachers and learners can speak on any themes or values. There are no areas in which one must be silent. We can talk about everything, and we can give testimony about everything

**2. Theory of Knowledge**

What is knowledge? How is it different from belief? How can knowledge be acquired? These are answered very differently by Freire.

Knowledge is a social construct. Knowing is a social process. However individual dimension of knowledge and knowing cannot be forgotten or even devalued. The process of learning has individual dimensions, which involves the whole conscious self, feelings, emotions, memory, affects, a curious mind and so on. The process of knowing focused on the object equally involves other thinking subjects. All are capable of knowing and curious. *This simply means that the relationship called "thinking" is not enclosed in a relationship "thinking subject – knowable object" because thinking extends to other thinking subjects.*

Freire discusses two types of knowledge, a) unconscious, sometimes practical knowledge and b) critical, reflective or theory knowledge. Beliefs are shaped into knowledge by discussion and critical reflection.

Knowledge should not be limited to logic and content, or emotions and superstitions. Knowledge should seek the connections between understandings and feelings. Paulo does talk at length that it is wrong to accept one side of any dichotomy.

### 10.2.1 Freire's Aversion to the Teacher-Student Dichotomy

The term dichotomy means division or segregation into two. A seeker of knowledge must never segregate cognition and emotion. Pupils do not separate commonsense knowledge and others. All knowledge the child gets is knowledge, not separate knowledge. One of the mistakes we often make is to dichotomise reading and writing as two separate processes for knowing or learning. Even from children's earliest steps in the practice of reading and writing, they are to conceive of these processes as detached from the general process of knowing. This dichotomy between reading and writing follows us forever, as students and as teachers. The dichotomy between teachers and students as separate teaching and knowing units is to be discouraged. They are not to be compartmentalized. Instead teacher and pupils should teach and learn together.

### 3. Theory of Human Nature

Human being is a separate identity, different from other species. The ability of humans to plan and shape the world for their future needs is what separates man from animals. But this 'planning and shaping' is done by the oppressors. The oppressed majority must be taught to imagine a better way so that they can shape their future and thereby become more human. There is difference in the concept of human nature between the elite and others. The elite (oppressors) naturally believe that they are better and anything else is naturally inferior.

'Growing' to humans is something more than growing to the trees or the animals. Growing to humans is a process in which they can intervene or get involved. The point of decision of human growth is not found in other species.

Man has a strong tendency to affirm that what is different from him is inferior. Freire says, 'We start from the belief that our way of being is not only good but better than that of others who are different from us. This is **intolerance**.' The dominant class believes it has the power to distinguish itself from the dominated class. This group first rejects the differences between them, second, does not pretend to be equal to those who are different; third, it does not intend that those who are different shall be equal. What it wants is to maintain the differences and keep its distance and to recognize and emphasize in practice the **inferiority** of those who are dominated.

There are many things that limit the success of the oppressed majority. Non-critical thinking (naive consciousness) is a source of many limitations. Some poor people see no way out of their conditions.

**4. Theory of Learning**

What is learning? How are skills and knowledge acquired? Freire gives a different view on this.

Freire talks about the misleading notion of looking at the education system like a bank, a large depository where students come to withdraw the knowledge they need for life. Knowledge is not a set commodity that is passed from the teachers to the students. Students must construct knowledge from knowledge they already possess. Teachers must learn how the students learn and understand the world.

Teachers must learn how the students understand the world so that the teacher understands how the student can learn. Teaching cannot be a process of transference of knowledge from teacher to the learner. The mechanical transference results in machinelike memorization. The teaching-learning process necessarily demands a critical way of comprehending and of realizing the learning content. Learning is a process where knowledge is presented to learner, then shaped through understanding, discussion and reflection. It is a way of **problem posing method**.

**The attraction of learning:** When a learner understands an object, rather than memorizing the profile of the concept of the object, he knows that object and produces the knowledge of that object. When there is only the profile memorization of concept, such knowing or learning will not happen. While the learner critically achieves an understanding of the object that the teacher talks about, the learner knows the meaning of the content and becomes co-producer of that content. The learner then will not speak of the content matter merely as someone who has heard about it. The learner has worked and reworked on the meaning of the object or content. Here lies the difficulty and the attraction in the act of learning.

> *One of the challenges to progressive educators, in keeping with their choice, is not to feel or to proceed as if they were inferior to dominant-class learners in the private schools who arrogantly mistreat and belittle middleclass teachers. But on the other hand, nor should they feel superior, in the public school system, to the learners from the slums, to the lower class children, to the children with no comforts, who do not eat well, who do not "dress nicely," who do not "speak correctly," who speak with their own syntax, semantics, and accent.*
>
> – Pedagogy of the Oppressed

Just as a bricklayer requires a collection of tools and instruments, without which he cannot build a wall, a learner also requires fundamental instruments, without which he cannot learn effectively. He requires sufficient learning aids, interpretation from different tutors and lot of social experiences. Studying is a challenging task, for which one requiring patience and perseverance.

## 5. Theory of Transmission

Who is to teach? By what methods? What will the curriculum be?

According to Freire teaching is a political process. It must be a democratic process. The teacher must learn about the student so that knowledge can be constructed in ways that are meaningful to the student. The teacher should learn the way that the students learn. The teachers must become learners and teaching and learning should become knowing and 're-knowing'. Freire wants us to think in terms of teacher-student and student-teacher; that is, a teacher who learns and a learner who teaches, as the basic roles of classroom participation.

Teachers need to know what happens in the world of the children with whom they work. They need to know the universe of their dreams, the language with which they skillfully defend themselves from the aggressiveness of their world, what they know independently of the school, and how they know it. This knowledge of teachers will help them to do effective teaching.

> *One of our tasks as progressive educators, today and yesterday, is to use the past that influences the present. The past was not only a time of authoritarianism and imposed silence, but also a time that generated a culture of resistance as an answer to the violence of power.*

**The school** should be democratic. Atmosphere and total method of interaction between students and teachers must be democratic in all sense. Freire says, 'School that we need is not one in which only the teacher teaches, in which only the student learns, and in which the principal is the all powerful commander'. Teachers must have humility, coupled with love and respect for their students. Humility helps teachers to understand a truth: No one knows all; no one is ignorant of everything. All know something; all are ignorant of something.

The humility that enables teacher to listen even to those considered less competent. Democratic teachers increasingly prepare themselves to be heard by learners. By listening to learners and learning to talk with learners, democratic teachers teach the learners to listen to them as well. It means listening is not the student's 'duty' alone, but teacher's too. The novice teacher must be attentive to everything, even to the most innocent movements on the part of the students: the restlessness of their bodies, a surprised gaze, an un-wanting sound, un-wanting comment or a more or less aggressive reaction on the part of this or that student. Freire had suggested that the teacher training should be oriented to make teacher a novice teacher in this way.

### 6. Theory of Society and Opportunity

Freire challenges the conventional assumption that there is equal opportunity in a democratic society. He affirms that education is a political process. Schools become tools that are used by parents, business and the community to impose their values and beliefs. While no intentional harm is intended, this process often results in the oppression of less privileged persons. Freire's entire education career is based on his desire to provide greater opportunity for the poor and oppressed people of the world, particularly in Brazil. The oppressed majorities should avail opportunities for education and development.

### 7. Theory of Consensus

There may not be life or human existence without struggle and conflict. Conflict shares in our conscience. All disagreements can be overcome through compromise. Priority and preference should be provided in accordance with the character of conflict or struggle.

Disagreement is normal and something to expect always. Disagreement can be an impulsion to reflection and a source of growth. When opinions and disagreements are suppressed in the name of control and authority it creates adverse effects. They have to be treated democratically.

**His Further Suggestions**

Freire's most well known work is *Pedagogy of the Oppressed* (1970). Throughout this book (and in subsequent books also) he argues for a system of education that emphasizes learning as an act of culture and freedom. He is most well known for concepts such as "Banking" Education. Freire tried to reveal certain views through his text that Banking Education: a) passive learners have pre-selected knowledge deposited in their minds b) there is no progressive education c) it is teacher dominated and no dialogue between teachers and learners

Freire suggested progressive education and problem-posing learning or problem-posing methods as the ways of education. In this method a learner reaches "Conscientization", a process by which the learner advances towards critical consciousness through the "Culture of Silence", in which dominated individuals lose the means by which to critically respond to the culture that is forced on them by a dominant culture.

## 10.2.2 Banking Concept of Education

Freire is best-known for his opinions on what he called the "banking" concept of education. Banking in education is a metaphor used by Freire to comment on existing education that suggests students are considered empty bank accounts that should remain open to deposits made by the teacher. According to him, in this approach the student was viewed as an empty account to be filled by the teacher or the educator making 'deposits' in the learner. This concept is a strong criticism of the transmission of mere "facts" as the goal of education.

Freire rejects this approach, claiming it results in the **dehumanization** of both the students and the teachers.

The banking approach stimulates oppressive attitudes and practices in society.

The teacher talks about reality or fact as if it were motionless, static, compartmentalized, and predictable. Or else he explains a topic completely strange to the existing experience of the students. His task is to 'fill' the students with the contents of his narration. It is from this kind of instructive teaching that Freire draws his metaphor of *banking* as a concept of education. In it, teachers make *deposits* of information which students are to receive, memorize, and repeat.

It is a way of transmission of knowledge from the knowledgeable to the know nothings... Transmission from subject to object. Freire says, "The more students work at storing the deposits entrusted to them, the less they develop the critical consciousness which would result from their intervention in the world as transformers of that world".

Banking education emphasizes the teacher's role as the active one and learner's role as passive and the teacher-learner relationship as an anti-dialogical approach. It serves the oppressor by denying the learner an active role in the learning. It does not engage students in critical thinking; instead, it requires the students to be passive and to adapt thereby serving the purposes of oppression. It inhibits creativity, it resists dialogue and it is laid-back in nature.

### 10.2.3 Progressive Education and Problem-Posing Methods

As banking education is a way of dehumanisation, Freire advocates for a more authentic education, which aims at **Conscientization**. According to him, this "authentic" approach to education must allow people to be aware of their incompleteness and strive to be more fully human. The attempt to use education as a means of consciously shaping the person and the society is called conscientization. Libertarian, progressive education needs to "begin with the solution of the teacher-student contradiction, by reconciling the poles of the contradiction so that both are simultaneously teachers *and* students". True education is that which is democratic and denies the banking method.

Progressive educators help students to reach conscientization. Conscientization means breaking through prevailing mythologies to reach new levels of awareness—in particular, awareness of oppression, of being an object in a world where only subjects have power. The process of conscientization involves identifying contradictions in experience through dialogue and becoming a *Subject* with other oppressed subjects—that is, becoming part of the process of changing the world.

Instead of banking methods, progressive educators employ problem-posing methods. "Problem-posing education does not and cannot serve the interests of the oppressor. "In problem—posing education, people develop their power to perceive critically *the way they exist* in the world *with which and in which* they find themselves; they come to see the world not as a static reality, but as a reality in process, in transformation" Teacher-students and student-teachers are continually reflecting on themselves and the world, establishing "an authentic form of thought and action".

### 10.2.4 Concept of Dialogics, Dialogical Cultural Action and Praxis

Freire viewed the essence of education as the practice of freedom and dialogue. He argues that words involve a radical interaction between reflection and action and true words are transformational. These words are the frame of dialogue. Dialogue has unique capacity to ensure freedom, enjoy liberalism in learning, develop critical thinking and reflective interaction in learning and protect cultural synthesis. Dialogue requires mutual respect and cooperation to not only develop understanding, but also to change the world.

"Dialogue cannot exist unless the dialoguers engage in critical thinking. Without dialogue there is no communication, and without communication, there can be no true education". Dialogue is a give and take of ideas, a sharing. A teacher cannot dialogue and attempt to impose his own ideas on learner. Teacher and learner can dialogue about their ideas and others – mutual give and take. This is against the banking education and oppression.

"Authentic" education, according to Freire, will involve a dialogue between the teacher and the student, mediated by the broader world context. He warns that the limits imposed upon both the colonizer (oppressor) and the colonized (oppressed) dehumanize everyone involved, thereby removing the ability for dialogue to occur, inevitably barring the possibility of transformation. He proposes 'dialogics' as an instrument to free the colonized, through the use of cooperation, unity and organization and cultural synthesis. Dialogue is the way to overcome problems in society to liberate human beings.

Freire's model of 'dialogics' must be rooted within social praxis, informed reflection and political action. Dialogic and social praxis are working together to break down oppression. They together also try to degenerate the structures and mechanisms of oppression. According to him freedom will be the result of 'praxis' when a balance between theory and practice is achieved. The praxis here is the informed action. Actually Praxis is the step to critical consciousness through critical reflection and action. Learner has to move from 'object' to 'subject'. For this, the learner is needed to be involved in dialogical action with the teacher. Dialogic action has two basic dimensions, reflection and action. (Action + Reflection = word(dialogue) = work = praxis).

Some human beings are submerged in the culture of silence. Some are ignorant in different social matters. Every human being, no matter how "ignorant" he or she may be, is capable of looking critically at the world in a dialogical encounter with others. It is not a traditional way of teaching and learning. There is no individual without limitations. All are incomplete. Understanding of these limitations and incompleteness is essential for dialogue with others. Then it will work against the interests of oppressors. Dialogue should not become a teacher-centered process. It should be democratic. The teacher should keep respect towards students. It is a form of cultural exchange. Dialogue is not from the teacher to student, but mutual. Problem with the 'teacher to pupil' form of dialogue is that, the teacher may think himself as the leader to **empower** students. Educators take the stand that they are *empowering* students through their attempt. Empowerment does not come from the educator to the learner. There should be critical reflection through dialogue. This dialogical cultural action leads to praxis and it is the step to critical con-sciousness through critical reflection and action.

**Specific Note on Freire's Theory**

Paulo Freire can be called the true educationist of the twentieth century. His educational concepts are widely accepted by developing and undeveloped countries.

He describes two classes of society, the oppressed and oppressor. There is oppressor–oppressed conflict. Oppressors always try to practice their interest. They are interested to dominate. They have their own framework to oppress others. Freire identified four techniques used to oppress the people as part of the framework

a) conquest
b) divide and rule
c) manipulation
d) cultural invasion

The alternative framework of the oppressed is based upon dialogical cultural action. Dialogue is the base of critical thinking and reflection. The oppressed people can make the following techniques as part of alternative framework

a) cooperation c) organization

b) unity for liberation d) cultural synthesis.

The learning process of the oppressed should keep in view their aim. Learning is not a teacher-centered empowering. It is based on dialogue between teacher and pupils. The learning materials for their dialogue, Freire suggest is:

— Organize the perception on content to be learned.

— Clear articulation of content and method to develop critical thinking.

— Planned and informed action (praxis).

— Reflective and effective execution.

The educational concept of Freire can be understood easily from a learner's point of view. He has certain revolutionary suggestions of learning and education as we discussed previously. Some major tenets of his educational ideology can be summarized as follows:

— Education is for political mobilization of the poor (oppressed).

— Learning is not a teacher centered process.

— Learning is not memorization of the profile of concepts. It is a process of involvement. It is critical thinking and reflective action.

— Dialogical cultural action is the base of the teaching-learning process. Dialogue with pupil is the first step in educational process.

— Dialogue is an encounter among men who name the world.

— Design of education should be done by oppressed.

— A leader is not an oppressor. He has to be a servant of the people; create values rather than receive them

- — Learning should be in democratic way. Freedom should be practiced.
- — Always try to recognize, interpret, discuss and refine pupils' understanding.
- — Advocate multi-sensory stimulation techniques.
- — The oppressor's view and mechanisms of oppression are to be degenerated. But he discourages ill will, malice, hatred or violence against oppressors.
- — He attacks the banking functions of education as it is a way of dehumanization. True education is education for conscious as it is the way of conscientization.
- — Acceptable is digestive or nutritive process of education.
- — Real solution to protect poor (oppressed) is unfolding their spirit, willpower, consciousness, ability to questioning, critical thinking and reflection, environmental awareness and attitudes. Dialogical cultural actions is the method to make use this solution.

Paulo Freire started his educational journey with the first step on adult education. Normally the poor are the sector of society who need deviated education and literacy programmes. Freire developed his concept based on this interest. Hence, we can justify his strong stand for adult education and informal education from his views.

Chapter

11

# Swami Vivekananda

Each soul is potentially divine", Vivekananda said. The goal of educational process is to manifest this divinity within, by controlling nature, external and internal.

Education is the manifestation of perfection already existing in man – is the popular quote of Vivekananda. He is a yogi who defined education in a different way.

To him right education was Man Making Education.

This chapter covers his educational contributions.

Chapter is provided content in the heads like:

*Vivekananda – Life Sketch*

*Philosophy*

*Educational Philosophy*

- *Concept of knowledge*
- *Concept of concentration*
- *Ideals of teaching and learning*
- *Ideas of women education*

**Swami** Vivekananda was a great figure in different fields; to him we can give a top place in education. He is known as a practical Vedanthi or a pragmatic monk. He was described as 'being young in years but eternal in wisdom'. He had a brief life less than forty years.

Vivekananda was an Indian reformer, missionary, and spiritual leader who propagated Indian religious and philosophical values, particularly the Hinduism in Europe, England, and the United States, founding the Vedanta Society and the Ramakrishna Mission.

He was considered most because of the spirit he possessed to tackle problems. His stress was on man himself – right kind of man. He called the youth to "arise, awake and stop not till the end is achieved" (*uthishtatha, jagratha and prapya varan nibodhadha*). He advised his followers to be holy, unselfish and have shraddha (faith and concentration).

He was a great orator and scholar. His birth day is observed as Youth Day in India.

## 11.1 A Brief Life Sketch

**Birth**: 12 January 1863

**Death**: 4 July 1902

**Family**: Vivekananda was born in the famous Datta Family in Shimla Pally, Kolkota (Calcutta), India. His father was Viswanatha Datta and mother was Bhuvaneswari Devi.

### Vivekananda – Life

The Datta family in which Vivekananda was born was very famous in Calcutta (Kolkotha). Real name of Vivekanada is Narendra Nath Datta. The attitude and attempts of father and mother gave a strong moral education background at his early age. He became rich in the knowledge related with Indian epics and Puranas and also developed a great fancy for wandering monks. It is noted that he had prodigious memory. He learned matters easily than other students and was interested to question every thing.

His primary education was at Metropolitan Educational Institution, which was founded by Iswar Chandra Vidyasagar. While at school, he was good at studies, as well as various games. During his school education, two years were not formal education because his father was shifted to Raipur. The Presidency College, Calcutta and General Assembly's Institution of Scottish General Missionary (Scottish Church College) were his centers of college education.

Vivekananda became interested in the writings and contributions of J S Mill, Hume, Herbert Spencer, Marx, Iswar Chandra Vidya Sagar, Tagore and Keshab Chandra Sen. It is said that his life motto was swiveled after his meeting with a 'spiritual ecstasy', Shri Ramakrishna of Dakshineswar. The influence of this Guru, Shri Ramakrishna, made him a monk.

After deciding to lead the life of a monk Narendra Nath Datta accepted a new name – Vividhishananda. Because of the advice of friends and well wishers like Maharaja of Khetri, he accepted *Vivekananda* as the name. Vivekananda embraced the wandering life and visited almost all part of India. He visited Europe and America to deliver lectures and to coordinate his spiritual and social organization. His speech in International Parliament of Religions held at Chicago in America in 1893 brought him great fame and appreciation. This wandering had a great educational value for him, as it did provide opportunities for original thought and observation.

After Sri Ramakrishna's death, Swami Vivekananda renounced the world and traveled India as a wandering monk. His mounting compassion for India's people drove him to seek material help from the West. Accepting an opportunity to represent Hinduism at Chicago's Parliament of Religions in 1893, Vivekananda won instant celebrity in America and a ready forum for his spiritual teaching.

For three years he spread the Vedanta philosophy and religion in America and England and then returned to India to found the Ramakrishna Math and Mission. Exhorting his nation to spiritual greatness, he awakened India to a new national consciousness.

Though he preached more on religion he had a firm conviction that it is futile to preach religion amongst the common people without first trying to remove their poverty and sufferings. His wandering brought him face to face with the dreadful poverty and sufferings of Indians and of other countries. Here he identified education is the solution to overcome poverty and sufferings. To satisfy the ideals and aims, Vivekananda with his fellow men established the Belur Math – a monastery – at Belur near to Calcutta (Kolkotta). The Ramakrishna Mission, which is one of the foremost educational organizations in India now, was established by Vivekananda in May 1897. Establishment of Ramakrishna Mission is being considered as his greatest contribution to the formal education scenario.

## 11.2 Vivekananda: Philosophy and Educational Philosophy

More than stipulating a separate educational ideology, Vivekananda had expounded his views on different educational issues and matters. The sum total of all these views can be illuminated as his philosophical concept of education.

Vivekanadha is a thinker who explained the social and political applications of advaita thought. He believed in the doctrine that 'Jiva is Shiva' – means each individual is divinity itself. His philosophical ideals also promoted the concept of 'manava seva madhava seva' – means service to humanity is service to Godliness. He coined the concept of daridra narayan seva – the service of God in and through poor human beings.

Each individual is unique and paragon. Each one has unity with Brahman – the ultimate Godliness and knowledge. The perfection is there in all human beings. God created all with perfect humanity. No one can be regarded as better or worse, or even as better-off or worse-off, than others. He strongly postulated the belief that "Aham Brahmasmi, Thathvamasi" –you possess Godliness, like I also. He stressed on the vedantic saying that renunciation should be a human spirit 'for one's own salvation and for the welfare of the world'. Man should be simple in all the walks of life. He insisted the ideal of simple living and high thinking.

Though he was religious in all aspects, he pleaded for strict separation between religion and government. Vivekananda did not feel that religion, or any force, should be used for forcefully developing an ideal society. Bringing about an ideal society, according to him, was something that would evolve naturally by individualistic change when the conditions were right.

Vivekananda believed that "education is the manifestation of perfection already existing in man". All knowledge, material or spiritual is in the human mind. The process of education is resembled with the growth of banyan tree. The big banyan tree which covers acres of land was in the little seed which was perhaps no bigger than mustard seed. This seed has the potential to grow to acres and acres. It has divine perfection and material perfection. If it availed proper environment – water and manure – it will grow itself, doesn't need others 'massage'. All that energy was there confined. Human mind is also like that. Each one of us has come out of one protoplasmic cell and all the powers one possesses were coiled up there. Vivekananda believed that human mind or intellect has all the capacities within. What education has to do is provide proper environment like the water and manure to the seed. The mind will grow to maximum of its potential ability itself. So education does not mean teaching, but it is the process of setting proper environment according to the abilities and powers of the learner. No teacher can teach a child any more than he can grow a plant. The child develops his own nature and potential and abilities. Liberty is the first condition of growth at early age of child.

Education is not the amount of information that is put in to the brain. Education is a digestive process. Education must have assimilation of ideas focused on life building, man making and character making. Education is not identical with information acquisition. He said, "If education is identical with information, the libraries would be the greatest sages in the world and encyclopedias the Rishis"

Vivekananda stood for **man making education**. The end of all education processes should be man making. Education should develop the willpower of the individual. He should be able to face all personal and social consequences. The essence of his educational philosophy, the man making education, can be read from his suggestion that, "we want that education by which character is formed, strength of mind is increased, and the intellect is expanded and by which one can stand on one's own feet. It is man making education all round that we want".

### 11.2.1 Concept of Concentration

Concentration is the most important element in method of teaching and learning. Concentration is the essence of educational process. Knowledge is acquired through the way of concentration. It is the best method for effective leaning. The success of a learner depends on his concentration on the process. Meditation and 'yoga' will help to develop concentration. Swami considered concentration – Shraddha – as the key to open the treasury of knowledge. He said, "The very essence of education is concentration of mind, not the collection of facts". The stronger the power of concentration, the better will be the learning.

Concentration is integrated with willpower and stability of mind – *sthitha prajna* and celibacy – *brahmacharya*. Vivekananda tried to associate concentration with the cognitive process. A big part of thought force is wasted by a man who lacks concentration on the work he does. If a man dominates in a particular area, that is the result of his concentration on the same. If mind is concentrated and turned back on itself, all forces within the man will function as servants to reach on the end. Otherwise the attempt may be scattered. The strength and force of the functions comes through concentration.

Vivekananda suggested the practice of yoga and meditation as methods that lead to mental concentration. Other than Yoga and meditation, he suggested acquisition of willpower; self-confidence and faith in own self as the methods of concentration. A learner must have concentration in all walks of learning. He advocated brahmacharya (celibacy) during the learning period. Complete continence gives great intellectual and spiritual power. The acquisition of these powers gives concentration. By brahmacharya or celibacy he meant chastity in thought, word, action and deed always and in all conditions. It is the abstinence from all mundane desires.

## 11.2.2 Concept of Knowledge

Swami Vivekananda believed in idealist epistemology. He believed no knowledge comes from outside. What we mean by acquisition of knowledge is just the eradication of ignorance and unfolding of already existing knowledge in the mind. Every man is capable of that. It is a divine ability. Only occasion is to be provided for the process to take place – the unfolding of knowledge. The function of education is the uncovering of knowledge hidden in mind. Education is not pouring in something but just bringing forth the existing perfection.

Actually a child does not learn but discovers or unveils. He says, 'what a man learns is really what he discovers, by taking the cover off his soul which is a mine of infinite knowledge.

The outward experiences function as occasions for the discovery and development of knowledge which already exists. What the children have to learn is to learn to apply their own intellect to the maximum ability he can.

There are three types of men; knowing man, ignorant and omniscient. The man from whom the darkness of ignorance is being lifted is the knowing man, the man upon whom it lies with thick covering is ignorant, and the man from whom the darkness of ignorance is entirely gone is all knowing, the omniscient. Knowledge acquisition that is uncovering of hidden knowledge is possible by any normal man because all have the divine capacity and perfection to do so.

> *Knowledge is inherent in man, no knowledge comes from outside; it is all inside. We say Newton discovered gravitation. Was it sitting anywhere in a corner waiting for him to be discovered. It was in his mind, it was his own ability; the time came and he found it out. All knowledge that the world has ever received come from the mind.*
>
> – View of Vivekananda

**Education for Character**

Vivekananda believed that 'we are what our thoughts have made us'. Thoughts formulate the character. Character is the aggregate of one's tendencies, the sum total of the bend of mind. It is the expression of repeated habits. Education should aim at character development.

Every experience leaves a mark of impression on mind. Sum total of these impressions determines man's character. If good impressions prevail, the character becomes good, if bad it becomes bad. If an individual continuously hears bad words, authentic commands, thinks bad thoughts, does bad actions, his mind will be full of bad impressions and it will lead to a socially undesirable character. Hence centers of education should protect individual from the experiences which lead to bad impressions and provide circumstances to avail good impressions.

To form a socially desirable character, a child should go through the social consequences too. In some cases misery is a greater teacher than happiness. A child should share the miseries of poverty, loneliness, etc to know the miseries of the world. Good and evil have equal share in moulding character. Hence, schools should provide experiences in this area too to students. Education should function to build up individual's character and manifest his real nature.

### 11.2.3 Concept of Teaching and Learning

Vivekananda developed the concept of teaching and learning based on Indian tradition and British educational practices in India. He pleaded for 'Gurugriha vasa', live with teachers as a resident learner – in education. (Many educational institutions run by Ramakrishna Mission follow the residential system; i.e. living with Guru). Without the personal life of teacher there is no good education.

A learner and teacher should follow certain conditions. A good learner must observe celibacy at the time of studentship. The other conditions are purity, a real thirst for knowledge, and perseverance. Learning is a type of sacred activity. Purity in thought, speech and act is necessary for effective and pure learning. None of men can get anything other than what he fixes his heart upon. Man gets whatever he wants. There must be a continuous struggle and constant fight to achieve the end. Hence, a learner must have thirst for knowledge and perseverance to find success.

A learner, at the time of studentship, must give up all desire for gain. He must be able to control internal and external senses. He also should possess great power of endurance. Mind must not be restless and out of control. So he should develop concentration. Learner must have faith in the teacher and the learning material.

A teacher must bear in mind that he is doing a divine function. Teaching is not the pouring in of knowledge. Before transacting the curriculum he must grasp its spirit. The hidden spiritual and moral idea behind the curriculum should be transacted to the pupils. Character and personality of a teacher is important. Purity should personify a good teacher. His work must be simply out of love, out of pure love for mankind at large. He teaches not for single learner or for a whole classroom, but for the entire humanity. A teacher must keep in mind a view that he is an inevitable part of the man making education.

A teacher should be able in communication. He must be aware of the level and ability to learn of the student. He also has to try to develop the spirit of purity, thirst after knowledge and perseverance in child. A good teacher has to focus on quality of learner's achievement, not the quantity.

The learner has to reach his ends himself. Here the teacher is a guide and supporter. He should try to develop his mental ability and willpower. A teacher must be democratic in approaches. Pupils must be given qualified freedom. A child needs free scope for growth. The teaching must be modified by teacher according to the needs of the taught.

A child educates himself. A teacher is the 'occasion provider' for this process. Teacher has to provide suitable opportunities to the learner to unfold the existing knowledge. A teacher can never 'teach'. Vivekananda believed that 'a teacher spoils everything by thinking that he is teaching'.

### 11.2.4 Concept of Education of Women

On the concept of women education Vivekananda was with the Indian tradition. He believed that one and same Spirit or Self is present in all human beings, both in men and women. So education must be same to all. But he advised separate institutions for girls and boys for certain period.

Design and execution of education must not be developed only by men only, women should get equal share. The attempts to turn women into mere manufacturing machines must be changed by the ways of education. Women have immense ability of manifestation of spiritual forces. He believed the preaching of Manu Smrithi that 'where women are respected, there the God delights and where they are not, there all work and efforts come to naught'.

He considered education as the magic process to solve all problems of women. To a certain extent he had a type of traditional views in the practice of women education.

Female education should be spread with religion as its center. Education should keep up heritage of culture. Education should train them in ideals of renunciation, life long virginity, truth and great well being of family and society. Certain basic training such as sewing, culinary art, rules of domestic work and upbringing of children shall also be taught to women.

General education to women should focus on the spread of religious education, spiritual and moral education, patriotic sense and value education. Women are the best teachers and they are the most able to convey the traditions and culture to the coming generation. If the women are educated, the culture, knowledge, power and devotion will awaken in the society; Vivekananda believed.

Vivekananda was not a full-time educationist. But, within his short span of life he contributed a lot to education both ideologically and practically. His words were extraordinarily brilliant. His attempts to spread education to the poor awakened the whole attempt in India to educate the poor. The awakening of indigenous education for poor and gathering of youth efforts towards this aim can be considered as premier in his contributions in the education scenario.

# Mahatma Gandhi

Gandhi stressed on life-centered education. He developed his educational ideals as a way of liberation of the poor, of India in particular. It deviated from the traditional views. It is an educational effort both of intellectual and bodily training. He strongly pleaded that bodily education is never to be considered inferior to the intellectual training.

This chapter covers

*Mahatma Gandhi – Life*

*Philosophical Ideals*

- *Brahmacharya*
- *Simplicity*
- *Silence*
- *Nonviolence*
- *Truth*

*Educational Philosophy*

*An Account of His Educational Experiments*

*Concept and Ideals of Basic Education (Nai Talim)*

**Gandhi** was a true man. One can find faults in his political endeavors; one may find points to deny in his religious attitudes, educational concepts and ideals. But nobody can blame Gandhi the man. He is 'supernatural'. On Gandhi, Einstein said' "the generations to come scarce believe that ever a man in flesh and blood walked up on this earth like this". There is no other man who is daring enough to tell the world "My life is my message".

He was a British-educated lawyer. But by fate he became a leader to throw out the British rule from India. Non-cooperation and peaceful resistance were Gandhi's 'weapons' in the fight against injustice. He followed the forceful ways of strike based on truth and nonviolence like Satyagraha, Upavasa (fasting), Muona vrutha (observing silence). It created wonderful effects not only in India but also all over the world among those who love humanity. He himself suggested that he had nothing new to give, whatever he had given are as old as mountains and oceans. What he gave this world is the infinite power and spirit of truth, honesty, simplicity, manliness, love, satyagraha, sarvodaya and ahimsa – nonviolence.

Mahatma Gandhi is recognized as the Father of Nation (Rashtrapitha) of India. Gandhi's date of birth, October 2 is being declared by UNO as the International Day of Non-Violence.

## 12.1 A Brief Life Sketch

**Born**: October 02, 1869, Porbandhar, Gujarat, India

**Died**: January 30, 1948, New Delhi, India (assassinated)

Mohandas Karamchand Gandhi was born into a Hindu Baniyan family in Porbandar, Gujarat. He was the son of Karamchand Gandhi, the Diwan (Prime Minister) of Porbandar, and Putlibai (she was Karamchand's fourth wife). Living with a devout mother in a pious family and surrounded by the Jain religious philosophy influences of Gujarat, Gandhi learned from an early age the tenets of non-injury to living beings, vegetarianism, fasting for self-purification, and mutual tolerance between members of various creeds and sects.

In May 1883, at the age of 13, Gandhi was married through his parents' arrangements to Kasturba Makhanji. They had four sons: Harilal Gandhi, Manilal Gandhi, Ramdas Gandhi, and Devdas Gandhi. (Kasturba Gandhi died in February 1944)

Gandhi was an average student in his schooling at Porbandar and later at Rajkot. Samaldas College at Bhavanagar, Gujarat was his first centre of college education. His family wanted him to become a barrister. At the age of 18 on September 4, 1888, Gandhi went to University College London to train as a barrister.

The sign of his spiritual urge and mental strength can be read from his effort to follow a vow he had made to his mother in the presence of the Jain monk Becharji, upon leaving India. The oath was that to observe the Hindu precepts of abstinence from meat, alcohol, and promiscuity. Although Gandhi experimented with adopting 'English' customs – taking dancing lessons for example – he could not even taste mutton, other meats and alcohol. He managed to find London's few vegetarian restaurants. First to go along with his mother's wishes, and later because of knowledge gain on it, he intellectually embraced vegetarianism. He joined the Vegetarian Society movement in London and was elected to its executive committee. He wrote a book on vegetarianism, 'The Moral Basis of Vegetarianism'.

In London days he read works of and about Hinduism, Christianity, Buddhism, Islam and other religions. Bhagavad-Gita also gained his attention during these days.

He returned to India in 1891 and managed establishing a law practice in Bombay (Mumbai). Later he had done some related works and teaching profession in Porbandar.

To earn a living; in 1893 he went to South Africa to start his career as a legal advisor. There itself he introduced the ideas of peaceful civil disobedience in the Indian community's struggle for civil rights. Gandhi came back to India in 1914. He took up the leadership of Indian national movement for freedom within a short while. The Chambaran Satyagraha, non-cooperation movements, Salt March and Satyagraha, Quit India movement and so on made Gandhi a national spirit throughout the Indian movement for Independence. He was imprisoned for many years on numerous occasions.

The incidents related with racial discriminations experienced in South Africa have been acknowledged by several biographers as a turning point in his life, explaining his later social activism. (He was thrown off a train at Pietermaritzburg, after refusing to move from the first class to a third class coach while holding a valid first class ticket. Once he was beaten by a driver for refusing to travel on the footboard to make room for a European passenger) It was through witnessing firsthand the racism, prejudice and injustice against Indians in South Africa that Gandhi started to question his people's status, and his own place in society. He followed the path of truth and nonviolence, so called 'Gandhian Path', throughout in his life and struggles.

On January 30, 1948, Gandhi was shot and killed while having his public walk on the grounds of the Birla Bhavan (Birla House) in New Delhi. The assassin was Nathuram Godse.

## 12.2 Philosophical Principles of Gandhi

It is quite difficult to take a brief look at Gandhi's philosophical principles of life in one or two pages. A brief of the ideals may not satisfy a beginner to understand Gandhi.

In his religious philosophy Gandhi was a pious Hindu. When he was asked whether he was a Hindu, he replied: "Yes I am. I am also a Christian, a Muslim, a Buddhist and a Jew." Love of fellow men was his religion.

According to him a man's life is a journey of dedication for the wider purpose of discovering truth, or Satya. The most important battle to fight in an individual's life was overcoming his own demons, fears, and insecurities. Discovery of truth is the ultimate goal of life and nonviolence is the means to that end.

God is there in every human being. Man who truly believes in God is a temple of humanity. To Gandhi, God was 'life, truth, light and love'. God is the ultimate and changeless reality in the universe. First he expressed his principle that 'God is truth' and later in 1931 he changed this opinion to 'Truth is God' Thus, Satya (Truth) in Gandhi's philosophy is 'God'. He believed in the oneness of God and oneness of humanity.

Gandhi wanted every human being to be a seeker after truth and must follow the harmony between thought, word and deed. In manasa – mental process, vacha – words and karmana – deeds, a man should be perfect and follow the principles of nonviolence.

His philosophical ideals in certain walks of life are noted below:

### 12.2.1 Brahmacharya

According to Gandhi, basics of Brahmacharya are the spiritual purity and practical purity. It is largely associated with celibacy and asceticism. For Gandhi, brahmacharya does not mean only the withdrawal from sexual urges but 'control of the senses in thought, word and deed'. It is the abstinence from all worse and bad thoughts that cling man with the mundane passions.

### 12.2.2 Simplicity

Gandhi earnestly believed that a person involved in social service including education should lead a simple life which he thought could lead to the practical observation of Brahmacharya. He should give up unnecessary expenditure and be able to embrace a simple lifestyle. One should keep his belongings tidy himself and wash his own clothes. He should be simple in life, interactions, approaches and relations.

### 12.2.3 Silence

Observation of silence will help to keep away from worldly affairs caused to create confusion, frustration, emotional imbalances and inner unrest. It is needed for man for better and effective delivery of his abilities for the humanity.

### 12.2.4 Nonviolence: Ahimsa

Gandhi believed in the concept of 'ahimsa paramo dharma' – nonviolence is the ultimate righteousness. Nonviolence to Gandhi is not 'a shield of the coward, but the sword of the courageous'. A man should keep nonviolence in all aspects of life – thought, words and actions.

### 12.2.5 Truth

Satya (Truth) is the highly valued human quality. A man should follow the truth in his life. Human mind is the seeker after truth. He undoubtedly said his view that 'truth is God'. Without this value human life is worst.

Gandhi dedicated his life to discovering truth, or Satya. He tried to achieve this by learning from his own mistakes and conducting experiments on himself. His autobiography is named 'The Story of My Experiments with Truth'.

It is only through the path of truth one can achieve the developed state of human personality. 'Truth alone triumphs' – 'satyameve jayathe' – was a beloved Upanishath wording to him.

We can grasp the strength of his belief in truth as a personal and social value from his words, "When I despair, I remember that all through history the way of truth and love has always won. There have been tyrants and murderers and for a time they seem invincible, but in the end, they always fall —think of it, always"

## 12.3 Educational Philosophy

It is said that Gandhi started his educational attempts at Tolstoy farm, South Africa. He operated an Indian school there, teaching with a pedagogical approach developed by him. It was a new way of teaching and an action against the racial discriminations at South Africa. Gandhi's educational philosophy was influenced by his educational experiments at South Africa (Tolstoy Farm), Sabarmathi and Sevagram. It was also influenced by dissatisfaction in the prevailing system of education imparted by British administration, and his philosophy of life.

Mahatma Gandhi considered education as a way for liberation of people from their bondages. Education is an essential factor for social freedom, economic freedom and political freedom. Through education he aimed at social, moral, political and economic regeneration of India. Literacy and knowledge acquisition were only means of education and not ends. His educational principles were based on the concept of life-centered education.

Education is a democratic process with idealistic principles. According to Gandhi, "education is the all-round drawing out of the best in child and man – body, mind and spirit." Harmonious interaction between body, mind and spirit is the symptom of right education. He valued that education which draws out and stimulates intellectual and physical faculties of children.

Education is an instrument that moulds the new generation. He had an opinion that the education could reflect a society's fundamental assumptions about itself and the individuals who compose the society. Role of education in man's struggle to live is vital. Manipulated knowledge and wrong way of education may enslave men, society and nation. Emancipation from manipulated culture is possible by right education. Education would mean real freedom for individual.

**Aims:** Education is a method for the fulfillment and refinement of human personality. According to him the major aims of education are Knowledge of God, Self-realization,

Spiritual uplifting of humanity and Oneness with God. Education should aim at the construction of a new social order based on truth and nonviolence. It should aim at developing the useful citizens and character formation. Education must have vocational aims to be achieved. Earning a living to lead life is important. Education must provide a vocation to the educand. The ultimate aim of education is liberation.

**Teachers:** Gandhi wanted to free teachers from interference from outside, particularly government or state bureaucracy. The teacher who had a prescribed job to do that was based on what the authorities wanted the children to learn, cannot be a teacher dedicated for humanity. A teacher should possess good character, habits, teaching skills, knowledge and values. He or she should get opportunities to share them with pupils and people also. A teacher who establishes rapport with the taught, becomes one with them, learns more from them than he teaches them. He who learns nothing from his pupils is worthless. A good teacher takes from learners more than he gives them. A true teacher regards himself as a student of his students. He should be democratic in all aspects.

A teacher in his attitude should be like a father to children. He or she should care the child in all needs. The teacher should possess and try to create in child the purity in thought, words and action.

Curriculum and method should be based up on the principles of learning by doing and activity-centeredness. Both curriculum and method should revolve on a basic craft that is selected according to the needs of the community. Educational system should not load the student with textbooks. Textbooks should bear true knowledge and as far as be simple. Teaching is best while the medium is mother tongue. Education must take place in a free atmosphere. The free will for learning and self activities of students must be permitted in learning. Discipline is self-discipline. An individual has to develop discipline as a spiritual necessity. The institution and teachers have to provide circumstances to develop the self-discipline. He believed that along with the craftwork an individual will emerge himself with self-discipline. He was against physical punishments or corporal punishments.

Though he followed idealistic principles in setting aims and practices of education he collected principles of naturalism and pragmatism for the same and in curricular activities and teachers role. We cannot bind his philosophical ideals to a single thought, yet it is eclecticism. The philosophical principles of Gandhi can be selectively called Gandhism. Gandhi's philosophy of education is appreciated as naturalistic in its setting, idealistic in its aims and pragmatic in its methods and programme of work.

**Characteristic features of Gandhi's educational principles**

Education should be utilitarian. It should reflect the cultural life of society. The inner culture must be reflected through daily contact. Education is a process for harmonious development of personality and it is a preparation for complete living.

The 'sarvodhaya' or manifestation of all abilities in the individual is the major programme of his educational system. By right education an individual should be able to control his body, senses and mind. He considered character formation and habit formation as essential characteristics of education. Purity in approaches and control over mind and senses are the basis of character formation. Citizenship training is also considered as an essential characteristic of education. A sound education should produce useful citizens.

Gandhiji wanted to convert school into communities. By that individuals will get plenty of opportunities for social contact and cooperation. It will help in the synthesis of social and individual aims of education. Individuals cannot develop in a social vacuum but should develop a spirit of service and sacrifice for the good of society. Education should reconcile individual freedom and social restraint. Individual freedom and social freedom are not contradictory but complementary.

**Specific Views:** Education should focus on human aspirations. Regarding education he was of the opinion that manual work should not be seen as something inferior to mental work. He felt that the work of the craftsman or labourer should be the ideal model for the 'good life'. Schools which were based around productive work for the benefit of all were carrying out education of the whole person – mind, body and spirit. Education is need-based rather than interest-based.

Gandhi intended to transfer state's power on education in designing curriculum, textbook, practices and designing teachers' role from the state to the village. Gandhi's basic education was, therefore, an embodiment of his perception of an ideal society consisting of small, self-reliant communities. In his concept, an ideal educated citizen is an industrious, self-respecting and generous individual living in a small cooperative community.

Lastly, it was an education that aimed at educating the whole person, rather than concentrating on one aspect. It is a highly moral activity for the development of whole of human personality.

Within this context of the need for an ideal society, Gandhi developed his ideas on the scheme of education. The core of his proposal was the introduction of productive handicrafts in the school curriculum. The idea was not simply to introduce handicrafts as a compulsory school subject, but to make the learning of a craft the centre piece of the entire teaching programme.

Gandhi proposal the introduction of productive handicrafts into the school system was not really as disgraceful as it may appear. What he really wanted was for the schools to be self-supporting, as far as possible. There were two reasons for this;

Firstly, a poor society such as India simply could not afford to provide education for all children unless the schools could generate resources from within. Secondly, the more financially independent the schools were, the more politically independent. What Gandhi wanted to avoid was dependence on the state. Above all else, Gandhi valued self-sufficiency and autonomy. We can observe the practical side of these ideas in Wardha scheme or basic education.

## 12.4 Gandhi's Educational Experiments

Gandihi's educational effort was the application of his philosophical principles aimed to protect the values of truth, goodness, virtue, dignity of labour and greatness of humanity. He started attempts from South Africa itself to flag his educational ideals. All these educational ventures continued till his death.

**Durban South Africa, 1897**

He did not send his children to European schools, where racial discrimination is too high. He himself taught them in Gujarati, their mother tongue. For this he started a center of education at Durban.

**Phoenix settlement South Africa, 1904**

Started a school to keep his own views and give life to his educational ideals. The school tried to focus on agriculture, painting and other crafts.

**Tolstoy farm, Transval, South Africa, 1911**

He set up an ashram and school with the help of a German friend, Hermann Kallenbach. This is being treated by many as Gandhi's first educational effort.

**Shantiniketan, Bengal, India, 1914**

He stayed with group from South Africa to learn the educational practices at Santiniketan. Gandhi said on several occasions that this experience helped him to develop educational principles.

**Satyagraha Ashram, Ahamedhabad, Gujarat 1915**

This ashram was established with educational interest and training was given to members to themselves for service.

**Sabharmadhi Ashram, Gujarat, 1916**

Due to outbreak of plague, Satyagraha ashram shifted to Sabharmadhi and continued educational practices. Crafts had been given importance. Weaving was made a principal activity. Six schools were started in six villages. People provided free food and accommodation for teachers.

**Foundation of Gujarat Vidyapeeth, 1920**

He declared that the spirit of the doctrine 'sa vidyaya vimukthaya' – education that emancipate us – as the aim of Gujarat Vidyapeeth's aim. The ultimate aim liberation does not mean spiritual liberation. It means freedom from all manner of bondages, burdens and ties of the present life.

**Sevagram Ashram & Wardha Scheme, 1937**

New educational scheme launched through 'Harijan', a periodical published by Gandhi. This scheme was led to the foundation of basic education.

## 12.5 Basic Education (Nai Talim)

Basic education is the outcome of Gandhi's educational philosophy. He developed the principles of basic education system as a method for the social, moral, political and economic regeneration of common people.

**Origin and Development of Basic Education Scheme**

The ideas and principles, and views of his educational intentions were revealed by Gandhi through the pages of 'Harijan'. The scheme of education, its intentions and aims were declared in the Educational Conference held at Wardha on 22nd and 23rd October 1937. Gandhi put forth his ideas as a systematic education plan. Because of it's launching in Wardha conference, it also known as Wardha scheme of education.

A discussion was held on the plan suggested by Gandhi. A committee under the chairmanship of Dr. Sakkir Husain was appointed to suggest a practical shape, including syllabus to Gandhi's scheme. This committee suggested modifications and set it up as a practical scheme. The Haripura session of Indian National Congress in 1938 accepted this plan which scripted Basic National Education (this name is popularized as Basic Education). To work out a practical programme, an All India Board of educational experts was formed with Sevagram as headquarters. This board was named Hindustani Talimi Sang (Indian education Board). Some provincial governments implemented basic education as an experimental measure. In 1944, all these educational outcomes were evaluated by Sargent Committee on education, which was formed by the government of British India for the post-War (2nd World War) reconstruction of education in India and accepted it as national scheme of education.

The committee under the leadership of BC Kher in 1940 and Central Advisory Board on Education in 1944 had made a number of recommendations and these were also accepted for the modification of Basic Education.

The educational conference convened at Wardha in 1945 suggested extending the scope of basic education scheme. In 1945 at a meeting of the Talimi Sang it was renamed Nai Talim – New Education. The scheme was classified into four sessions; pre-basic, basic, post-basic and adult education. Nai Talim or New Education extended its scope to the whole span of life from birth to death of individual.

Basic Education was considered a medium of effecting social, economic and psychological changes in Indian society. As National System of education it was extended for almost two decades in free India.

**Basic Education: Principles and Practice**

Basic education can be adjudicated 'basic' because it is

— based on Indian culture

— based on basic interests and social needs of the children

— based on basic occupation (basic craft) of the community.

Basic education was not just a way of meeting the educational needs of the masses. It combined everyday processes of living and working with formal training. It is designed to develop all abilities of pupils. The training given has to be integrally related to the environment of the child and needs of the community. It was a self-supporting scheme of education that will help one to be self-supporting in later life. It was even proposed that this scheme of education will produce enough to meet the teachers' salaries!

The major characteristics of the basic education scheme can be summed up as follows:

a) The system seeks to give free and compulsory education to all children for seven years or up to fourteenth year of the age.

b) Medium of instruction should be mother tongue.

c) Education has to be self-supporting. Each center of education has to be self-supporting. (Basic education system will be able to cover gradually even the remuneration of teachers).

d) The process of education throughout the period of education should center round some form of manual productive work. This productive work or basic craft is the main focus of education system.

e) Curriculum has to built around three integrally related cores:

Physical environment

Social environment

Craftwork or manual productive work

In this system, ideal citizenship is emphasized. Character development of the pupil is important than literary achievement. Dignity of labour should be appreciated. Basic education is life-centered education. It has definite social orientation. It helps in promotion of livelihood and inculcation of civic responsibility of individuals. Textbooks have less importance in the implication of basic crafts. It seeks development of moral qualities.

In a basic school the aim of teaching has shifted from subject matter to serving the child's needs. It is the education for community development. It keeps the principle of individual differences throughout the practice.

In basic education, instruction of different subjects is not compartmentalized. There is coordination and correlation in methods of teaching. The different subjects in the curriculum such as history, geography, science, mathematics, language and painting are taught in their mutual correlation and relation with life.

**Basic craft** may be any work that is based on the needs of the community; for example in a locality where rubber taping is giving a livelihood, for the children that can be accepted as a basic craft. It may be spinning, weaving, gardening, cooking, book craft, leather work, wood work, carpentry, clay work , fishing and home craft.

Basic craft will stimulate the interest of children without allowing them to degenerate into mere excitement or pleasure. It involves learning by doing. Basic craft in basic education is not a vocational training going by the side of general education stream. It is not separate training with some designated periods. The craft is the medium of education and not a vocational craft. Entire teaching learning processes are to be revolved on the basic craft learning. It is the soul of the ideals of basic education. It is the core of the process. Teaching of it should be scientific. The craft in a school may not be same to all.

The school in basic education system should set up situations which provide constant practice in social and cooperative living and the child should be made aware of the purpose of education he is experiencing. Education must emphasize cooperative action instead of competitive individualism. The social uplifting and community development must be achieved by education itself. It is the totality of the means and end to the achievement of 'sarvodhaya'. The government's intervention in educational practices must be discouraged as far as possible. These can be achieved by the self-supporting, self-sufficient and self-governing institutions. Here lies the significance of Gandhiji's educational ideals and principles.

# Contributions of Great Educators

Pestalozzi, was a pious man who lived for orphans and tried to make education psychological,

Froebel, who is the Father of Kindergarten movement,

Montessori, the first Italian lady doctor and founder of Montessori Method in early education,

Tagore, the famous Indian poet and Nobel Prize winner who made education a retreat to peace – Santhinikethan *and*

Aurobindo, the great yogi and educational philosopher of India...

...are some of the great figures who significantly contributed to the development of education. Their contributions are highly acknowledged by educational practitioners all over the world.

This chapter gives a sketch of

*Their Life,*
*Educational Philosophy,*
*Specific Educational Contributions*

## 13.1 Johann Heinrich Pestalozzi

Pestalozzi can be called as the pioneer educationist who tried to psychologize education. He was a man who loved poor and children. More than forty children lived in his house and in his farmhouse at a time. He alone fed them and gave them clothes. More than an educationist, he was a lover of humanity.

Even his educational ideals were an extension of his attitude towards common people.

He was a man of commitment to social justice and tried to protect the poor throughout his life. He was interested in everyday forms and the innovations in schooling and educational practices.

Pestalozzi was highly influenced by Rousseau's works, particularly by Emile and Social Contract.

**Life Sketch**

**Born**: January 12, 1746

**Died**: February 17, 1827

Pestalozzi was born in Zurich, Switzerland. His father died when he was five, and he was raised in a loving home by his mother. He did not enter school until he was nine. It is said that his elementary school record was not so good because of his tendency to daydream. After school he completed his studies at the University of Zurich.

His early years were spent in schemes for improving the condition of the poor people and devoted himself to education. He did some businesses and farming but failed. Later he had opened his farmhouse as a school for orphans. He married at twenty-three. Pestalozzi and his heroic wife had sacrificed all their property for his schemes for poor. Sometimes they lacked bread and fuel, and illness added to their suffering. Sympathizing with the poor peasantry, Pestalozzi developed a plan for uplifting their condition through education.

His early experiments in education at Neuhof ran into difficulties but his attempts came to fruition later. In 1798 Pestalozzi was made the head of an institution at Stanz in which the orphans were to be trained. He established a school at Yverdon 1805. It was a success and the Yverdon School functioned for 20 years.

Pestalozzi learned his teaching methods from his experiences in teaching his son, Jacobi; this was the influence of Emile.

Pestalozzi's career is almost a puzzle. All his undertakings proved failures. There was nothing attractive in his external appearance and educational experiments. He had read very few books, possessed neither philosophical diffusion nor mastery of method, and entirely lacked talent for organization. In spite of all these drawbacks, he exerted a profound influence on modern education. It was due chiefly to his self-sacrificing love for children, his enthusiasm for educational work, and his sincere and influential attempts for uplifting the poor. He created a new educational spirit, interest in education, and a new school atmosphere, namely, unconditional love for the children.

**Works**

The Evening Hours of a Hermit (1780) – a series of thoughts and reflections.

Leonard and Gertrude (1781) – an account of the gradual reformation, first of a household, and then of a whole village, by the efforts of a good and devoted woman, and a pastor.

He published two books 'Fables' and 'Inquiry' in 1791, Fables was a collection of animal stories with simple morals. "Inquiry" was a philosophical work.

How Gertrude Teaches Her Children (1801): an exposition of his ideas on education.

Swans Song (1825): his last work

**Educational Ideals and Attempts**

Pestalozzi's ideals of education were formed in contrast with education system of his period. During his time the church was the supreme power in educational system. Privileged classes were the dominant group in society and they feared to enlighten the poor. There were no real concerns for the improvement of poor classes. It was this social condition and his life experiences that shaped Pestalozzi's educational ideals.

He had strong faith in education as effective means for individual and social improvement. He had the opinion that education is a right of every individual. Education should reach all members of the society, to the poorest, with all democratic values.

Education is not the transmission of ideals. It is the process of organic development. The education which encourages memorizing the holy script or the catechism is to be discarded. It needs psychological way of teaching. There is the need of religious education and moral education but it is deeper than dogmas and memorizing.

### 13.1.1 Educational Philosophy

Heinrich Pestalozzi's educational philosophy is developed based on the strong support toward love of children and love of poor.

He extended Rousseau's naturalism by giving concrete suggestions to be carried out in the schools. Pestalozzi evolved the principle that children must be educated as children before they become adults. He organized his schools on the pattern of the family, maintaining that there should be no difference between the school and the home.

The major contribution of Pestalozzi was pupil-activity, constructive and creative work, and pupil discussion in educational process. Instead of dealing with words, he argued, children should learn through activity and through things. They should be free to pursue their own interests and draw their own conclusions.

He placed a special emphasis on spontaneity and self-activity. He was against giving readymade solutions and answers to the problems of children. Children should not be given readymade answers but should arrive at answers themselves. Their own powers of seeing, judging and reasoning should be cultivated and their self-activity should be encouraged to reach on their own answers and solutions.

The aim of education is to educate the whole child. Intellectual education is only part of a wider plan of education. He aimed to keep equilibrium in three elements – hands, heart and head by education.

Pestalozzi asserted that the teacher must earn the trust of the children. He advocated a policy of 'thinking love' in handling children. The classroom must possess the atmosphere of a loving 'Christian family'. A teacher must recognize that education is nothing more than the polishing of each single link in the great chain that binds humanity together and gives it unity. Once a teacher knows this fact he or she can love students without any conditions.

Pestalozzi believed that thought began with sensation and that teaching should use the senses. He possessed a principle that children should study the objects in their natural environment. Holding this idea he developed the so-called **'object lesson'.** Object lesson involved exercises in learning form, number, and language. Pupils determined and traced an object's form, counted objects, and named them. Students progressed from these lessons to exercises in drawing, writing, adding, subtracting, multiplying, dividing, and reading

He wanted to establish a 'psychological method of instruction' that was in line with the laws of human nature. Love is the undercurrent of educational process, he recognized. So kindness ruled in Pestalozzi's schools. He abolished beating and other corporal punishments – much to the amazement of outsiders.

He saw education as central to the improvement of social conditions. He wanted the school to combine education with work. The school was to be a production unit so that children could finance their own learning – and in so doing they would be under no obligation to anyone (later we can see this idea in Gandhi's ideals of education).

He wished to entrust education to the eternal powers of nature and to the light God. By education, he said that children should grow up in favour with God and with men.

Following are the major principles can be found from the ideals of learning and education of Pestalozzi:

- Personality is sacred. This constitutes the inner dignity of each individual.
- As 'a little seed contains the design of the tree', so in each child is the promise of his potentiality. The teacher should care that the outward influence shall never disturb nature's march of developments.
- Teaching should be based upon psychological principles and build up child's mind from clear sense perceptions.
- Method was based on immediate experience of object and situations.
- All beneficent powers of man are due to nature and education should bring them out.
- He associated training in gardening, farming spinning and house work with instruction and reading.
- Love is the foundation of educational work. 'Without love, neither the physical nor the intellectual powers will develop naturally'.
- To get rid of the 'verbosity' of meaningless words Pestalozzi developed his doctrine of direct concrete observation, often inadequately called 'sense perception' or 'object lessons' (intuition). No word was to be used for any purpose until adequate perception and observation of object had

proceeded. The thing or distinction must be felt or observed in the concrete. This sense impression is the intuition that child gets. (various sayings in education are contributed from this: e.g, from the known to the unknown, from the simple to the complex, from the concrete to the abstract)

- To perfect the perception got by the observation of the thing that must be named, an appropriate action must followed to know it more.

*The other specific principles are:*

Education is the unfolding of the natural powers and faculties latent in every human being.

The purpose of education is both social and individual. Education provides the means for the social regeneration of humanity.

The moral, social, emotional and intellectual development of each individual unfolds through education.

While individuals achieve their full potential society is also improved.

'Along with the perception of concrete acts and with the experiencing of emotional responses, education begins', he says. Sense impression or intuition is the fact that makes learning effective. Effective thinking is depending up on clear observation of actual object. Words and ideals become meaningful when it related to concrete things.

He tried to define education as 'progressive, harmonious development of all powers of human beings'. Education is nothing but the development of innate tendencies which express themselves from within.

The following are the chief points of Pestalozzi's method of education:

a. Child-centered.

b) Method of direct experience: The teacher must never teach by words when a child can see, hear or touch an object for himself. Nature can teach the child better than man can. Language teaching must be linked with observation of objects.

c) Principle of activity-centeredness. The child is expected to be continually active in seeing for himself, making and correcting mistakes, describing his observations, analyzing objects and satisfying his natural curiosity.

d) Initiation and self-stimulation. The child must observe, learn to express his impressions of concrete objects perceived by the senses and must learn to formulate new generalizations for himself.

e) No books to early education: Early elementary education needs direct and concrete experience rather than books. In this way the child proceeds from the concrete to the abstract.

f) Principle of simplify all subjects: All subjects are reduced to their simple elements. The child proceeds, through experiencing the simple parts, to formulate more abstract generalizations.

g) Pestalozzi believed home is the ideal educational institution and mother is the best teacher. Hence school should provide homely atmosphere in all aspects. School and home should have an air of love, kindness and sympathy.

h) Teacher should respect the individuality of the child.

Pestalozzi was the first to make systematic observation of child's growth. Once he said, "I want to teach beggars to live like man..." He loved poor. He worked for their reformation. He attempted to democratize education by suggesting that education is the absolute right of every child. Only education can transform the personality of the child. It is believed that he introduced slates, pencils and the abacus in teaching to the European education.

## 13.2 Friedrich Wilhelm August Froebel

Friedrich Wilhelm August Froebel (1782–1852), a German educator, is well known as the father of the kindergarten concept in education. He was neglected in his early years and his memories of the sufferings of those years made him want to help others to lead happier lives. Froebel created a new respect for the individuality of the child. He advised the world to give up the rigid discipline and traditional formality of the school atmosphere. He suggested developing the dynamic and active qualities of child's nature by education. Froebel's kindergarten had been declared to be 'by far the most original, attractive and philosophical form of infant development the world has yet seen'. His so-called attitude towards children and their education can be intensively read from these words, "Children are like tiny flowers; they are varied and need care, but each is beautiful alone and glorious when seen in the community of peers."

He was influenced by Rousseau and Pestalozzi in developing his educational ideals. In many aspects we can see the origin of Froebel's theories in both Pestalozzi and Rousseau.

### Life Sketch

**Born**: April 21, 1782

**Died**: June 21, 1852

Froebel was born at Oberweissbach, in Thuringia, Germany. His father was a pastor, by name Johann Jakob Fröbel. He was the youngest and sixth son of his parents.

By all accounts he had a difficult childhood. His father left him to his own devices. Froebel's mother died when he was nine months old. His early education was in a village school for old girls. It was quite an adverse experience to the young boy. His father did not pay sufficient attention to him. His life with stepmother faced difficulties. In 1792, Froebel went to live with his uncle, a gentle and affectionate man. At the age of fifteen

Froebel, who loved nature, became the apprentice to a forester. In 1799, he left his apprenticeship and studied mathematics and botany in Jena University. After his study in Architecture at Frankfurt University, in 1805 Froebel began to teach in a school at Frankfurt. He worked with Pestalozzi from 1808 for two years at Yverdon School, Switzerland where his ideas further developed. Meeting with Pestalozzi changed Froebel's life attitude to a large extent.

In between the life at university, he had done military service for two years. Army taught him the value of discipline in life and strength of united actions. After two years of army service he joined as curator of the Museum in Berlin.

In 1818 Froebel married Henriette Wilhelmine Hoffmeister. After her death he married second time in 1851.

Froebel established at Blankenburg, Germany a Play and Activity Institute in 1837 which he renamed in 1840 Kindergarten. It was the first Kindergarten in the world.

His career life was full of uncertainty. He moved from one job to another, but kept the fire of educational interest uncovered. Throughout the life he never gave up his ambition and spirit on destination – education.

**Works**

The Education of Man (1826)

Mutter und Koselieder (1843), a series of songs designed to help mothers provide sensory stimulation and educational play for children from the first months of life

### 13.2.1 Philosophical Views and Educational Philosophy

Froebel's philosophy of education was based on Idealism. But his educational practices are influenced by the principles of naturalism to a great extent. His idealist view of education was closely related to religion. He takes man in his eternal being, in his eternal existence. Philosophically, he believed that all objects, material and ethereal take their origin from one source. There is an eternal unity between all objects in this universe. The core of his philosophical views is the conception of unity – the unity of mind and matter. Both have origin from the same source. Every object has two fold aspects; a form of unity in itself and the unity of wholeness. For example, the hand is a unit in and by itself, at the same time it is a part of the whole body. Specifically, the major aim of education according to Froebel was enabling the individual to comprehend the universal unity of objects

He believed that every human being had a spiritual essence and that every person had spiritual worth and dignity. Like Idealists, he also believed that every child had within him all he was to be at birth. The proper educational environment is needed to encourage the child to grow and develop in a most favorable manner. The purpose of education is to encourage and guide man as a conscious, thinking and perceiving being in such a way that he becomes a pure and perfect representation of the divine inner law. For this development, education should be through his own personal choice. Education must show him the ways and means of attaining that goal. He served education with a sound philosophical base and organized and systematized the methods of early childhood education.

Froebel's educational philosophy postulated the following facts:

a) education is a process of evolution. It is the element in the process of cosmic evolution.

b) effective education is based upon self-activities of the child

c) education is the process of participation in the life around.

d) by education individual becomes able to interact harmoniously with nature and society.

e) education is the process by which the individual develops self-consciousness, manhood, and harmonious functioning in relation to nature and society.

His educational philosophy rested on four basic ideas: free self-expression, creativity, social participation, and motor expression. Froebel believed in children's potential for good. He advised the need to provide a place in which children could be nurtured and developed through experiences with the natural environment and caring people. In such an environment a child can develop the acquisition of self-confidence and self-consciousness, which are also the aims of education.

Froebel's educational attempts with Pestalozzi for two years at Yverdon had helped him to develop the basic principles of education: liberal school atmosphere, emphasis on nature, and the object lesson. He believed true education originated in activity and that play was an essential part of the education process. Education must develop the values related with physical life and social life. Child acquires social and personal values like courage, tolerance, love, perseverance, politeness, prudence, enthusiasm, industry simplicity, friendliness, gentleness, justice, truthfulness loyalty, respect and etc through the way of play as a method of education.

His idea of education was to help children learn while they were playing. He believed that they learned best by doing rather than by direct teacher instruction. According to educational philosophy humans are essentially productive and creative – and fulfillment comes through developing these in harmony with God and the world. He believed in introducing play as a means of engaging children in self-activity for the purpose of externalizing their inner natures and a way of imitating and trying out various adult roles. Froebel characterized "play" as the "work" of childhood and described it as "the purest, the most spiritual, product of man at this (childhood) stage."

To attain the aims of education described in his philosophy of education, Froebel developed the learning experiences with Gifts and Occupations. The Kindergarten movement was also an attempt reach the aim of education as he designed in his ideals.

**Concept of Common Origin**

He believed that just as the different branches of a tree come from the same origin, all things in the world, though they seem to be different have one common origin (which he considered God). Unity of substance, unity of origin and unity of purpose are the three fold unity of nature and its creature.

### 13.2.2 Specific Principles Lead to Froebel's Method of Education

Education is a process by which man a biological animal becomes a social animal. For that the child needs continuous contacts and interactions. It is through self-activity that the child realizes his own nature and develops his own individuality and becomes capable of seeking perfection. Human being is essentially dynamic or productive and not merely receptive. Man is a self-generating force and not sponge (to absorb knowledge). Man is able because he is the most perfect product in the process of evolution.

The gifts and occupations are the effective method to move with continuous contacts and interactions. A child has to acquire ability to cooperate in communal purposes. For that he suggested the following principles as his ways of education:

a) education must based upon the natural evolution of child's activities

b) real development of child shoots from inner self-activity. So self-activity must be encouraged

c) the essential process of early childhood education is 'play'

d) an educationist should bear in mind that mankind is always in the making or in the process of development

e) education essential means for the future evolution of mankind

f) education of women is very important because development of human race largely depends up on women

g) knowledge is not an end but a means of functions in relation to the activities of the organism.

h) Freedom is the breath of educational process.

Training in expression for children had to be given in three ways namely – song, movement and instruction. A child should not be introduced to any new subject until he is ripe for it. The educational system should keep a principle that education is to bring out more rather than pouring into the man. Main purpose of instruction is not to acquire knowledge but to build habits, skills and powers of will and character.

**Regarding Teachers**

A teacher must consider and respond to the originality of responses from learners. No pressure should be put on pupils to achieve and develop more. Teachers must stress on relaxed and democratic classroom environment. It should not be a teacher-dominated classroom. A teacher is not a mere lecturer or instructor. He is a stage setter and guide. He is a helper to promote pupil achievement. He should follow the concept that which is good within; the person must come out by learning in terms of products, actions and activities. A teacher also encourages play way method in instruction, because play is the most beautiful activity.

**Gifts and Occupations**

Froebel's Kindergarten had a series of gifts and occupations designed by Froebel himself. He divided young child's learning into gifts and occupations. A gift was an object given to a child to play with—such as a ball. The gift helped the child to understand the concepts of shape, dimension, size, and their relationships. Gifts were intended to teach kindergarten children about the principles of geometry and the discipline of design.

The occupations were items such as paints and clay which the children could use to make what they wished. Through the occupations, children externalized the concepts existing within their minds.

Gifts were objects that were fixed in form such as blocks. The purpose was that in playing with the object the child would learn the underlying concept represented by the object. Occupations allowed more freedom and consisted of things that children could shape and manipulate such as clay, sand, beads, string etc. There was an underlying symbolic meaning in all that was done.

Block play is open-ended, and its possibilities are limitless. Even as children grow and develop new interests and abilities, blocks remain an active, creative learning tool. These blocks are known as manipulatives and by them children can develop skills in design, representation, balance and stability.

Gifts consisted of common objects and materials – balls, blocks, sticks, paper, pencils, and clay – that were used to teach concepts in nature, science, and aesthetics. Through directed play, trained teachers encouraged children to draw analogies between the gifts and other forms, such as the body and other natural objects like nuts or the sun, and even abstract concepts, such as self, unity, perfection, and color. Using a single gift, children learned to pick out similar shapes in nature, to manipu-late the gift in basic arithmetic operations and in representations of geometric concepts, and to explore aesthetic issues.

Froebel developed a specific set of twenty gifts and occupations (somebody said that Froebel developed only five set of gifts and others are developed by his followers). Some of them are:

1. ball on string
2. sphere, cube and cylinder
3. eight cubes
4. eight rectangular blocks
5. more cubes,
6. more rectangular blocks,
7. parquetry tiles
8. lines
9. rings

In Froebel's words, "the gifts are intended to give the child from time to time new universal aspects of the external world, suited to a child's development. The occupations, on the other hand, furnish material for practice in certain phases of the skill. The gift leads to discovery; the occupation to invention. The gift gives insight; the occupation, power."

**Kindergarten**

Kindergarten is a form of preschool education in which children are taught through creative play, social interaction, and natural expression. The kindergarten served as a transitional stage from home to school. It is a system which encourages fun and play based learning

Froebel states that in nature we allow plants and animals space and time to grow because their internal laws suggest they will develop properly only in this manner. He strongly advocates the extension and application of this rule to the education of children. Kindergarten is the live example for this idea.

Froebel wanted his school to be a garden where children unfolded as naturally as flowers. Like Pestalozzi he felt that natural development took place through self-activity, activity deriving from and continued by the interests of the child himself. The kindergarten provided the free environment in which such self-activity could take place.

He was against to the contemporary European concept that child can learn from the age seven or eight. He argued learning is possible at the earliest. For that a systematic, scientific and free atmosphere is needed. Kindergarten was nothing but this atmosphere. This is the preschool education.

Method of teaching and learning in kindergarten was a new experience. Froebel recognized that children began to learn as soon as they began to interact with the world, and he reasoned that since the interaction was mostly in the form of play, the way to educate children was through play. Play was the core of his all educational practices in kindergarten. He believed play is the highest expression of human development in childhood. It alone is the free expression of what is in a child's soul. The significance of play – it is both a creative activity and through it children become aware of their place in the world.

In kindergarten, group activities were balanced with individual play, direction from teachers was balanced with periods of freedom, and the studies of nature, mathematics, and art were balanced by exploring them through a single medium – the gifts.

Children being engaged with blocks in different shapes and sizes led the child to observe, compare and contrast, measure, and count. Materials for handwork – such as drawing, coloring, modeling, and sewing – helped develop motor coordination and encourage self-expression.

Froebel created the word kindergarten for the Play and Activity Institute he had founded at Blankenburg for young children. The Play and Activity school was renamed by him in 1840 as Kindergarten. The name Kindergarten signifies both a garden for children, a location where they can observe and interact with nature, and also a garden of children, where they themselves can grow and develop in freedom. Activities in the kindergarten included singing, dancing, gardening and playing with the Froebel Gifts. The major educational objectives of the Kindergarten are

— to ensure children's physical and mental health,
— to train children to form good habits,
— to enrich children's living experience,
— to reinforce children's ethical concepts
— to make effective socialization
— to make children cooperate with others.

The kindergarten was essentially created on new educational method and philosophy based on structured, activity-based learning which has ensured three factors'

— toys for sitting creative play (these Froebel called gifts and occupations)
— games and dances for healthy activity
— observing and nurturing plants in a garden for stimulating awareness of the natural world

Substantial value in the exercises of the Kindergarten are bringing out the active powers of the children – their powers of observation, judgment, and invention – and make them at once apt in doing as well as learning.

## 13.3 Maria Montessori

The Italian educator and physician Maria Montessori (1870–1952) was the originator of the Montessori Method of education for young children. Maria Montessori is recognized as one of the pioneers in the development of early childhood education. She was influenced a lot by Eduardo Seguin, a French psychologist who is recognized as the founder of the modern approach to special education and Itard, Rousseau, Pestalozzi and Froebel. Along with educational works she was an active supporter of various social re-form movements and was a highly regarded guest speaker throughout Europe on behalf of children's rights, the women's movement, peace education, and the importance of League of Nations.

Montessori's educational method is in use today in a number of public as well as private schools throughout the world. Association Montessori International is the famous organization that spread her educational ideals all over the world.

**Life Sketch**

**Born**: 31 August 1870

**Birthplace**: Chiaravalle, (Ancona) Rome, Italy

**Died**: 6 May, 1952 (Maria Montessori died in Noordwilk aan zee, Holland (Netherlands)

**Born to**: Alessandro Montessori and Renilde Stoppani.

Maria Montessori was, in many ways, ahead of her time. In 1894 she graduated with highest honors from the Medical School of the University of Rome, becoming the first woman physician in Italy. She was the first woman to receive a medical degree in Italy.

Her entry to the field of education was somewhat vital. She was not trained to be a professional educationist, but was a doctor. Maria Montessori's first appointment was as an assistant doctor in the psychiatric clinic of the University of Rome, where she had her first contact with mentally challenged children. As a doctor, her clinical observations led her to analyze how children learn. She came to a conclusion that the children build themselves from what they find in their environment. This observation envisaged her spirit in educational findings. Shifting her focus from the body to the mind, Montessori decided to lean more about education of child. She returned to the university in 1901, this time to study psychology and philosophy. In 1904, she was made a professor of pedagogical anthropology at the University of Rome.

In 1906 she gave up both her university professorship and her medical practice to work with a group of sixty young children of working parents who lived in slums in the San Lorenzo district of Rome. It was there in 1907 that she founded the first institution – Children's House-Casa dei Bambini – (This day care center or house had been built as part of a slum redevelopment). The Montessori Method of education was developed in this school based upon Montessori's scientific observations of these children's ability to absorb knowledge from their surroundings, as well as their untiring interest in manipulating materials.

Maria Montessori got support to her efforts from great figures like Alexander Graham Bell and his wife Mabel, Thomas Edison and Helen Keller, when she visited USA. The first Montessori school of USA was established (1912) in New York.

Though she was well approved by Spanish, US and London society and was appointed a government inspector of schools in Italy, she was forced to leave Italy in 1934 because of her opposition to Mussolini's policies. She traveled to Barcelona, Spain and Netherlands. She opened the Montessori Training Centre in Laren, Netherlands, in 1938, and founded a series of teacher training courses in India in 1939.

She was nominated for the Nobel Peace Prize three times—in 1949, 1950, and 1951.

**Major Works**

The Montessori Method (1912)
Pedagogical Anthropology (1913)
The Advanced Montessori Method (1917)
The Secret of Childhood (1936).
The Absorbent Mind (1949)

### 13.3.1 Educational Philosophy

Montessori is one among the educationists who brought psychological tendencies to education. Her educational ideals generated great discussion not only in Europe but all over the world. It was a rival attempt against the existing system of educational works.

Her entire educational methods are based on the observation of the self-creating process of the child. The major principles of her educational practices can be summarized as follows:

- — Every child is a problem in itself
- — Advocated method is individualized method.
- — Collective method of observation and study is not suitable to child; each child must be observed and studied in a different manner.
- — For a teacher, a child is not 'one in the class', but each child is a 'teaching unit'.
- — Education must aim at normal expansion of the nature, abilities and capacities of the child
- — Education is a process of unfolding of child's hidden powers.
- — Education must provide active help to child, to its expression of capacities and powers
- — The process of mental development of child has to take place according to child's own initiatives and not according to the dogmatic directions of teacher.
- — Education system must provide proper and amiable environment to develop child's personality.

Montessori defined early education as a process of auto education. Teacher is a director at this stage. Under the supervision of this director children are to be left themselves to do deviated activities according to their interest and correct themselves when they are wrong. Through this way of education a child will become self-reliant to acquire more concentration and initiation. They develop themselves self-reliance and industry in this way than develop the habit of obedience and dependence. The processes of auto education will actively help the child to acquire the spirit of self-respect and self-confidence. First the education of the senses, then the education of the intellect is the basis of Montessori's popular vision and method. Her educational philosophy stresses the need of sensory training.

Montessori's philosophy of education is affirmed upon one ideal – children teach themselves. This simple but thoughtful truth inspired Montessori's lifelong pursuit of educational reform, methodology, psychology, teaching, and teacher training.

According to Montessori's educational philosophy the teacher is the 'keeper' of the environment. While children are engaged with their activities the teacher's task is to observe and to intervene from the side-line. She believed that the observation and study of a child's activities will teach the teacher how to teach the child. She often said, "I followed children, studying them, studied them closely, and they taught me how to teach them."

Montessori argued that the teacher's job is to serve the child, determining what each individual student needs to make the greatest progress. A child who fails in school should not be blamed, any more than a doctor should blame a patient who does not get well fast enough. It is the teacher's job to facilitate the natural process of learning.

The major contributions to educational thought by Montessori can be specifically summarized as follows:

— post the children as natural learners

— division of children to the sensitive periods of development (example: Birth–3, 3–6, 6–9, and 9–12)

— considered children as competent beings, encouraged to make maximal decisions

— observation of the child's exercises for skill development and information accumulation in the environment can be taken as the basis for ongoing curriculum development

— small, child-sized furniture and creation of child-sized environment, creation of self-running small children's world and creation of free atmosphere are the basic requirements of child's learning centers

— her educational philosophy explains the limitless motivation of the young child to achieve competence over his or her environment. With this competence child tries to perfect his or her skills and understandings as they occur within each sensitive period.

— self-correcting 'auto-didactic' materials are the major outcome of Montessori's educational outlook.

Dr. Maria Montessori is a theorist of child romance. Her methods of child education were based on her work with the mentally deficient. She trained her children to work but there was no imposition of work, there were no rewards and no punishments. Work in the prepared environment is the reward and encouragement to children. According to her words "Every stupid child and every stupid man is the product of discouragement" – that sums up her thesis.

**Concept of Discipline**

Montessori was against to the traditional beliefs of discipline. Keeping silence and obedience are not the symptoms of discipline. She said, "Discipline must come through liberty. We do not consider an individual disciplined only when he has been rendered as artificially silent as a mute and as immovable as a paralytic. He is an individual annihilated, not disciplined." Self-discipline emerges out of the independence of the atmosphere of learning. She saw self-discipline as something that emerges as a result of natural law.

**Montessori Method – a Practical Expansion of Educational Philosophy**

"If education is always to be conceived along the same antiquated lines of a mere transmission of knowledge, there is little to be hoped from it in the bettering of man's future. What is the use of transmitting knowledge if the individual's total development lags behind?" This ideal is the basis of Montessori's educational method. She believed that child must be active in the learning in all aspects. The practice of Montessori Method vitalized the ideals of child's auto education.

The method was nurtured from her experience with the Children's House established to care the children from slums. Dealing with culturally deprived children, she used what she termed a 'prepared environment' to provide an atmosphere for learning. The practice of the method suggested small chairs and tables instead of rows of desks. It was the first attempt in the field of education to make infrastructure and furniture arrangements to child size!

The basic features of the method are

— development of the child's initiative through responsible individual freedom of behavior

— improvement of sense perception through training

— development of bodily coordination through games and exercise.

— child should avail complete liberty for manifestation and utilization of his or her natural energy

— schools should provide proper and prepared environment for free and natural manifestation of child's inner energy.

The function of the teacher is to provide didactic material, such as counting beads or geometric puzzles to learners, and act as an adviser and guide, staying as much as possible in the background. Teacher should keep a record of physiological, psychological and mental development of each child.

The Montessori Method is based on her view of the nature of the child. She suggested that children go through a series of 'sensitive periods' with 'creative moments,' when they show natural interest in learning. It is then that the children have the greatest ability to learn. These sensitive periods and creative moments should be utilized to the fullest so that the children learn as much as possible. At this time they should not be held back by non-natural curricula or classes. There is no necessity for rewards for learning. Work, she believed, is its own reward to the child.

The Montessori system is based on belief in children's creative potential, their drive to learn, and their right to be treated as individuals. It relies on the use of 'didactic apparatuses' to cultivate hand-eye coordination, self-directed-ness, and sensitivity to pre-mathematical and pre-literary instruction. Montessori Method also stresses physical exercise because motor abilities should be developed along with sensory and intellectual capacities.

The chief components of the Montessori Method are self-motivation and auto education. Montessori Method believes that a child will learn naturally if put in an environment containing the proper materials. These materials, consisting of "learning games" suited to a child's abilities and interests, are set up by a teacher-observer who intervenes only when individual help is needed. Montessori teachers try to reverse the traditional system of an active teacher to a passive class. The typical classroom under Montessori Method consists of readily available games and toys, household apparatus, plants and animals that are cared for by the children, and child-sized furniture.

### Practical steps of Montessori

She developed a teaching programme that enabled 'defective' children to read and write. She wanted to teach skills not by having children repeatedly try it, but by developing exercises that prepare them. These exercises would then be repeated: for example, Looking becomes reading; touching becomes writing.

Montessori's The *Casa dei Bambini* (Children's house) was established in Rome in 1907.This house was designed to provide a good environment for children to live and learn. An emphasis was placed on self-determination and self-realization. Exercise in daily living and other exercises, developed in The House were to function like a ladder – allowing the child to pick up the challenge and to judge their progress. It was from there the Montessori Method came out through various experimentations and observations.

## 13.4 Rabindra Nath Tagore

Rabindranath Tagore was a great poet, philosopher, artist, playwright, novelist, composer and social and cultural activist. He was a great educator of the East who contributed to the theory and practice of education. Tagore can be called India's true naturalist educationist, with idealistic outlook, who loved children most. He turned against the contemporary educational practice. He stood for the emancipation of the child and emphasized child's right to live on his own. He asserted that teachers must possess an international cultural outlook of humanity in their attitude and thought. Tagore happens to be the first educator in the world who felt that the teacher will have to play a new role in the international sphere because most of the problems a teacher faces on human cultural perspective are international.

**Life Sketch**

**Born**: 7 May 1861-in the family Jorasanko mansion, Kolkota (Calcutta), India

**Died**: 7 August 1941Kolkota.

**Born to**: He was born the thirteenth of fourteen children of Debendranath Tagore and Sarada Devi.

Rabindra Nath Tagore was born in an economically sound, aristocratic family of Kolkota. Though reared with high reputations, he experienced loneliness in early days. He was interested to sit alone watching the nature and dreaming about it.

At the age of eleven, on February 1873, Tagore and his father left Calcutta to tour India for several months. He visited his father's Santiniketan estate, Amritsar and The Himalayan hill station of Lord Dalhousie. During this time Tagore read biographies, studied history, astronomy, modern science, and Sanskrit, and examined the classical poetry of Kalidasa, the great poet.

Seeking to become a barrister, Tagore enrolled at a public school in Brighton, England in 1878. After that he studied at University College London, but returned to Bengal in 1880 without a degree.

In December 1883 he married Mrinalini Devi; they had five children. (Two of whom later died before reaching full adulthood). His wife also left him before time during his efforts to establish Visva-Bharati at Santiniketan.

In 1890, he began to manage his family's estates in Shilaidaha (a region now in Bangladesh) and Santiniketan.

In 1901, Tagore found an ashram at Santiniketan, and an experimental school with groves of trees, gardens, and a library.

Tagore, who also known by the name Gurudev, had won the 1913 Nobel Prize in Literature. He was the first Asian who received it. Tagore also accepted knighthood from the British Crown. (He renounced his knighthood in protest against the 1919 Jallianwala Bagh Massacre).

In 1921, Tagore and agricultural economist Leonard Elmhirst set up the Institute for Rural Reconstruction (which Tagore later renamed Shriniketan—'Abode of Peace') in Surul, a village near the ashram at Santiniketan.

He was thinking of a new type of university in which he desired to blend all culture of this world harmoniously. Keeping the dream to "make Santiniketan the connecting thread between India and the world, a world center for the study of humanity, somewhere beyond the limits of nation and geography", he established Visva-Bharati. Visva-Bharati—had its foundation stone laid on 22 December 1918; it was later inaugurated on 22 December 1921. Now it is a unique university in the world of its kind.

**Works**

Tagore's works included numerous novels, short-stories, collection of songs, dance-drama, political and personal essays. Some of them are Bhikharini (1877; The Beggar Woman—the Bengali language's first short story) and Sandhya Sangit (1882) Naivedya (1901) and Kheya (1906).

The major works are:

The Ideal One – Manasi (1890)

The Sacrifice – Visarjan (1890)

The Golden Boat – Sonar Tari (1894)

The Broken Nest – Nastanirh (1901)

Fair-Faced – Gora (1910), Song Offerings – Gitanjali (1910)

The Post Office – Dak Ghar (1912), The Immovable – Achalayatan (1912),

Wreath of Songs – Gitmalya (1914)

The Flight of Cranes – Balaka (1916)

The Waterfall – Muktadhara (1922)

Crosscurrents – Yogayog (1929), and

Biographies – My Reminiscences – Jivansmriti (1912) and My Boyhood Days – Chhelebela (1940)

### 13.4.1 Educational Philosophy

Tagore was not a full-time educationist. His educational thinking and practices are the efforts to fulfill his intentions he expressed in his poems and essays.

Tagore developed his educational ideals on the basement of Eastern – specifically Indian – concept of education and culture. At the same time he purposely blended it with Western philosophical outlook and practices. His inter-pretations on idealistic and naturalistic principles possessed genuine clarifications of his own way of thought, which are extremely different from other naturalists and idealists. As far as his educational philosophy is concerned we can call him a rue naturalist.

He emphasized education to self-help and intellectual uplift of the masses. To cure the "political symptom of India's social disease", he suggested a solution that was steady and purposeful education. He was against the rote-oriented education. A child must be able to contribute to his own learning. Education is a natural development.

In education he aimed at the development of man's love of nature and harmony with nature's creations. He strongly believed in the Indian concept of unity of creations and man's relationship with nature. Man has kinship with nature's creations. Realization of this kinship is the aim of education. To acquire this, he suggested education should be carried on in natural surroundings.

Education is not a process of giving and taking knowledge. It is not a communication process, but an interaction process. In this interaction 'mind' of the teacher, which has strong kinship with nature and its creations, descends in the mind of the pupil. In true education significance is not to the curriculum, textbook, organization and infrastructure or equipments but to the living contact and interaction between teacher and pupils. Education is a common venture for individual's harmonious development by organizers, teachers and significantly of students.

Education must emphasize the commitment of each individual to the community, each community to the nation, and each nation to the world or to this nature. Service to community is considered as a major aim of education by Tagore.

Education, Tagore believed, is not a programme to build sound scholars: it is a process to develop a sound man. A sound man should come before a sound scholar. What is the use of a scholar if he does possess no humanity? This question is the fundamental explanation to Tagore's ideals of educational practice. World of humanity needs no scholar but 'men'. He founded Santiniketan School – The Peace Retreat, Sriniketan and Visva Bharati as live examples to his educational ideals.

**Principles and Scheme of Education**

The educational ideals suggested for the conduct of Santiniketan can be considered the practical side of Tagore's educational philosophy.

Visva-Bharati was the extension of the ideals he tried to practice through the ashram and school at Santinekatan. He considered it a centre of worldly culture. Tagore implemented a brahmacharya pedagogical structure employing *Gurus* to provide individualized guidance for pupils at Visva-Bharathi.

Tagore said that every teacher should know every pupil and every pupil should know his or her teachers and fellow pupils. It is a must for hearty contact and interaction between teacher and pupils.

School should provide a family spirit. Santiniketan ensured such a spirit in its atmosphere. The delinquency and disobedience of the pupils must be treated with a family spirit. No child is treated as wrong child; only what he has done is treated as wrong. A child who committed a mistake must be well informed about the mistake he had done, and on what ground it is a mistake. On his confession and promise of reform he should be forgiven. If there is the need of punishment, there must be adjudication by boy court and boy judge formed in the school.

Education should ensure development of self-confidence, strong ambition to withstand, strong willpower and stability of mind. If it does not develop these qualities, it is not education at all.

The other practical principles he suggested are:

a) No one religion taught or practiced. He advocated universal religion aiming at the unification of mankind

b) He advocated vernacular language as the medium of instruction. Knowledge is better while it is absorbed in mother tongue.

c) Education should emphasize on culture of humanity, irrespective of national barriers.

d) Provisions for contact and interaction with nature, opportunities for the aesthetic expressions like painting, music, dance, performing arts, festivals, rituals, etc should be the criteria of education.

e) Highest aim of education that is unification of mankind should be associated with each step in education.

f) Child possesses godliness or child is the purest

g) Discipline must develop in family spirit.

h) Discipline is the attitude towards good behaviour, social acceptance, self-respect, respect for others, orderliness, cleanliness, honesty, modesty and etc.

i) Student deserves love and respect from others. He should be rendered with them without disparity. Individual attention should be paid to each individual.

Tagore suggested a new scheme of education to the world's humanity. It is really a deviated one and unique in all aspects. That is why he is treated as an educationist rather than a poet and writer.

## 13.5 Aurobindo

Sri Aurobindo is regarded as one of the greatest Yogis of all time in Hindu history. He was a teacher, principal, editor, politician, nationalist, scholar, poet, mystic, evolutionary philosopher, seer, yogi and guru and a Hindu scholar who originated the philosophy of cosmic salvation through spiritual evolution. During solitary imprisonment for almost a year as an 'under trial' prisoner in Alipore jail (Kolkota) he had a number of fundamental spiritual experiences which convinced him of the truth of the 'Sanatana Dharma' – the ancient spiritual knowledge and practice of India.

According to CR Das he is to be looked upon as the poet of patriotism, as the prophet of nationalism and lover of humanity. It may be observed that Sri Aurobindo's education in England gave him a wide introduction to the culture of ancient or mediaeval and of modern Europe. He was a brilliant scholar in Greek and Latin. He had learned French from his childhood in Manchester and self-learnt German and Italian. He studied Kalidasa, Goethe and Dante in the original tongues. He was a scholar in Indian literature too. His life account shows journey of a brilliant, intelligent, educated extremist to a yogi.

**Life Sketch**

**Birth**: August 15, 1872 Kolkata (Calcutta), India

**Death**: December 5, 1950, Pondicherry

**Born to**: His father was Dr K. D. Ghosh and his mother Swarnalata Devi.

Aurobindo Akroyd Ghosh was born in a rich and well-known family. His father was an admirer of European lifestyle and intended his children to live a European way of life. He sent Aurobindo and his siblings to the Loreto Convent School at Darjeeling for schooling. In 1879, at the age of seven, he was taken with his two elder brothers to England for education. There, they were placed with a clergyman and his wife, a Mr and Mrs.Drewett, at Manchester. He got admission into St Paul's School in London. At St. Paul's Aurobindo mastered Greek and Latin. During this time he got several scholarships and prizes. In 1890 he managed to achieve a senior classical scholarship to King's College, Cambridge, where he studied for two years. In 1890 he passed the open competition for the Indian Civil Service, but at the end of two years of probation failed to present himself at the riding examination and was disqualified for the Service. He lived in England for fourteen years and returned to India in 1893.

Aurobindo worked for thirteen years, from 1893 to 1906, in the Baroda Service. He was Vice-Principal in the Baroda College for a short period. In 1906 he joined as Principal of the Bengal National College, which was established as an effort of nationalist movement. This placement helped him to move on with his political attempts.

The Bengal Partition, which is a notable incident in British Indian history, was the omen he received after his stepping into politics. From 1905, he became a leader of the group of Indian nationalists known as the Extremists. He was one of the founders of Jugantar Party, an underground revolutionary outfit. He was the editor of a nationalist Bengali newspaper Vande Mataram.

In May, ·1908, he was arrested in the Alipore Conspiracy Case (another page in the history of British India). No evidence of any value could be established against him. After detention of one year as an under-trial prisoner in the Alipore Jail, he was released in May, 1909.

After a short political career as one of the leaders of the freedom movement of India, Sri Aurobindo turned to the development and practice of a new spiritual path. It is said that his conversion from political action to spirituality occurred while he was the prisoner. During this time he was inspired by the Hindu scripture the Bhagavad-Gita and the path of Yoga. His meeting with a Maharashtrian yogi called Vishnu Bhaskar Lele, who convinced him to explore the ancient Hindu practices of yoga, also motivated this conversion.

After imprisonment he started two magazines and tried to run along with Indian national movements. It was noticed by British administrators. He intended to keep away from politics for a solitary life. Finally in April 1910 he went to Pondicherry, then a French colony. Most of his literature works including poetry came out in this period. Aurobindo wrote on his spiritual philosophy and practice, on social and political development, on Indian culture, and translations of ancient Indian scriptures.

He withdrew completely from politics and devoted himself to spiritual attempts. In 1914, after four years of silent practice of Yoga, he began the publication of a philosophical monthly, the Arya. He established an ashram and received disciples to experience his spiritual path.

**Works**

Most of his works appeared serially in the philosophical periodical, Arya.

His works are largely concerned with the Yoga and spiritual life. Others were concerned with the spirit and significance of

Indian civilization and culture (The Foundations of Indian Culture), the true meaning of the Vedas (The Secret of the Veda), the progress of human society (The Human Cycle), the nature and evolution of poetry (The Future Poetry), are some of them.

Chaotic literary output includes philosophical pondering, poetry, plays, and other works. His works are The Life Divine (1940), The Human Cycle (1949), The Ideal of Human Unity (1949), On the Veda (1956), Collected Poems and Plays (1942), Essays on the Gita (1928), The Synthesis of Yoga (1948), and Savitri: A Legend and a Symbol (1950).

### 13.5.1 Philosophical Ideals of Aurobindo

Aurobindo's philosophical notions are deep explanations of Indian culture and traditions and are the spiritual explanations of Hindu philosophy.

He called his path the 'integral yoga.' The aim of integral yoga was the evolution of human life on earth by establishing a high level of spiritual consciousness. Path of integral yoga would represent a divine life.

Human life is integration. It is the integration of body, soul, spirit and life. Man has last resort to God only. Integral yoga is not the practice of artificial concentration or physical postures. It is the complete surrendering of man before the God. It is the hug with spirituality and godliness.

Yogic illumination surpasses both reason and intuition. Achievement of spiritual reason and intuition leads to the freeing of the individual from the bonds of individuality. It is the release from all bondages of all mankind. Yogic illumination of inner spirituality and intuition will eventually help the individual to achieve moksha (liberation).

One of Aurobindo's main philosophical achievements was to introduce the concept of evolution into Vedantic thought. Aurobindo rejected the materialistic tendencies of both

Darwinism and Samkhya, and proposed an evolution of spirit rather than matter. Man is the integral being and the result of this spiritual evolution.

The created world is the scene of a spiritual evolution. Mind is the highest term yet reached in the evolution. Mind has four layers of process – memory, thought perception by sensory impressions, intellect and intuition. There is a 'Supermind' (or eternal Truth-Consciousness) above the mind. It is the high-level spiritual consciousness. This 'supermind' in its nature is the self-aware and self-determining light and power of a Divine Knowledge. 'Supermind' is a self-existent Knowledge harmoniously manifesting its forms and forces. At the same time mind is an unawareness seeking after Truth. It is only by the conquering of the 'supermind' that the perfection of humanity can come.

Because of the development of Mind, individual human beings can use their will and intelligence for self-discovery and self-exploration for knowledge acquisition. This knowledge gives an optimistic and dynamic world-view and cosmic unfolding of individuality. Self-attempt through spiritual path helps to recognize power of light and bliss, discover one's true self, and remain in constant union with the Divinity. Spiritual path helps the transformation of mind and life and body. To realize this possibility has been the dynamic aim of Sri Aurobindo's integral Yoga.

### 13.5.2 Educational Philosophy: Concept of Integral Education

Education is a revolutionary movement. It is process to ensure the revival and liberation of the people. Education is each individual's and society's return to the progress of human civilization. Education is forming the outer basis of a fairer, brighter and nobler life for all mankind.

Education should support the process of yogic illumination and recognition of inner spirituality. Thus education is a spiritual process carrying out as a medium between mankind and Godliness. Education is an attempt to help individual to achieve moksha or liberation. By education, one should be able to recognize that he is a spiritual being. According to Aurobindo, "to help the growing soul to draw out that in itself which is best and make it perfect for a noble use" is the main aim of education.

Training to senses and training to mind for perfect perception are a must. Mind must be trained to the highest possibility. Without perfect training to mind education will remain incomplete. 'Reform the mind before reforming the world' is the slogan of education.

**Integral Education**

The educational ideals of Aurobindo are collectively called integral education. Integral education is the philosophy and practice of education for the whole child: his body, emotions, mind, soul, and spirit.

According to the concept of integral education, education should activate individual's memory, should develop judgment and creative power, should stress on observation and experiment. He insisted on education in mother tongue.

Prosperity of mental, spiritual and physical being of man should be achieved by education. He associated yoga with integral education. Yogic illumination of spirituality is one of the major aims of integral education. Moral education is an inevitable part of integral educational system. Moral and religious education helps man to keep his civilization. The components of moral nature like emotions, formed habits, associations and innate nature are to be nurtured properly by education. Education should cultivate right emotions, right habits, right associations and right actions. Moral discipline of individuality is the aim of moral education. For that he suggested the purification of mind of child through the path of yoga in education.

Integral education is based on the teachings in education of Sri Aurobindo and especially The Mother. It has been taught and refined over half a century at the Sri Aurobindo International Centre of Education in Pondicherry, India.

**The Mother and Auroville**

Aurobindo's spiritual collaborator, Mirra Richard was known as The Mother. She was born in Paris on February 21, 1878, to Turkish and Egyptian parents. She came to Pondicherry in March, 1914. Aurobindo considered her his spiritual equal and collaborator.

After 1926, when Aurobindo retired into solitude, he left the growing Sri Aurobindo Ashram to her. Because of her spiritual attempts and preaching she was called the Mother. It was she who established the Sri Aurobindo International Centre of Education. When Sri Aurobindo died in 1950, the Mother continued the spiritual work and directed the Ashram and guided the disciples. In the mid 1960s she started Auroville, an international township sponsored by UNESCO to further human unity near the town of Pondicherry. Auroville earned fame to be a place where men and women of all countries are able to live in peace and progressive harmony above all creeds, all politics and all nationalities. It is centre of humanity. The community in Auroville follows the spiritual path taught by Aurobindo.

It was inaugurated in 1968 in a ceremony in which representatives of 121 nations and all the states of India placed a handful of their soil in an urn near the center of the city.

The Mother stayed in Pondicherry until her death on November 17, 1973.

❖ ❖ ❖

## Author Index

Numbers in bold denote that the name can be found in next pages continuously for details see subject index also.

## Subject Index

**E**



**F**